The Great Treatise on the Stages of the Path to Enlightenment

The Lamrim Chenmo Translation Committee

José Ignacio Cabezón
Daniel Cozort
Joshua W. C. Cutler
Natalie Hauptman
Roger R. Jackson
Karen Lang
Donald S. Lopez, Jr.
John Makransky
Elizabeth S. Napper
Guy Newland
John Newman
Gareth Sparham
B. Alan Wallace
Joe B. Wilson

THE GREAT TREATISE ON THE STAGES OF THE PATH TO ENLIGHTENMENT

by

Tsong-kha-pa

Volume Two

Translated by

The Lamrim Chenmo Translation Committee

Joshua W. C. Cutler, Editor-in-Chief

Guy Newland, Editor

Snow Lion Publications
Ithaca, New York
Boulder, Colorado

Snow Lion Publications
605 West State Street
P. O. Box 6483
Ithaca, NY 14851
(607) 273-8519
www.snowlionpub.com

First edition USA 2004

Printed in Canada on acid-free, recycled paper.

ISBN 1-55939-168-5

Library of Congress Cataloging-in-Publication Data

Tsoṅ-kha-pa Blo-bzaṅ-grags-pa, 1357-1419.
[sKyes bu gsum gyi rnyams su blaṅ ba'i rim pa thams cad tshaṅ bar ston pa'i byaṅ chub lam gyi rim pa/ Lam rim chen mo. English]
The great treatise on the stages of the path to enlightenment / by Tsong-kha-pa; translated by the Lamrim Chenmo Translation Committee ; Joshua W. C. Cutler, editor-in-chief ; Guy Newland, editor.
p. cm.
Includes bibliographical references and index.
Volume 1 ISBN 1-55939-152-9 (alk. paper)
Volume 2 ISBN 1-55939-168-5 (alk. paper)
Volume 3 ISBN 1-55939-166-9 (alk. paper)
1. Lam-rim—Early works to 1800. I. Title.

BQ7950.T754.L34413 2000
294.3'444—dc21

00-044664

TABLE OF CONTENTS

DEDICATION

We dedicate this translation to
His Holiness the Fourteenth Dalai Lama
and the people of Tibet.

Editor's Preface

This book is the second volume in a three-volume translation of the *Great Treatise on the Stages of the Path to Enlightenment* (*Byang chub lam rim che ba*). It brings to a conclusion a project initiated by the Tibetan Buddhist Learning Center (TBLC) in 1992. Volume one was published by Snow Lion Publications in 2000 and volume three in 2002. Just as the location of this volume between the other two indicates, this middle volume is the heart of the *Great Treatise*. It covers the spirit of enlightenment (*bodhicitta; byang chub kyi sems*) and the deeds of the bodhisattvas, the great beings whose deeds are motivated by this altruistic spirit.

The Lamrim Chenmo Translation Committee has followed the same procedure and format that was used for volumes one and three, except for giving in the notes on the citations the Sanskrit reference and Tohoku catalogue (Ui et al. 1934) reference (identified by the abbreviation D) as supplied by Tsultrim Kelsang Khangkar's critical edition of the Tibetan text. The committee members who worked on this volume were Natalie M. Hauptman, Gareth Sparham, Daniel Cozort, and John Makransky. These translators again used the Tso-ngön (mTsho-sngon) edition of the *Lam rim chen mo* published in Zi-ling by Tso Ngön People's Press in 1985 (bracketed numbers appear throughout this work). They also referred to the commentary *Four Interwoven Annotations (Lam rim mchan bzhi sbrags ma)* and used it consistently to interpret citations. The editors again had the invaluable assistance of the eminent contemporary Tibetan Buddhist scholars Denma Lochö Rimbochay and Loling Geshe Yeshe Tapkay to read through the text and discuss difficult passages. Over the twelve years of this project the editors have come to appreciate what rare and precious treasures these two persons are.

While I was working on this translation project, I was often under the illusion that I was doing everything myself. However, as mentioned in this book, the distinction between self and other is not as sharp as we naturally think. Therefore, I would like to acknowledge the great contributions of others who have been as essential as myself in bringing this project to completion. In the prefaces to the other two *Great Treatise* volumes I have already thanked many people, and I hold their continued help in highest esteem. Yet I would be remiss if I did not give special thanks to a number of people whose contributions were especially beneficial to me over the past two years it took to complete this final volume.

I especially express my deepest gratitude to His Holiness the Dalai Lama, my constant source of inspiration for this work. His Holiness's activities embody the lofty ideals described in this book, such that he is the light of hope for those who desire peace in this strife-torn world. In response to my request His Holiness has said that He will give teachings at TBLC on the entire *Great Treatise,* and I pray that this great honor can soon become a reality. I am also continually grateful to my guru the late Geshe Ngawang Wangyal, whose profound effect upon my life has made him an ever-present source of support. As always, I greatly appreciate the efforts of the above-mentioned translators and Tibetan scholars. I would like to mention the two Tibetan scholars in particular. Geshe Yeshe Tapkay first proposed this project to me and has subsequently given his invaluable assistance without hesitation. Denma Lochö Rimbochay has given me constant guidance and support. I am most indebted to the great kindness they both have shown me. Among the translators I especially appreciate all the extra efforts of Gareth Sparham, who edited the original manuscript, entered all the citation notes, and put together the bibliography. I am also very grateful to Guy Newland, whose cogent suggestions brought clarity to the translation. I am also thankful to Gray Tuttle and Brady Whitton for their thoughtful editing suggestions. And I am most grateful to Snow Lion editor Susan Kyser for all her kind efforts at doing a very careful job to avoid any discrepancies in the text. In addition, I thank Snow Lion's Steven Rhodes for bibliographic help, and Jeff Cox and Sidney Piburn for their support and encouragement.

Also I would like to extend my great appreciation to all the family, friends, students, and supporters of TBLC who have given from their hearts to make this work possible: to my parents, Eric and Nancy Cutler, whose inestimable kindness I can never repay; to Buff and Johnnie Chace and their son, Ben, for their valued friendship and financial support; to my other friends and supporters—Alexander Levchuk, Martha Keys, Pierroluigi Squillante, Mukesh and Sepna Sehgal, Sharon Cohen, Frank and Raksha Weber, Chip and Susan Carlin, Harvey Aronson and Anne C. Klein, Elizabeth S. Napper, Thao and Gai Nguyen, Al Bellini, Victoria Jenks, Jim and Bonnie Onembo, Nick and Shelley Guarriello, Pence and Joanie Ziegler, David and Victoria Urubshurow, Frank and Khady Lusby, Jane Bullis, Jim Mershon, Vera Krivoshein, Sally Ward, Chot and Armen Elliott, and Louise Duhaime; to some of the TBLC students for their support—Amy and John Miller, Jennifer Collins, and Thomas Santomartino; and to the TBLC doctors—Peter Beskyd, James Goodwin, Frank Viverette, Jerry Cohen, David and Ming Ming Molony, Davis Smith and Kendra Lawrence, and Robert Blease.

There is one person whose collaboration on this project has made everything possible. The nature of my responsibilities at TBLC are such that I would not have been able to put my fingers on the keyboard if it were not for my wife, Diana. Since the inception of this project, she has selflessly shouldered more and more of the duties that keep TBLC running smoothly, as well as helped me on this translation project whenever needed. Over the twelve years of this project it has been very difficult for me to keep on track, and it has only been possible because of Diana's deep dedication to our guru Geshe Wangyal's vision, her boundless energy and enthusiasm, a consistent ability to put her own interests second, and a very practical intelligence. Just as an infant grows up in dependence upon the affection and support of its mother, so Diana has been the mother of this translation. For this I am eternally grateful.

Joshua W.C. Cutler
Tibetan Buddhist Learning Center
Washington, New Jersey

1

The Stages of the Path for Persons of Great Capacity[1]

3) Training the mind in the stages of the path for persons of great capacity
   a) Showing that developing the spirit of enlightenment is the only entrance to the Mahāyāna
   b) How to develop the spirit of enlightenment
      i) How the spirit of enlightenment depends on certain causes to arise
         a′ The development of the spirit through the four conditions
         b′ The development of the spirit through the four causes
         c′ The development of the spirit through the four strengths

Respectfully I bow down at the feet of those excellent and revered persons who have great compassion. **[281]**

After such extended meditation on the faults of cyclic existence from various perspectives, you will see all of cyclic existence as a pit of blazing fire. Then you will be completely consumed with the desire to attain liberation, the elimination of suffering and the afflictions. If you learn the path of the three precious trainings, you will attain liberation, which is free of cyclic existence and is indeed irreversible, unlike the glory of high status within cyclic existence. However, your elimination of faults and attainment of good qualities will be incomplete. Thus, you will not have accomplished your own aims and can only accomplish the purposes of others in a limited way. Eventually, a buddha will exhort you, and you will have to enter the Mahāyāna. Because of this, intelligent persons should enter the Mahāyāna from the beginning. As Āryaśūra's *Compendium of the Perfections* (*Pāramitā-samāsa*) says:[2]

> Once you have abandoned forever the two lower vehicles,
> Which possess no power to provide the welfare of the world,
> Enter the vehicle which the Conqueror Śākyamuni compassionately taught—
> This consists only of helping others. **[282]**

And also:

> When people see that joy and unhappiness are like a dream
> And that beings degenerate due to the faults of delusion,
> Why would they strive for their own welfare,
> Forsaking delight in the excellent deeds of altruism?

When you see that beings have fallen, just as you have, into the ocean of existence and are stumbling, unable to walk in a safe direction, because the eye of wisdom—which distinguishes what to adopt and what to discard—for them is closed, is it not better to care for others and to strive for their welfare, you who are in the Conqueror's lineage? That same text says:[3]

> Why wouldn't anyone who is in the Conqueror's lineage and
> Who works for the welfare of the world
> Have compassion for those stumbling with their eyes of wisdom closed
> And joyously persevere so as to clear away such confusion?

Here, you should use a great person's joy, charisma, and strength to shoulder the responsibility of others' welfare, for focusing only on your own welfare is a trait shared even with animals. Consequently, the fundamental orientation of a great person is to focus solely on achieving the happiness and benefit of others. Candragomin's *Letter to a Student* (*Śiṣya-lekha*) says:[4]

> Domestic animals eat a mouthful of easily found grass,
> And when tormented by great thirst, they happily drink water they find.
> Here, those who make an effort at working for the welfare of others
> Do so out of charisma, joy, and surpassing strength.
>
> The sun's great rays shine everywhere, traveling like a horse-drawn chariot.
> The ground supports the world without calculating the burden—

> Such is the nature of persons of great capacity, who lack any self-interest;
> They are consumed with whatever brings happiness and benefit to the world.

One who sees beings tormented by the above-mentioned suffering and who hastens to act for their welfare is called a "person of great capacity" and an "adept." **[283]** The same text says:[5]

> Those who see beings disturbed by the smoke cloud of ignorance that enshrouds the world,
> Helplessly fallen into the blazing fire of suffering,
> And hastily make effort as if their own heads were on fire
> Are here called "great persons" and "adepts."

Therefore, the Mahāyāna is the origin of all the good of self and others; the medicine that alleviates all troubles; the great path traveled by all knowledgeable persons; nourishment for all beings who see, hear, remember, and come into contact with it; and that which has the great skill-in-means that engages you in others' welfare and thereby indirectly achieves your own welfare in its entirety. One who enters it thinks, "Wonderful! I have found what I am looking for." Enter this supreme vehicle with all of the "strength of an excellent person" that you have. The *Compendium of the Perfections* states:[6]

> This supreme vehicle is realized by genuine wisdom.
> From it the omniscience of the Great Sage arises.
> He is like the eye of the world,
> His radiance like the rays of the rising sun.

Thus, enter the Mahāyāna after you have developed great respect for it induced by seeing its good qualities from various perspectives.

3) **Training the mind in the stages of the path for persons of great capacity**

Training the mind in the stages of the path for persons of great capacity is presented in three sections:

1. Showing that developing the spirit of enlightenment is the only entrance to the Mahāyāna
2. How to develop the spirit of enlightenment (Chapters 1-6)
3. How to learn the bodhisattva deeds after developing the spirit of enlightenment (Chapters 7 and on)

a) **Showing that developing the spirit of enlightenment is the only entrance to the Mahāyāna**

Question: Given that you should enter the Mahāyāna in the above-mentioned manner, what is the entrance?

Reply: The Conqueror taught that there are no Mahāyāna vehicles other than the perfection vehicle and the tantra vehicle. Whichever of these two you enter, the only entrance is the spirit of enlightenment. Once you have generated this spirit in your mind, you are recognized as a Mahāyāna practitioner even though you may not have generated any other good quality. **[284]** When you separate from this spirit, no matter what other good qualities you may have—such as the knowledge of emptiness, etc.—you lapse from the Mahāyāna, falling to the level of a *śrāvaka* and the like. This point is taught in many Mahāyāna scriptures and is also proved by reason.

The initial entrance into the Mahāyāna is determined by the development of this spirit alone. A subsequent departure from the Mahāyāna is determined by its loss alone. Hence, being a Mahāyāna practitioner or not is contingent upon the existence or nonexistence of this spirit. You become a conquerors' child immediately after generating this spirit. As Śāntideva's *Engaging in the Bodhisattva Deeds (Bodhisattva-caryāvatāra)* says:[7]

> The moment helpless beings, bound in the prison of cyclic existence,
> Develop this spirit of enlightenment
> They are called "children of the *sugatas*"...

And also:

> Today I have been born in the buddhas' family;
> I have become a child of the buddhas.

Thus it says that once you have generated this spirit, you are called "a bodhisattva." Moreover, the *Life of Maitreya* (*Ārya-maitreya-vimokṣa*) speaks of persons being bodhisattvas if they have this spirit even though they have not trained in the bodhisattva deeds:[8]

> O child of good lineage, although a precious diamond breaks, it still outshines all special ornaments of gold. It does not lose its name "precious diamond," and it still removes all poverty. O child of good lineage, similarly, those who have developed the precious diamond which is the spirit of enlightenment and the aspiration to omniscience, although they lack its application, still outshine all the golden ornaments which are the good qualities

of the *śrāvaka* and *pratyekabuddha.* They do not lose the name "bodhisattva," and they still remove all the poverty of cyclic existence.

Also the protector Nāgārjuna in his *Precious Garland* (*Ratnāvalī*) says:[9]

If you and the world
Wish to obtain unexcelled enlightenment,
Its root is the spirit of enlightenment,
Firm as the king of mountains.

Further, the *Tantra Bestowing the Initiation of Vajrapāṇi* (*Vajrapāṇy-abhiṣeka-mahā-tantra*) says:[10]

"O great bodhisattva, Mañjuśrī, this tantric maṇḍala is exceedingly secret, unfathomable, very profound, and vast. It is unsuitable to teach it to sinful beings." **[285]**

"Vajrapāṇi, you say this maṇḍala is very rare. Since I have not heard about it, to whom should it be explained?"

Vajrapāṇi replied, "O Mañjuśrī, once those who have entered meditation on the spirit of enlightenment have attained it, Mañjuśrī, these bodhisattvas who practice the bodhisattva deeds—the door to tantra—should enter into the tantric maṇḍala of the great sublime wisdom initiation. However, those who have not fully attained the spirit of enlightenment should not enter it. They should not even enter and see the maṇḍala. Moreover, do not teach them the gestures and mantras."

Therefore it is not sufficient that the teaching be a Mahāyāna teaching; it is crucial that the person be a Mahāyāna practitioner. Furthermore, functioning as a Mahāyāna practitioner depends solely on realizing the spirit of enlightenment. Hence, if you have only an intellectual understanding of this spirit, then you likewise have only an intellectual understanding of what it means to be a Mahāyāna practitioner. If the spirit is completely perfect, then the Mahāyāna practitioner is genuine, so strive for this.

In regard to this the *Array of Stalks Sūtra* (*Gaṇḍa-vyūha-sūtra*) says:[11]

O child of good lineage, the spirit of enlightenment is like the seed of all the buddha qualities.

Because you must fully comprehend this statement, I will explain it. When water, manure, warmth, earth, etc., combine with a rice seed, they act as the causes of the rice sprout. If they combine with the seeds of wheat, peas, etc., they act as the causes of these types of sprouts. Therefore these factors are the general causes of the sprouts. But it is impossible for a barley seed, though it combines with those conditions, to be the cause of a sprout of rice, and so on. **[286]** Thus a barley seed is the specific cause of a barley sprout, and the water, manure, and so forth, that are linked with that seed become the general causes of the barley sprout. Likewise, the spirit of unsurpassed enlightenment is like the seed, the specific cause among the general causes of the sprout of buddhahood. The wisdom that knows emptiness is the general cause of the three types of enlightenment [the *śrāvaka, pratyekabuddha,* and bodhisattva], just as water, manure, etc. are the general causes of the sprouts. Hence Maitreya's *Sublime Continuum* (*Uttara-tantra*) also states that:[12]

> Aspiration to the supreme vehicle is the seed;
> Wisdom is the mother for generating the buddha qualities.

Thus the spirit of enlightenment is like the seed of the father, and the wisdom which knows selflessness is like the mother. For example, since a Tibetan father cannot have a boy who is Indian, Mongolian, and so forth, he is the specific cause of the child's lineage, whereas a Tibetan mother can give birth to a variety of boys and is therefore the general cause of her child. And the *śrāvakas* and *pratyekabuddhas* also depend on wisdom, for the protector Nāgārjuna, in the *Praise of the Perfection of Wisdom* (*Prajñā-pāramitā-stotra*) says:[13]

> The path of liberation upon which the buddhas,
> *Pratyekabuddhas*, and *śrāvakas* definitely rely
> Is just this.
> It is certain that there are no others.

The perfection of wisdom is the mother of both Hīnayāna and Mahāyāna disciples, for it is also spoken of as "mother." Consequently, do not distinguish Hīnayāna and Mahāyāna by the wisdom that knows emptiness but by the spirit of enlightenment and the greatly effective bodhisattva deeds. Nāgārjuna's *Precious Garland* says:[14]

> Since the aspirational prayers, deeds,
> And complete dedications of the bodhisattva
> Are not explained in the *śrāvaka* vehicle,
> How then could you become a bodhisattva through it?

Thus he says that you differentiate these vehicles not by philosophical view but by deeds. If, in this way, even the wisdom that knows emptiness is not a specifically Mahāyāna path, it goes without saying that there are other shared paths as well. **[287]** Hence it is a clear indication that you have very little familiarity with the teachings when, after you have taken the spirit of enlightenment to be the crucial instruction, you do not practice it, but, after recalling it at the beginning of a session only in words, you intently make great effort at some single, small portion of the path.

In general, just as both father and mother are needed to have a child, you need the entire complement of method and wisdom to have a complete path. In particular, you need the main method—the spirit of enlightenment—and the main wisdom—the knowledge of emptiness. If you only meditate on one of them and diligently seek merely to be liberated from cyclic existence, then you have to meditate on the meaning of emptiness—selflessness—without mistaking meditative serenity for insight. Nonetheless, if you claim to be a Mahāyāna practitioner, then you must be practicing the spirit of enlightenment as well. Why? You need wisdom to prevent falling into the extreme of cyclic existence, and you need compassion to prevent falling into the extreme of peace [nirvāṇa], so wisdom does not prevent you from falling into the extreme of peace. As the venerable Maitreya says in his *Ornament for Clear Knowledge* (*Abhisamayālaṃkāra*):[15]

> Through knowledge you do not abide in cyclic existence.
> Through compassion you do not abide in peace.

If you are a Mahāyāna practitioner, you must practice the spirit of enlightenment because even in the Hīnayāna you do not fall into the extreme of cyclic existence and the main thing to be prevented on the bodhisattva path is falling into the extreme of peace.

When the conquerors' children, who validly interpret the commentaries on the Conqueror's intended meaning, generate just this precious spirit in their minds, they are amazed and think, "Such a marvelous path has arisen." However, they do not have this same feeling when they attain a slight good quality pleasing to ordinary persons. *Engaging in the Bodhisattva Deeds* says:[16]

> This altruistic spirit which is not born
> In others even for their own sake,
> Is a special jewel of the mind,
> Bringing an unprecedented wonder.

And also:

> Is there any virtue equal to this?
> Is there any such friend?
> Is there any such merit?

And also:

> I bow down to the body of anyone
> Who has generated this sacred jewel of the mind. **[288]**

And:

> It is the quintessential butter
> Churned from the milk of the sublime teaching.

Thus the spirit of enlightenment is the supreme instruction, extracting the quintessence of the scriptures.

Therefore, although the glorious Atisha held the Madhyamaka view and his teacher Ser-ling-ba (gSer-gling-pa) held the Satyākāravādin view,[17] Atisha attained the spirit of enlightenment by depending on him and therefore took him to be the kindest of his gurus. If those who know the core of the scriptures look at this part of Atisha's biography, they will gain a great understanding of a key point of the path.

If you generate this spirit in an uncontrived manner after making much effort, you will be imbued with the spirit of enlightenment and then even giving a tiny morsel of food to a crow will be considered a bodhisattva deed. However, if you lack this spirit, even offering a universe of three billion world systems filled with jewels will not be considered a bodhisattva deed. Likewise, actions such as the perfections from ethical discipline through wisdom, as well as meditation on yourself as a deity and meditation on the channels, winds, drops, etc., will also not be considered bodhisattva deeds.

If your precious spirit has not actualized the key point of the practice, no matter how long you try to cultivate virtue, you will not accomplish much. It is like cutting grass with a very dull sickle. If your spirit of enlightenment has actualized the key point of the practice, however, it is like cutting the grass and sharpening the sickle—even when you are not cutting the grass, you will be sharpening the sickle, and when you set to cutting, you cut a large amount even in a short time. Likewise, with this fully actualized spirit of enlightenment, in each instant you are able to easily clear away obscurations and accumulate the collections of merit and sublime wisdom. Even small virtues become extensive, and those that would otherwise be lost after a certain period of time do not end. *Engaging in the Bodhisattva Deeds* states:[18]

> The force of sin is great and extremely intense;
> Besides the spirit of perfect enlightenment,
> What virtue can overcome it?

And also:

> Like the fire at the end of an eon,
> It will instantly consume grave sins. **[289]**

And also:

> If even those who think, "I'll clear away
> Just the headaches of living beings,"
> Have such a beneficial intention
> That they receive immeasurable merit,
>
> Then what is there to say
> Of one who aspires to clear away
> The immeasurable unhappiness of each being
> And to endow each with immeasurable good qualities?

And also:

> All other virtues are like the plantain tree—
> After bearing fruit they perish.
> But this spirit of enlightenment, like a wish-granting tree,
> Always bears fruit and never dies, but flourishes.

b) **How to develop the spirit of enlightenment**

How to develop the spirit of enlightenment is explained in four parts:

1. How the spirit of enlightenment depends on certain causes to arise
2. The stages of training in the spirit of enlightenment (Chapters 2-4)
3. The measure of producing the spirit of enlightenment (Chapter 4)
4. How to adopt the spirit of enlightenment through its ritual (Chapters 5-6)

i) How the spirit of enlightenment depends on certain causes to arise

How the spirit of enlightenment depends on certain causes to arise is explained in three parts:

1. The development of the spirit through the four conditions
2. The development of the spirit through the four causes
3. The development of the spirit through the four strengths

a′ The development of the spirit through the four conditions

1. You develop the spirit of enlightenment either by seeing for yourself the inconceivable power of buddhas or bodhisattvas, or by hearing about them from a reliable person, and then thinking, "This enlightenment in which they abide or which they pursue is very powerful."

2. Although you may not have seen or heard of such power in this way, you can develop the spirit by listening to the scriptural collections which take unsurpassed enlightenment as a point of departure, and then aspiring to the sublime wisdom of a buddha.

3. Although you may not have heard the teachings, you can develop the spirit by understanding that the excellent teaching of the bodhisattvas is about to disappear, and then thinking, "I will definitely develop the spirit of enlightenment so that the bodhisattva teaching will remain for a long time, because the existence of such teaching removes suffering from innumerable living beings."

4. Although you have not seen the decline of the teaching, you think, "It is difficult to generate the spirit of enlightenment of even a *śrāvaka* or *pratyekabuddha* in these terrible times in which there is a preponderance of ignorance, shamelessness, lack of embarrassment, jealousy, stinginess, and the like. Then what need is there to mention developing the spirit of highest enlightenment? If I were, at some point, to develop the spirit of enlightenment, others would surely follow." Thus, you generate the spirit of enlightenment through seeing the difficulty required to develop it. **[290]**

Concerning *how* the spirit of enlightenment arises from these four conditions, it is said that they inspire you to attain great enlightenment, so a desire to attain enlightenment arises. The ways in which this happens are as follows:

1. After you see or hear about supernormal powers, you are awed, thinking, "I will attain such an enlightenment," and then generate the spirit of enlightenment.

2. Through hearing about the good qualities of a buddha from an instructor, you first develop faith and then there arises a desire to attain these qualities.

3. On finding the thought of the decline of the Mahāyāna teaching unbearable, you develop the desire to attain a buddha's sublime wisdom.

In regard to this last point, you see that if the teaching does not disappear, the suffering of living beings can be stopped. So even though your objective is indeed to remove suffering, nevertheless, the principal condition for the spirit of enlightenment arising is your inability to bear the fact that the teaching might disappear. Otherwise, this way of developing the spirit would repeat the explanation (presented later on in this text) of how the spirit arises in dependence on compassion.

4. After you see how rare this most purposeful spirit is, you develop a desire to attain buddhahood, spurred on principally by this awareness.

With regard to the two components of the spirit of enlightenment—the desire to attain enlightenment and the aim of the welfare of all beings—this fourth development of the spirit of enlightenment is established in terms of producing a desire to attain enlightenment, and is not established in terms of the aim.

Without the desire to attain buddhahood that comes from cultivating faith in a buddha's good qualities, you cannot overcome the sense of contentment that thinks peace [nirvāṇa] alone is sufficient to fulfill your own aims. The desire to attain buddhahood on account of training in love and compassion and seeing the fulfillment of others' aims as a necessity can eradicate the sense of contentment that thinks your peace alone is sufficient to fulfill *others'* aims, but cannot stop the sense of contentment that thinks peace is enough for *your own* aims. Besides this desire to attain buddhahood that comes from cultivating faith in a buddha's good qualities, there is no other way to stop the sense of contentment that thinks your peace alone is sufficient to fulfill your own aims. Indeed, you do need to overcome the sense of contentment that peace alone is enough to accomplish your own welfare because (1) Hīnayāna practitioners, who are merely liberated from cyclic existence, have only a partial elimination of faults and a partial knowledge, and thus lack the perfect fulfillment of their own aims; (2) these practitioners are liberated from the problems of cyclic existence but not from the problems of peace; and (3) the perfect fulfillment of one's own aims, it is said, is a buddha's embodiment of truth. **[291]** Therefore, once you cultivate faith in the good qualities of a buddha, you will see that you must attain buddhahood to accomplish even your own aims, let alone the aims of others. Understanding this is important for causing you not to turn back toward the Hīnayāna.

Among the four developments of the spirit of enlightenment explained above, the first two are not induced by compassion and love. In other scriptures and treatises as well there are many explanations of the development of the spirit of enlightenment as the desire to attain buddhahood induced by just seeing the good qualities of a buddha's embodiment of truth and embodiment of form. The determination to establish all beings in buddhahood is also said to be the development of this spirit. So you must consider each of these two to be counted as simply "developments of the spirit of enlightenment." With regard to developing a completely perfect spirit of enlightenment, however, it is not sufficient merely to have the desire to attain buddhahood upon seeing the necessity of fulfilling others' aims. You must have the desire to attain buddhahood that sees that it is indispensable even for your own aims. Furthermore, this intention must not neglect others' welfare but be for others' sake as well, because the *Ornament for Clear Knowledge* talks about both the intention to attain enlightenment and the intention to accomplish others' welfare:[19]

> The development of the spirit of enlightenment
> Is the desire for perfect enlightenment for others' welfare.

b′ **The development of the spirit through the four causes**

You develop the spirit of enlightenment through relying on:

1) a perfect lineage;
2) being sustained by a teacher;
3) compassion toward living beings;
4) not being disheartened by the difficulties of cyclic existence.

c′ **The development of the spirit through the four strengths**

You develop the spirit through relying on the four strengths:

1) the strength of yourself—the desire to attain perfect enlightenment through your own power;
2) the strength of others—the desire to attain perfect enlightenment through others' power; **[292]**

3) the strength of the cause—developing the spirit by having been familiar with the Mahāyāna and now merely hearing praise of buddhas and bodhisattvas;
4) the strength of application—in this life, being accustomed for a long time to such virtuous activities as relying upon an excellent being and reflecting on the teachings you have heard.

Furthermore, Asaṅga's *Bodhisattva Levels* (*Bodhisattva-bhūmi*) says[20] that after you depend on the four causes and four conditions (whether individually or collectively), you generate a firm spirit of enlightenment if you develop it from your own strength or from the strength of the cause. It is not firm if you develop it from others' strength or from the strength of application.

Once you have understood well that the teaching in general and the Mahāyāna teaching in particular are about to disappear, and that this time is particularly degenerate, you realize that a spirit of enlightenment developed from the depths of the heart is extremely rare. Rely on an excellent teacher and make an effort to practice—studying and reflecting, etc. upon the Mahāyāna scriptural collection—and plant the root for the development of the spirit from the depths of your heart, not forced by others, nor mindlessly following others, nor through the habit of custom, but through your own strength. All the bodhisattva deeds are necessarily based on it.

2

COMPASSION, THE ENTRANCE TO THE MAHĀYĀNA

ii) The stages of training in the spirit of enlightenment
a′ The training based on the seven cause-and-effect personal instructions in the lineage descended from the Great Elder [Atisha]
1′ Developing certainty about the order of the stages
a″ Showing that the root of the Mahāyāna path is compassion
1″ The importance of compassion in the beginning
2″ The importance of compassion in the middle
3″ The importance of compassion at the end
b″ How the six other personal instructions are either causes or effects of compassion
1″ How the first four personal instructions—recognition of all living beings as your mothers through the development of love—act as causes of compassion
2″ How wholehearted resolve and the spirit of enlightenment are the effects of compassion

ii) **The stages of training in the spirit of enlightenment**

The training in the spirit of enlightenment has two parts:

1. The training based on the seven cause-and-effect personal instructions in the lineage descended from the Great Elder [Atisha] (Chapters 2-3)
2. The training based on the teachings of the conquerors' child Śāntideva (Chapter 4)

a′ The training based on the seven cause-and-effect personal instructions in the lineage descended from the Great Elder

The seven causes and effects are: [7] the spirit of enlightenment from which perfect buddhahood arises; this spirit arises from [6] the wholehearted resolve; this resolve arises from [5] compassion; compassion arises from [4] love; love arises from [3] the wish to repay your mothers' kindness; the wish to repay their kindness arises from [2] recollecting their kindness; and the recollection of their kindness arises from [1] recognizing all beings as your mothers.

The training based on the seven cause-and-effect personal instructions has two sections:

1. Developing certainty about the order of the stages
2. The gradual training (Chapter 3)

1′ Developing certainty about the order of the stages

Developing certainty about the order of the stages has two sections:

1. Showing that the root of the Mahāyāna path is compassion
2. How the six other personal instructions are either causes or effects of compassion

a″ Showing that the root of the Mahāyāna path is compassion

Showing that the root of the Mahāyāna path is compassion has three parts: **[293]**

1. The importance of compassion in the beginning
2. The importance of compassion in the middle
3. The importance of compassion at the end

1″ The importance of compassion in the beginning

Once your mind is moved by great compassion, you will definitely make the commitment to free all living beings from cyclic existence. If your compassion is weak, you will not. Therefore, compassion is important in the beginning because feeling responsible to free all beings requires great compassion and because, if you do not take on this responsibility, you are not ranked as a Mahāyāna practitioner. In this vein, the *Teachings of Akṣayamati Sūtra* (*Akṣayamati-nirdeśa-sūtra*) states:[21]

> Furthermore, Venerable Śāriputra, the great compassion of the bodhisattvas is inexhaustible. Why? Because it is the prerequisite. Venerable Śāriputra, just as the movement of the breath is the pre-

> requisite for the life force of a human being, the great compassion of the bodhisattvas is the prerequisite for correctly reaching the Mahāyāna.

Also the *Foremost of Gayā* (*Gayā-śirṣa*) states:[22]

> "Mañjuśrī, what is it that motivates the bodhisattva deeds? What is its object?" Mañjuśrī said, "Devaputra, great compassion motivates the bodhisattva deeds; its object is living beings."

Thus compassion is the basis of engaging in the deeds because when you see that you will not live up to your commitment without training in the two vast collections, you set about the difficult work of amassing these vast collections.

2″ The importance of compassion in the middle

You may develop the spirit of enlightenment at one time and then engage in the bodhisattva deeds. But when you see that living beings are innumerable and act improperly, that the training is very difficult and limitless, and that you need an immeasurable length of time, you may lose heart and fall into the Hīnayāna. However, by accustoming yourself to increasingly greater compassion that is not just a one-time development, you become less concerned with your own happiness or suffering and are not discouraged at providing others' welfare. Therefore you easily accomplish all the collections. **[294]** Kamalaśīla's first *Stages of Meditation* (*Bhāvanā-krama*) states:[23]

> Because bodhisattvas are moved by great compassion, they diligently strive to be very helpful to others without considering themselves. Consequently, they engage in accumulating the two collections, which is very difficult, tiring, and requires a long period of time. As the *Seal of Engaging in Developing the Power of Faith Sūtra* (*Śraddhā-balādhānāvatāra-sūtra*) says:[24]
>
> > One who has great compassion will always take on a life of suffering and will always give up a happy life in order to help all living beings to mature.
>
> If bodhisattvas engage like this in something that is extremely difficult to do, they will fully and quickly complete the collections. They will definitely attain the high state of omniscience. Therefore the sole root of a buddha's qualities is compassion.

3″ The importance of compassion at the end

Based on the power of great compassion, buddhas, even when they reach their goal, do not abide in peace like Hīnayāna practitioners, but continue to work for the welfare of beings as long as space remains. For, without compassion buddhas would be like *śrāvakas*. Kamalaśīla's second *Stages of Meditation* says:[25]

> Since the *bhagavan* buddhas are imbued with great compassion they remain until the end of the realm in which beings dwell, even though they have attained the complete perfection of their own aims.

And also:

> The sole cause of the non-abiding nirvāṇa of the *bhagavans* is great compassion.

The glorious Candrakīrti taught that just as seeds, water, and ripening are important in the beginning, middle, and end of a harvest, similarly compassion is important in the beginning, middle, and end of the harvest of buddhahood. His *Commentary on the "Middle Way"* (*Madhyamakāvatāra*) states:[26]

> Compassion alone is regarded as the seed of a conqueror's
> excellent harvest,
> As water for its development,
> And as the maturation in a state of long enjoyment.
> Therefore at the beginning I praise compassion. **[295]**

With this powerful idea in view, the *Compendium of the Teachings Sūtra* (*Dharma-saṃgīti-sūtra*) says:[27]

> Bhagavan, bodhisattvas should not learn many teachings. Bhagavan, if bodhisattvas grasp and know one teaching, they will have all of the Buddha's teachings in the palm of their hand. What is this one teaching? It is great compassion.
>
> Bhagavan, with great compassion all the Buddha's teachings are in the bodhisattvas' palm. For example, Bhagavan, wherever the precious wheel of a universal sovereign is, there also is the assembly of his battalions. Likewise, Bhagavan, wherever the bodhisattvas' great compassion is, there are all the Buddha's teachings. For example, Bhagavan, once there is a life force, all the other sensory faculties will exist. Bhagavan, similarly, once great compassion exists, all the other bodhisattvas' qualities will appear.

Once you become convinced that compassion is the excellent key to the path through such proof as reason and limitless scriptures, why would you not hold the spirit of enlightenment together with its root—compassion—to be the supreme instruction? The teacher Shang-na-chung (Zhang-sna-chung) said, "Even though I asked for instructions from the Great Elder [Atisha], he said nothing except: 'Renounce the world; cultivate the spirit of enlightenment.'" Upon hearing this, Geshe Drom-dön-ba (dGe-bshes 'Brom-ston-pa-rgyal-ba'i-'byung-gnas) was embarrassed for him and said, "You received the Great Elder's ultimate instruction!" Geshe Drom-dön-ba understood the core of the teaching.

This conviction is very difficult to achieve, so you must seek a stable and certain knowledge by repeatedly clearing away sins, accumulating merit, and reading scriptures such as the *Array of Stalks Sūtra* and the commentaries. The glorious Mātṛceṭa's *Praise in One Hundred and Fifty Verses* (*Śata-pañcāśatka-stotra*) says:[28]

> Only you, O hero [Buddha], know your precious spirit,
> The seed of perfect enlightenment,
> To be the quintessence;
> No one else can reach this certainty. **[296]**

b" **How the six other personal instructions are either causes or effects of compassion**

The explanation of how the six other personal instructions are either causes or effects of compassion has two parts:

1. How the first four personal instructions—recognition of all living beings as your mothers through the development of love—act as causes of compassion
2. How wholehearted resolve and the spirit of enlightenment are the effects of compassion

1" **How the first four personal instructions—recognition of all living beings as your mothers through the development of love—act as causes of compassion**

In general, if you repeatedly consider the sufferings of living beings, you of course develop a simple desire to free them from suffering. However, to develop this attitude easily, strongly, and firmly, you must first cherish these beings and have affection for them. For, at present you cannot bear for your friends to suffer; you are pleased with your enemies' suffering; and you are indifferent to the suffering of persons toward whom you have neutral feelings, who are neither enemies nor friends.

You have the first attitude because you are fond of your friends. Commensurate with your cherishing of them, you cannot bear for them to suffer. When you cherish friends to a small or medium degree, you are only able to bear their suffering slightly. When you cherish friends a great deal, you clearly cannot bear for them to suffer at all, even if they suffer just a little.

When you see enemies suffer, not only do you *not* develop a desire to free them from it, but you also think, "May they not be free from suffering and suffer even more." This is due to your lack of affection for them. Your lack of affection for enemies is commensurate with your pleasure at their suffering.

Being neither unable to bear nor pleased with the sufferings of persons toward whom you have neutral feelings results from your having neither affection nor lack of affection for them.

Consequently, in order to have affection for living beings, cultivate the view that they are close to you, like friends or relatives. Since your mother is the closest person to you, cultivate a recognition of all beings as your mothers. Also, recollect their kindness as your mothers and develop the wish to repay their kindness. These three steps are how you learn to cherish and have affection for living beings. The result of these three steps is a love that considers living beings to be beloved, just as a mother considers her only child. This love gives rise to compassion. **[297]**

The causal relationship between compassion and the love that is the wish for beings to have happiness is not definite. These three objectives—recognizing all beings as your mothers, recollecting their kindness, and wishing to repay this kindness—are the basis for both the love that wishes beings to have happiness and the compassion that wishes them to be free from suffering, so you must make effort to cultivate these three. The masters Candrakīrti, Candragomin, and Kamalaśīla explained that cultivating the view that living beings are your friends or relatives is the cause of developing the spirit of enlightenment.

2″ How wholehearted resolve and the spirit of enlightenment are the effects of compassion

Qualm: Once you develop compassion through a gradual training of the mind, you generate the desire to attain buddhahood for the sake of all living beings. This should be enough. Why is it necessary to have the step of developing wholehearted resolve in between developing compassion and generating the spirit of enlightenment?

Reply: Although *śrāvaka*s and *pratyekabuddha*s have the immeasurable love and compassion whereby they think, "If only beings could have happiness and be free from suffering," these non-Mahāyāna followers do not think, "I will take on the responsibility to remove the suffering and to provide the happiness of all living beings." Therefore, you must develop wholehearted resolve that surpasses all other courageous thoughts. It is not enough to think, "If only all living beings could have happiness and could be free from suffering." You must also wholeheartedly assume the responsibility of producing this yourself. Consequently, you should distinguish between these ways of thinking. The *Questions of Sāgaramati Sūtra* (*Sāgaramati-paripṛcchā-sūtra*) states:[29]

> Suppose, Sāgaramati, a householder or a merchant had only one son, and this son was attractive, beloved, appealing, and pleasing. Suppose that because the son was young and playful, he fell into a pit of filth. When his mother and relatives noticed that he had fallen into it, they cried out, lamented, and grieved, but they did not enter the pit and take him out. **[298]** When the boy's father arrived and saw that his son had fallen into this pit of filth, however, his only thought was to save him, and without revulsion, jumped into the pit of filth and pulled him out.

To make the connection between the meaning and the parts of the analogy, the pit of filth represents the three realms; the only child represents living beings; and the mother and other relatives represent *śrāvaka*s and *pratyekabuddha*s who see beings fall into cyclic existence, grieve and lament, but are not able to save them. The merchant or householder represents the bodhisattva. Hence this is saying that *śrāvaka*s and *pratyekabuddha*s have the compassion which is like that of the mother for her beloved only son who has fallen into a pit of filth. Therefore develop a wholehearted resolve that assumes the responsibility of liberating all beings based on compassion.

Once you intend to liberate all beings, you realize that in your present condition you cannot fulfill the aims of even a single being. Moreover, even if you attain the high state of the two arhats [*śrāvaka* and *pratyekabuddha*], you will still only be able to fulfill the aim of liberation for merely a few living beings and will be unable to establish them in omniscience. Therefore, if you think, "Who can fulfill all the temporary and final aims of limitless living beings?" you will realize that only a buddha has this ability. Then you will develop the desire to attain buddhahood for the sake of these beings.

3

The Seven Cause-and-Effect Personal Instructions

2′ The gradual training
a″ Training the mind to be intent on others' welfare
1″ Establishing the basis for developing this attitude
(a) Achieving impartiality toward living beings
(b) Having affection for all beings
(i) Cultivating a recognition that all beings are your mothers
(ii) Cultivating a remembrance of their kindness
(iii) Cultivating the wish to repay your mothers' kindness
2″ The development of the attitude of being intent on others' welfare
(a) The cultivation of love
(b) The cultivation of compassion
(c) The cultivation of wholehearted resolve
b″ Training the mind to be intent on enlightenment
c″ Identifying the spirit of enlightenment, the fruit of the training

2′ The gradual training

The gradual training has three sections:

1. Training the mind to be intent on others' welfare
2. Training the mind to be intent on enlightenment
3. Identifying the spirit of enlightenment, the fruit of the training

a″ **Training the mind to be intent on others' welfare**

Training the mind to be intent on others' welfare has two parts:

1. Establishing the basis for developing this attitude
2. The development of the attitude of being intent on others' welfare

1″ **Establishing the basis for developing this attitude**

Establishing the basis for developing this attitude has two parts:

1. Achieving impartiality toward living beings
2. Having affection for all beings **[299]**

(a) **Achieving impartiality toward living beings**

I have previously explained the stages of the preliminary practices and so forth in the context of the persons of small and medium capacities. Practice these preliminary practices here as well and then sustain your meditation.

From the outset establish an even-minded attitude, eliminating the bias which comes from attachment to some living beings and hostility to others. Otherwise, any love or compassion you feel will be biased; you will never feel unbiased love or compassion. So, cultivate impartiality. There are three kinds of impartiality: (1) equanimity with respect to application,[30] (2) the feeling of impartiality, and (3) immeasurable impartiality. In this section, impartiality refers to the last one. Immeasurable impartiality is said to have two types: (1) wishing that living beings were free from such afflictions as attachment and hostility, and (2) being even-minded yourself after you have become free of attachment or hostility toward living beings. In this section, impartiality refers to the latter.

The steps for cultivating immeasurable impartiality are as follows. Since you can easily be impartial to a person toward whom you have neutral feelings, first take as the object of your meditation such a person, someone who has neither helped nor harmed you. Achieve an even-mindedness toward this person, removing your attachment and hostility.

Once you have attained this, then cultivate even-mindedness toward a friend. Your lack of even-mindedness toward this friend is either because of the degree of your attachment for him or her or because of the bias from your attachment and hostility.

After you achieve an even-mindedness toward this friend, cultivate it toward an enemy. Your lack of even-mindedness toward this person is due to your hostility, viewing him or her as totally disagreeable. After you are even-minded toward this person, finally cultivate it toward all living beings.

Question: Well then, what meditation eliminates attachment and hostility toward these three persons?

Reply: Kamalaśīla's second *Stages of Meditation* offers[31] two approaches: (1) Contemplate as follows, "From living beings' viewpoint, all equally want happiness and do not want suffering. Therefore, it is inappropriate to hold some close and to help them, while keeping others at a distance and harming or not helping them." **[300]** (2) Contemplate as follows, "From my viewpoint, if I have continuously been reborn since beginningless time, all beings have been my friends hundreds of times. To whom should I be attached? To whom should I be hostile?"

Furthermore, with regard to attachment to friends the *Daughter Like the Finest Moon's Discourse Sūtra* (*Candrottama-dārikā-vyākaraṇa-sūtra*) says:[32]

> Formerly I have killed all of you,
> And you have slashed and dismembered me.
> All of us have been mutual enemies and killed one another.
> How could you be attached?

In accordance with my previous explanation in the section on the fault of uncertainty,[33] think about how all friends and enemies can quickly change. By thinking in this way, stop both hostility and attachment.

In this context your contemplation requires you to make the distinction between friend and enemy. It is not the notion of friend or enemy that you need to stop but the bias that comes from attachment and hostility, which are based on the reason that some people are your friends and others your enemies.

(b) **Having affection for all beings**

Kamalaśīla's second *Stages of Meditation* states:[34]

> Moistened by love, your mind becomes like friable, fertile soil. When you plant the seed of compassion, it grows easily and bountifully. Therefore, after you infuse your mind with love, cultivate compassion.

The love mentioned here views living beings with affection, as if they were your dear children. By cultivating impartiality you eliminate the unevenness in attitude that comes from the bias of your attachment and hostility, and your mind becomes like a good field. Kamalaśīla says here that if you moisten your mind with the water of love which views all living beings with affection, and you then plant the healthy seed of compassion, you will easily generate great compassion. Understand this to be an extremely important point.

(i) **Cultivating a recognition that all beings are your mothers**

Because cyclic existence is beginningless, your births are also without beginning. Therefore you have died and been reborn time and time again. There is absolutely no kind of body which you have not assumed in cyclic existence. **[301]** There is absolutely no place where you have not been born, and there is no person who has not been a relative such as your mother. Asaṅga's *Levels of Yogic Deeds (Yoga-caryā-bhūmi)* cites a sūtra as follows:[35]

> I have difficulty seeing a place wherein you have not been born, gone to, or died in the distant past. I have difficulty seeing any person in the distant past who has not been your father, mother, uncle, aunt, sister, master, abbot, guru, or someone like a guru.

Moreover, all beings have not only previously been your mothers but will also be your mothers in the future a limitless number of times. Reflect upon this and become convinced that all beings have been your mothers. Once you develop this conviction, you will then easily remember their kindness and so forth. If you do not develop it, you will have no basis for remembering their kindness.

(ii) **Cultivating a remembrance of their kindness**

Bo-do-wa (Po-to-ba) said that after you have recognized that all living beings are your mothers, you will quickly remember their kindness if at first you cultivate a remembrance of your mother's kindness in this lifetime. Do so in accordance with his presentation, as follows.

Imagine your mother clearly in front of you. Think the following a few times: "Not only has she been my mother at present but she has been so an incalculable number of times throughout beginningless cyclic existence." As your mother, she protected you from all harm and provided you all benefit and happiness. Particularly in this lifetime she carried you for a long time in her womb. Then, when you were a helpless, newborn infant, she held you to the warmth of her flesh and bounced you on the tips of her ten fingers. She suckled you at her breast, used her mouth to give you soft food and to remove mucus from your nose, and used her hand to wipe away your excrement. So in various ways she nurtured you tirelessly.

Moreover, when you were hungry and thirsty, she gave you food and drink; when you were cold, clothes; when you were poor, she gave from her wealth those things which were very dear to her. Even more, what she gave to you were not things that she had obtained easily but that she had secured through great hardship while engaging in wrongdoing and receiving ill repute and suffering. **[302]**

If you suffered from illness, pain, or the threat of death, your mother made the choice from the depths of her heart that she would rather be sick than you be sick, she would rather be in pain than you be in pain, she would rather die than you die. By putting this feeling into action, she did what was needed to alleviate these troubles. In short, contemplate one-pointedly how your mother provided help and happiness and cleared away harm and suffering to the best of her knowledge and ability.

By cultivating a remembrance of your mother's kindness, you will not remember it just in words. Once you have given rise to such a remembrance, recognize that other friends and relatives such as your father are your mothers and cultivate a remembrance of their kindness. Then do the same with persons toward whom you have neutral feelings. Once you have produced an attitude toward them which is similar to how you feel toward your friends, recognize that your enemies are your mothers and cultivate a remembrance of their kindness. When you have an attitude toward your enemies that is like the one you have toward your mother, recognize that all beings in the ten directions are your mothers, and then gradually and with increasing extensiveness cultivate a remembrance of their kindness.

(iii) **Cultivating the wish to repay your mothers' kindness**

These beings, your kind mothers (whom you do not recognize due to the process of death and rebirth) are suffering and have no refuge. There is nothing more shameful than to do your best to liberate yourself from cyclic existence while considering these beings, your mothers, unimportant and abandoning them. Candragomin's *Letter to a Student* states:[36]

> While you see that your relatives are engulfed in the ocean of
> cyclic existence,
> And are as if fallen into a pit of fire,

> There is nothing more shameful than to work for your own liberation,
> Neglecting those whom you do not recognize due to the process of death and rebirth.

Therefore, reflect, "If abandoning such kind beings is unsuitable even for disreputable persons, how could it be appropriate in my case?" and then assume the responsibility to repay their kindness. The same text states:[37]

> The infant on the mother's lap cannot do anything
> And suckles milk which flows through love,
> While through that same love the mother endures many hardships.
> Who, even among the very disreputable, would like to abandon his or her mother? **[303]**
>
> Who, even among the most disreputable, wants to leave
> And abandon those who provided a home,
> Who carefully looked after the child with compassion,
> And who are afflicted, without refuge, and suffering?

Triratnadāsa's *Praise of Infinite Qualities* (*Guṇāparyanta-stotra*) states:[38]

> "It is not my way to liberate myself while abandoning these beings
> Whose blind ignorance ruins their intelligence
> And who are my fathers and children, serving and lovingly helping me."
> Thinking this, I made aspirational prayers to liberate these protectorless beings.

Qualm: How can you repay their help?

Reply: No matter how much wealth and happiness your mothers obtain in cyclic existence, it all deceives them. Thus you must repay their help, thinking, "Formerly, my mothers were seriously wounded because the madness of the afflictions possessed them. Then, I produced a variety of further sufferings for these beings who were already suffering, as if I had applied sea salt to their deep wounds. Now I will establish these beings, who lovingly helped me, in the happiness of liberation, nirvāṇa." Bhāvaviveka's *Heart of the Middle Way (Madhyamaka-hṛdaya)* states:[39]

> Furthermore, like applying salt
> To the wounds of those who have been possessed

By the madness of their afflictions,
I created suffering for those sick with suffering.

Now, what else is there other than nirvāṇa
To repay the help of those
Who in other lives
Helped me with love and service?

It is said that a kindness unrepaid weighs more than the heavy burden of the ocean together with Mount Meru and that repaying others' kindness occasions the praise of the learned. The *Verses from the Nāga King's Drum* (*Nāga-rāja-bherī-gāthā*) says:[40]

The ocean, Mount Meru, and the earth
Are not a burden to me. **[304]**
Whereas not repaying others' kindness
Is a great burden to me.

The learned praise persons
Whose minds are not excited,
Who recognize and repay others' deeds,
And who do not waste others' kindness.

In brief, your mother is crazed, unable to remain composed. She is blind, has no guide, and stumbles with every step as she approaches a frightful precipice. If she cannot place hope in her child, in whom can she place hope? If her child does not take responsibility for freeing her from this terror, who should take responsibility? Her child must set her free. Likewise, the madness of the afflictions disturbs the peace of mind of living beings, your mothers. Thus they are crazed because they have no control of their minds. They lack eyes to see the paths to high status [rebirth as a human or deity] and certain goodness [liberation or omniscience]. They have no true teacher, who is a guide for the blind. They stumble because their wrongdoing cripples them at each moment. When these mothers see the edge of the precipice of cyclic existence in general and the miserable realms in particular, they naturally take hope in their children, and the children have a responsibility to get their mothers out of this situation. Therefore, with this in mind, repay your mothers' kindness by definitely causing them to emerge from cyclic existence. Śāntideva's *Compendium of Trainings* (*Śikṣā-samuccaya*) states:[41]

Crazed by the afflictions, blinded by ignorance,
Stumbling with each step
On a path with many a precipice,

> You and others are always subject to sorrow—
> All beings have similar sufferings.

Although it is said that it is improper to look for others' faults and that it is wonderful to notice even a single virtue, here it is appropriate to consider how others are helpless.

2″ The development of the attitude of being intent on others' welfare

The development of the attitude of being intent on others' welfare has three parts:

1. The cultivation of love
2. The cultivation of compassion
3. The cultivation of wholehearted resolve

(a) The cultivation of love

In order to understand the cultivation of love you must know the following topics. *The object of love* is living beings who do not have happiness. *The subjective aspects* are thinking, "How nice it would be if beings were happy," "May they be happy," and "I will cause them to be happy." **[305]**

With respect to the benefits of love, the *King of Concentrations Sūtra (Samādhi-rāja-sūtra)* states:[42]

> Always offering to superior beings
> As many countless offerings
> As there are in billions of lands does not equal
> A portion of the benefit of a loving attitude.

It says that the benefit of love has far greater merit than continually making vast offerings to the highest recipients [buddhas and bodhisattvas]. Also, the *Array of Qualities in Mañjuśrī's Buddha-realm* (*Mañjuśrī-buddha-kṣetra-guṇa-vyūha-sūtra*) states:[43]

> In the northeast is the land of the Conqueror Buddheśvara called "Decorated by a Thousand Universes." There living beings have a happiness which is like the bliss of a monk who experiences a cessation. If you generate a loving attitude here in Jambudvīpa toward all living beings for merely a snap of the fingers, the merit produced greatly surpasses the merit gained by keeping pure conduct there for one trillion years. Is there any need to mention the merit of abiding in a loving attitude both day and night?

Moreover, Nāgārjuna's *Precious Garland* states:[44]

To offer three hundred small pots of food
Even three times a day
Does not equal a portion of the merit
Of a fraction of an instant of love.

Even if you are not liberated through love
You will attain its eight good qualities:
Deities and humans will love you,
They will also protect you.

You will have joy and much physical pleasure;
Poison and weapons will not harm you.
You will attain your aims effortlessly,
And be reborn in the world of Brahmā.

If you have love, deities and humans will love you and will naturally gravitate toward you. Moreover, the Conqueror defeated Māra's armies with the power of love, so love is the supreme protector, and so forth. Thus, although love is difficult to develop, you must strive to do so. The *Compendium of Trainings* says that you should think wholeheartedly about the verses of the *Sūtra of the Golden Light* (*Suvarṇa-prabhāsa-sūtra*) which discuss the cultivation of love and compassion.**[306]** It further says that you should at least recite and meditate on the following verse from this sūtra:[45]

Through the sound of the sacred Golden Light's great drum
May the sufferings of miserable realms, the sufferings brought on by the Lord of Death,
The sufferings of poverty, and all suffering be extinguished
In the three realms of the universe of three billion world systems.

The stages of cultivating love are as follows. First, cultivate love toward friends. Then, cultivate love for persons toward whom you have neutral feelings. Next, cultivate love toward your enemies. Then, cultivate it gradually toward all beings.

The way to cultivate love is as follows. Just as you can develop compassion once you have repeatedly thought about how living beings are made miserable by suffering, develop love by thinking repeatedly about how living beings lack all happiness, both contaminated and uncontaminated. When you become familiar with this, you will naturally wish for beings to be happy. In addition, bring to mind various forms of happiness and then offer them to living beings.

(b) **The cultivation of compassion**

In order to understand the cultivation of compassion you must know the following topics. *The object of compassion* is living beings who experience misery through any of the three kinds of suffering. *The subjective aspects* are thinking, "How nice it would be if living beings were free from suffering," "May they be free from suffering," and "I will cause them to be free from suffering." *The steps of cultivating compassion* are first to cultivate it toward friends, then toward those beings for whom you have neutral feelings, and next toward enemies. When you have equal compassion for your enemies and friends, cultivate it gradually toward all living beings in the ten directions.

Kamalaśīla, following the discourses on knowledge, set out this way of gradually cultivating impartiality, love, and compassion while distinguishing specific objects of meditation.[46] It is an extremely important point. If you train in these attitudes of impartiality, love, and compassion without distinguishing and taking up specific objects of meditation, but only using a general object from the outset, you will just seem to generate these attitudes. Then, when you try to apply them to specific individuals, you will not be able to actually generate these attitudes toward anyone. But once you have a transformative experience toward an individual in your meditation practice as explained previously, you may then gradually increase the number of individuals you visualize within your meditation. Finally, take all beings in general as your object of meditation. **[307]** When you sustain this practice in meditation, you will generate these attitudes correctly, whether you are dealing with individuals or a group.

The way to cultivate compassion is as follows. Consider how these living beings—your mothers—experience general and specific sufferings after falling into cyclic existence. I explained these sufferings earlier.[47] Moreover, if you have developed an awareness of your own general and specific suffering by training in the path of a person of medium capacity, you will assess your own situation and cultivate compassion toward others. By following this method, you will easily generate compassion. Considering your own suffering creates the determination to be free. Thinking about others' suffering creates compassion. However, if you do not first consider your own suffering, you will not reach the key point of the practice.

These are simple illustrations of how to meditate. Intelligent persons should meditate in detail on the one hundred and ten sufferings that are observed with compassion. These are explained in the *Bodhisattva Levels*.[48]

Furthermore, it is said that the bodhisattvas' thoughts of suffering during their cultivation of compassion are more numerous than *śrāvakas*' thoughts, which perceive suffering with an attitude of disenchantment—the final and actual knowledge of the truth of suffering for the *śrāvakas*. If you reflect from limitless viewpoints on how beings lack happiness and have suffering, you will develop much love and compassion. Moreover, if you think about this for a long time, your love and compassion will be strong and steady. Therefore, if you are satisfied with just a little personal instruction and neglect to familiarize yourself with the explanations of the classical texts, your compassion and love will be very weak.

Moreover, after you have thoroughly distinguished the objects of meditation according to the previous explanations—how compassion is the root, how the development of the spirit of enlightenment is the entrance to the Mahāyāna, and so forth—you must then analyze these explanations with discerning wisdom and elicit the experience produced after sustaining them in meditation. You will not achieve anything with the unclear experiences that come when you make a short, concentrated effort without precisely clarifying the topic with your understanding. Know that this is true for other kinds of practice as well. **[308]**

Kamalaśīla's first *Stages of Meditation* gives the measure for the development of compassion:[49]

> When you spontaneously feel compassion which has the subjective wish to completely eliminate the sufferings of all living beings—just like a mother's wish to remove her dear child's unhappiness—then your compassion is complete and is therefore called great compassion.

Here Kamalaśīla says that when you spontaneously feel compassion for all beings commensurate with a mother's compassion for her very dear and small suffering child, then you have completely perfect great compassion. Through this, understand the measure for the development of great love as well.

Taking that passage as point of departure, Kamalaśīla says:[50]

> When you have committed yourself to being a guide for all living beings by conditioning yourself to great compassion, you effortlessly generate the spirit of enlightenment which has the nature of aspiring to unexcelled perfect enlightenment.

Here he says that great compassion, which he explained above, is a necessary cause for developing the aspirational spirit of enlightenment. Understand from this too the measure for the development of the spirit of enlightenment. Furthermore, this statement pertains not just to the development of the spirit of enlightenment for someone who has reached a high path, but to a beginner's initial generation of the spirit of enlightenment as well. Asaṅga's *Mahāyāna Compendium* (*Mahāyāna-saṃgraha*) states:[51]

> That which has the attributes of goodness,
> The power of wishing, and firm aspiration
> Always initiates the bodhisattva's
> Three immeasurable eons.

So even a bodhisattva who is at the start of the three countless eons of practice must develop such a spirit of enlightenment.

So, suppose that you are not anywhere near these objectives and that you give rise to the mere thought, "I will attain buddhahood for the sake of all living beings, and in order to do this I will cultivate this virtue." You may make the great error of entertaining the false conceit "I have attained it" with regard to something you have not attained. If you then hold that the spirit of enlightenment is the core personal instruction, yet instead of training in it you search for something else and work on that, then you are only making a claim to have passed through many of the levels of attainment. **[309]** If those who know the key points of the Mahāyāna see you doing this, they will ridicule you. Many books say that the excellent conquerors' children train in the spirit of enlightenment for many eons, holding it as their most important practice. So what need is there to mention that it could not be attained by those who have nothing more than a superficial understanding? This is not to say it is unsuitable to meditate on other paths, but it is to say you must hold the training in the spirit of enlightenment as the core instruction and then sustain it in meditation.

There are those who, even without having gained the experiences as explained above,[52] know about the Mahāyāna trainings and have firm conviction in the Mahāyāna. They first develop the spirit of enlightenment and take the vow through the ritual, and then train in the spirit of enlightenment. For instance, in *Engaging in the Bodhisattva Deeds*[53] first there is a description of adopting the spirit of enlightenment and taking the vow and then a detailed explanation of how to practice the spirit of enlightenment in the context of meditative stabilization (a section within the six perfections, which are the trainings subsequent to generating the spirit of enlightenment). However, even in order to establish yourself as a proper recipient for these practices, you must first train in many kinds of earlier attitudes. After you have trained your mind by thinking of the benefits, by practicing the seven branches of worship, and by going for refuge, and after you have come to understand the trainings, then you develop the desire to maintain the spirit of enlightenment.

Some say rightly, though merely uttering the words, that in order to progress on the path you must go on increasing your knowledge of emptiness. In order to progress on the path you must likewise first sustain the spirit of enlightenment in meditation and then increase it in an ever more special way the higher you go, but those persons do not even merely utter these words. This is the one way traveled by all the conquerors, the twenty-two kinds of spirit of enlightenment taught in the *Ornament for Clear Knowledge*.[54] Understand this from the great trailblazers' explanations concerning how to progress on the path by means of these two, the spirit of enlightenment and the knowledge of emptiness. **[310]**

(c) The cultivation of wholehearted resolve

At the conclusion of meditating on love and compassion think, "Alas, these dear living beings for whom I feel affection are deprived of happiness and tormented by suffering; how can I provide them happiness and free them from suffering?" Thinking in this way, train your mind in at least this thought in order to take on the responsibility to liberate living beings. Even though this thought was described in the context of the practice of repaying your mothers' kindness, here it indicates that it is insufficient to have the compassion and love which merely think, "How nice it would be if they had happiness and were free from suffering." For, the thought that assumes responsibility shows that you must develop the compassion and love which have the power to induce the resolve, "I will provide happiness and benefit to all living beings." It is very effective if you practice this continuously, being mindful of it in all of your physical activities during the period of post-meditation and so on, not just during the meditation session. Kamalaśīla's second *Stages of Meditation* says:[55]

> Cultivate this compassion toward all beings at all times, whether you are in meditative concentration or in the course of any other activity.

Here compassion is just one example; you must do the same when sustaining any meditation. The great master Candragomin states [in his *Praise of Confession (Deśanā-stava)*]:[56]

> Since beginningless time the tree of the mind
> Has been moistened with the bitter juice of the afflictions
> And you are unable to sweeten its taste.
> How could a drop of the water of good qualities affect it?

Thus he says, for example, that you cannot sweeten the very bitter and large trunk of the *Tig-ta* tree by pouring just one drop of sugarcane juice onto it. Similarly, the mind-stream which has been infused since beginningless time with the bitter afflictions will not change at all from just a short cultivation of the good qualities of love, compassion, and so forth. Therefore you must sustain your meditation continuously.

b″ Training the mind to be intent on enlightenment

Once you have been inspired by the aforementioned process and have seen that you need enlightenment for the sake of others' welfare, you develop the wish to attain it. **[311]** However, this is not enough. First, increase your faith as much as possible by contemplating the good qualities of the Buddha's body, speech, mind, and enlightened activities as previously explained in the section on going for refuge.[57] Then, as it is taught that faith is the basis of aspiration, develop the desire to attain those good qualities from the depths of your heart and induce a certainty that it is absolutely necessary to attain omniscience even for your own welfare.

Although there are many causes for the development of the spirit of enlightenment, the *Concentration of the Tathāgata's Sublime Wisdom Gesture Sūtra (Tathāgata-jñāna-mudrā-samādhi-sūtra)*, cited in the first *Stages of Meditation*, says that it is most special to develop it on your own, overcome by compassion.[58]

c″ Identifying the spirit of enlightenment, the fruit of the training

The general definition of the spirit of enlightenment follows the meaning of that given in the *Ornament for Clear Knowledge* ["The development of the spirit of enlightenment is the desire for perfect enlightenment for others' welfare"] cited earlier.[59] With respect to its subdivisions, *Engaging in the Bodhisattva Deeds* follows the *Array of Stalks Sūtra* and says that it is both aspirational and engaged:[60]

> Just as one distinguishes
> Between wishing to go and going,

> Similarly the learned should understand the division
> Of these two in accordance with this sequence.

Although there are many disagreements about what these two are, know that the aspiration is either "May I become a buddha" or "I will become a buddha" for the sake of all beings and that as long as you have not taken the [bodhisattva] vows it is the aspirational spirit that is present, whether or not you are training in the deeds of generosity, etc. Once you have taken the vows, the spirit present is the engaged spirit of enlightenment. The first *Stages of Meditation* states:[61]

> The aspirational spirit of enlightenment is the initial intent, "May I become a buddha in order to benefit all beings." The engaged spirit is present once you have taken the vows and engaged in accumulating the collections of merit and sublime wisdom.

There are many arguments over this, but I will not elaborate on them here. **[312]**

4

EXCHANGING SELF AND OTHER

b′ The training based on the teachings of the conquerors′ child Śāntideva

The training based on the teachings of the conquerors′ child Śāntideva has three parts:

1. Contemplating the benefits of exchanging self and other and the faults of not exchanging self and other
2. The ability to exchange self and other if you accustom yourself to the thought of doing so
3. The stages of meditating on how to exchange self and other

1′ Contemplating the benefits of exchanging self and other and the faults of not exchanging self and other

Engaging in the Bodhisattva Deeds says:[62]

> Whoever wishes to quickly protect
> Self and other
> Must exchange self for other.
> Practice this excellent secret.

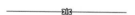

And:

> Whatever worldly joy there is
> Arises from wishing for others' happiness.
> Whatever worldly suffering there is
> Arises from wishing for your own happiness.
>
> What need is there to say more?
> Look at the difference between these two:
> Ordinary persons act for their own welfare;
> The Sage acts for others' welfare.
>
> If you do not genuinely exchange
> Your own happiness for others' suffering,
> You will not achieve buddhahood,
> And even in cyclic existence, you will have no joy.

Consider how being self-centered is the door to all suffering and being other-centered is the basis of all excellence.

2′ The ability to exchange self and other if you accustom yourself to the thought of doing so

Take the example of your enemy becoming a friend. At first, when you heard even the name of your enemy, fear arose. Later you were reconciled and became such close friends that when this new friend was absent you were very unhappy. This reversal resulted from familiarizing your mind with a new attitude. So likewise, if you become habituated to viewing yourself as you presently view others [with an attitude of neglect] and to viewing others as you presently view yourself [with a cherishing attitude], you will exchange self and other. *Engaging in the Bodhisattva Deeds* says:[63]

> Do not turn away from this difficulty.
> Although you were frightened upon hearing someone's name,
> Now, due to the power of conditioning,
> You dislike that person's absence.

And also:

> It is not difficult to consider my body
> With the perspective I have toward another's body.

Qualm: Since someone else's body is not your body, how can you develop the same attitude that you have toward your own?

Reply: Your body was produced from your father's semen and your mother's blood.[64] Even though it was produced from a portion of someone else's body, you conceive it to be your own by the influence of previous conditioning. **[313]** Similarly, if you become accustomed to cherishing another's body as you presently do your own, you will view it with the same perspective that you now have toward your own body. *Engaging in the Bodhisattva Deeds* says:[65]

> Therefore just as you conceived "I"
> With respect to the drops of semen
> And blood of others, so you can be conditioned
> To cherishing others as you do yourself.

Reflect thoroughly on the benefits of being other-centered and the faults of being self-centered. Thereby you will produce from the depths of your heart a great delight in meditating on the exchange of self and other. Then recognize that you can actually generate it once you have become habituated to it.

3′ **The stages of meditating on how to exchange self and other**

The phrases "exchanging self and other" and "making oneself others and others oneself" do not indicate a training in an attitude which thinks "I am others" or "Others' eyes, etc., are mine." They indicate a change in the orientation of the two states of mind of cherishing yourself and neglecting others, wherein you develop the attitude of cherishing others as you presently do yourself and neglecting yourself as you presently do others.

Therefore Śāntideva's statement above that you must "exchange your own happiness for others' suffering" means to view cherishing yourself as the enemy and then to stop emphasizing your own happiness. In addition, you must view cherishing others as a good quality, stop neglecting others' suffering, and instead emphasize the removal of their suffering. In brief, this statement means that you remove others' suffering while disregarding your own happiness.

There are two obstacles to training in this attitude of exchanging self and other:

1. You make a categorical differentiation between people who are happy or suffering—yourself and others—making them as different as blue and yellow. Then, you accomplish your happiness and remove your suffering because you think of them as "mine," and you neglect others' happiness and suffering because you think of them as "belonging to others."

Therefore, the remedy for this is not to make a categorical distinction between self and other as being essentially different. Rather, understand that self and other are mutually dependent such that when you are aware of self, you are aware of other; and when you are aware of other, you are aware of self. It is like being aware of near mountains and distant mountains, for example. Relative to your being here, you think of a mountain there in the distance as being a distant mountain, yet when you go to this distant mountain, you think of it as a near mountain. **[314]** So the awareness of self and other is not like the awareness of a color, for, regardless of what color blue is related to, you are aware of just blue and are not aware of some other color. Moreover, Śāntideva's *Compendium of Trainings* states:[66]

> By becoming accustomed to the equality of self and other,
> The spirit of enlightenment becomes firm.
> Self and other are interdependent.
> Like this side and the other side of a river, they are false.
>
> The other bank is not in itself "other";
> In relation to someone else it is "this bank."
> Similarly, "self" does not exist in its own right;
> In relation to someone else it is "other."

Thus Śāntideva indicates that self and other are merely posited in relation to a particular reference point and do not essentially exist.

2. You must remove the obstacle of thinking, "I will not make an effort to dispel others' suffering because others' suffering does not harm me." It would be like not accumulating wealth in your youth out of fear of suffering in your old age because you think that your suffering in old age does no harm to you in your youth. Or, as stated in *Engaging in the Bodhisattva Deeds*,[67] it would be like not alleviating the pain in your foot with your hand, because your foot is "other." Old age and youth (or similarly, former and future lives) are just illustrations; this principle applies also to morning and evening, former and later days, and so forth.

Qualm: But old age and youth are one continuum and the foot and hand are one collection; therefore they are not the same as self and other.

Response: "Continuum" and "collection" are designated to many moments and to many parts; they do not have a self-sufficient essence. The "self" of yourself and the "self" of others must be posited to a collection and a continuum, so self and other are not established by way of an essence that can be posited independently.

However, since beginningless time you have found your own suffering unbearable because you have been conditioned to self-cherishing. Therefore, if you become conditioned to cherishing others, you will give rise to an attitude of finding others' suffering unbearable.

After you have eliminated the obstacles to exchanging self and other in this way, the actual way to meditate is as follows. **[315]** Out of attachment to self, your self-cherishing attitude has produced all sorts of undesirable things throughout the beginningless time of cyclic existence up to now. Although you wanted to make things perfect for yourself, you emphasized your own welfare and engaged in improper methods. You have spent countless eons at this, but have not at all accomplished your own or others' aims. Not only have you not achieved these, you have been tormented only by suffering. If you had replaced concern for your own welfare with concern for others' welfare, you would certainly have already become a buddha long ago and would have completely and perfectly accomplished your own aims as well as those of others. As you did not do this, you have spent your time uselessly and laboriously.

Make a firm determination by thinking, "Now I understand the faults of self-cherishing and the benefits of cherishing others. With great effort, relying on mindfulness and vigilance, I will discontinue the present self-cherishing, my greatest enemy, and I will not allow any potential self-cherishing to arise." In this way frequently stop self-cherishing. *Engaging in the Bodhisattva Deeds* says:[68]

> Self-cherishing has harmed me in all
> My myriad lifetimes in cyclic existence.
>
> You, O mind, though you spent countless eons
> Wanting to accomplish your own welfare,
> Through such great hardship
> You have accomplished only suffering.

And also:

> If formerly you had acted for others' welfare,
> This condition which lacks
> The perfect happiness of buddhahood
> Could not possibly have occurred.

Thus, neither be self-centered nor support self-centered tendencies. You must train again and again in the attitude of freely giving to all beings your own body, resources, and roots of virtue, and you must work for the welfare of those to whom you give these things. It is wrong to do the opposite, so stop the attitude which sees your own body, resources, and roots of virtue as being for your own purposes. *Engaging in the Bodhisattva Deeds* says:[69]

"I am controlled by others";
You, O mind, know this for certain.
Now do not think of anything
Other than the welfare of all beings. **[316]**

It is wrong to achieve my own aims
With my eyes, etc. that are under others' control.
Therefore, it is incorrect to do wrong to others
With my eyes, etc. that are for their welfare.

If you lose the thought that your body, etc. are for others' welfare and think that they are for your own benefit, or if you see them as agents of physical, verbal, or mental harm to others, then stop this way of thinking by contemplating how this previously brought you limitless harm and how you are still mistaken with regard to its appearance of helpfulness, which is false. If you are controlled by this wrong way of thinking, it produces only unbearable suffering. *Engaging in the Bodhisattva Deeds* says:[70]

When you [self-cherishing] ruined me before,
That was another time.
Now I recognize you; where will you go?
I will destroy all your arrogance.

Dispel the thought,
"I still have my own welfare."
I have sold you [my mind] to others.
Do not be dispirited; offer your energy.

If I become careless
And do not give you to beings,
You will certainly give me over
To the guardians of hell.

Thus you gave me over
To long periods of suffering.
Now I remember my grudges;
I will destroy your selfish thoughts.

Similarly, when you repeatedly reflect on the benefits of cherishing others, you produce powerful enthusiasm from the depths of your heart. Discontinue your present attitude of disregarding others and keep your potential disregard of others from arising. Through affectionately viewing others as dear and beloved as much as you can, develop an attitude that cherishes others to the degree to which you previously cherished yourself—"Cherish others as you do yourself."[71]

To produce the attitude that cherishes beings in this way, you must remember their kindness or recognize that they help you. For example, once farmers see that through sowing healthy seeds they will reap a good and abundant harvest, they value a fertile field. [317] Likewise, once you are certain that you will accomplish all temporary and final well-being through sowing the seeds of generosity and so forth in the field of living beings, you will cherish others. Reflect on this. *Engaging in the Bodhisattva Deeds* states:[72]

> Living beings and conquerors are similar—
> From them you achieve a buddha's qualities.
> How is it that you do not respect living beings
> Just as you respect conquerors?

In reference to this, killing living beings leads you to the three miserable realms. If you save others from being killed, you go to a happy realm and have a long life there. In the same way, stealing or giving away your resources, being hostile or cultivating love and compassion, will produce results such as leading you respectively to a miserable realm or to a happy realm. Contemplate especially that you need to focus on living beings as you develop the spirit of enlightenment, and that by accomplishing the bodhisattva deeds for the sake of living beings, you reach buddhahood—so these too depend on living beings. Also, reflect on bringing generosity, etc. to perfection in dependence on living beings as taught in the verses on the necessity of making living beings happy. Nāgārjuna's *Essay on the Spirit of Enlightenment (Bodhicitta-vivaraṇa)* states:[73]

> The desirable and undesirable effects—
> A life in the happy or miserable realms in this world—
> Arise through the benefit and harm
> You do to living beings.
>
> If you attain unexcelled buddhahood
> In dependence on living beings,
> Why be at all amazed that in these three realms,
> The resources of deities or humans
>
> Relied upon by Brahmā, Indra, Rudra,
> And the worldly protectors
> Are also brought about by
> Just helping living beings?
>
> All of the many sufferings
> Living beings experience
> As animals, hungry ghosts, and hell beings
> Come from harming living beings.

The sufferings of hunger,
Thirst, violence, and torture,
Which are difficult to reverse and inexhaustible,
Are the results of harming living beings. **[318]**

The *śrāvaka*s' goal is inferior because they do not emphasize others' welfare, whereas buddhas attain the final goal because they stress others' welfare. It is said that once you have contemplated the principle here, you should not for even an instant be attached to your own welfare. The *Essay on the Spirit of Enlightenment* states:[74]

With effort eliminate as a poison
Your lack of care for living beings.

Don't *śrāvaka*s attain an inferior enlightenment
Because they lack caring?
By not forsaking living beings
Perfect buddhas attain enlightenment.

Once bodhisattvas ascertain the effects
Arising from helping and not helping,
How can they remain even for a moment
Attached to their own welfare?

Therefore, after conquerors' children understand that full absorption in others' welfare and the goal of enlightenment arise from the sprout of the spirit of enlightenment, and after they see that its root is compassion, they are very intent on cultivating compassion. They become thoroughly conditioned to it so that their compassion and spirit of enlightenment become firm. Thereupon they cannot help but engage in the deeds of the great undertaking that is most challenging. The *Essay on the Spirit of Enlightenment* states:[75]

The fruit of enlightenment solely for others' welfare
Grows from the sprout of the spirit of enlightenment
Which has a root of firm compassion.
This is what conquerors' children cultivate.

One who stabilizes this through conditioning,
Though initially terrified by the suffering of others,
Later gives up even the bliss of meditative stabilization
And enters the Unwavering Hell.

This is amazing! This is praiseworthy!
This is the superior way of excellent beings.

Now also develop certainty about these methods by means of the sayings of excellent beings, as follows:

Atisha said, "Tibet recognizes 'bodhisattvas' who do not know how to train in love and compassion." Someone then asked, "Well then, how should bodhisattvas practice?" He replied, "They must learn in stages from the beginning." **[319]**

Lang-ri-tang-ba (Glang-ri-thang-pa) said, "Sha-bo-ba (Shva-bo-pa) and I have eighteen human strategies and one horse strategy for a total of nineteen.[76] Our human strategy is simply to develop the spirit of highest enlightenment and then learn to do whatever we do for the sake of living beings. Our horse strategy is this: since self-cherishing keeps that spirit of enlightenment which has not arisen from arising, and destabilizes that which has arisen and prevents its increase, train by keeping self-cherishing away and doing what you can to damage it. Cherish living beings and do whatever you can to help them."

Nal-jor-ba-chen-bo (rNal-'byor-pa-chen-po) explained to Geshe Drom-dön-ba that he had this and that meditative concentration wherein the energy balances and absorbs, and so forth. Geshe Drom-dön-ba replied, "Even if you have a meditation undisturbed even by the beating of a large drum close to your ear, if you do not have love, compassion, and the spirit of enlightenment, you will be reborn in a place that to avoid you must now confess day and night." Drom-dön-ba thinks that Nal-jor-ba-chen-bo is proceeding so as to cause his rebirth in a state lacking leisure, such as rebirth as an ordinary being of the formless realm or the like.

Kam-lung-ba (Kham-lung-ba) said, "Through our disinterest in living beings, who are what is most important, they will also do the same [i.e., not bring the benefit of virtues] to us."

Whether you plant the roots of the Mahāyāna or not, or whether you have genuinely entered the Mahāyāna or not, is all founded upon this [love, compassion, cherishing others, and the like]. Therefore always consider what you should do to develop these. It is excellent if you do develop them; if you have not, do not let it remain that way. Always rely on a teacher who gives this kind of teaching. Always associate with friends who are training their minds in this way. Constantly look at the scriptures and their commentaries which describe these. Amass the collections as causes for these. Clear away the obstructions which prevent these. Moreover, if you train your mind in this way, you will definitely acquire all the seeds for developing these, so this work is not insignificant; take joy in it. The Great Elder [Atisha] said:[77]

> One who wishes to enter the door of the Mahāyāna teachings
> Should develop through effort over eons
> The spirit of enlightenment, which is like the sun that clears away darkness
> And the moon that quells the torment of heat. **[320]**

iii) **The measure of producing the spirit of enlightenment**[78]

Understand the measure of producing the spirit of enlightenment as previously explained.[79]

5

The Ritual for Adopting the Spirit of Enlightenment

iv) How to adopt the spirit of enlightenment through its ritual
- a′ Attaining that which you have not attained
  - 1′ The person before whom you adopt the spirit of enlightenment
  - 2′ The persons who adopt the spirit of enlightenment
  - 3′ How to take part in the ritual of adopting the spirit of enlightenment
    - a″ The preparation for the ritual
      - 1″ Performing the special practice of going for refuge
        - (a) After decorating the place of the ritual and setting up representations of the three jewels, arranging the offerings
        - (b) Supplications and going for refuge
        - (c) Stating the precepts of refuge
      - 2″ Amassing the collection of merit
      - 3″ Purifying your attitude
    - b″ Actual ritual
    - c″ The conclusion of the ritual

iv) **How to adopt the spirit of enlightenment through its ritual**

The Great Elder said:[80]

> Those who wish to train after they generate the spirit of enlightenment
> Cultivate with effort for a long time
> The four bases of Brahmā—love, and so on.[81]
> Thereby they clear away attachment and jealousy
> And produce the spirit of enlightenment through the correct ritual.

Once you have trained your mind in this way and have firm certainty about developing the spirit of enlightenment, take part in the ritual for adopting it.

The explanation of how to adopt the spirit of enlightenment through its ritual has three parts:

1. Attaining that which you have not attained
2. Maintaining and not weakening what you have attained (Chapter 6)
3. The method of repairing the spirit of enlightenment if you do weaken it (Chapter 6)

a′ **Attaining that which you have not attained**

Attaining the spirit of enlightenment which you have not attained has three parts:

1. The person before whom you adopt the spirit of enlightenment
2. The persons who adopt the spirit of enlightenment
3. How to take part in the ritual of adopting the spirit of enlightenment

1′ **The person before whom you adopt the spirit of enlightenment**

Aside from saying in his *Stages of the Activities of the Guru* (*Guru-kriyā-krama*)[82] that the person before whom you adopt the spirit of enlightenment should be "a master who is qualified," the Great Elder did not elucidate any further. Former teachers asserted that it was not sufficient for the person before whom you adopt the spirit of enlightenment just to have the aspirational spirit of enlightenment and to be maintaining its precepts, but he or she must have the vows of the engaged spirit of enlightenment. This accords with Jetāri, who said, "After you have come before a teacher who has the bodhisattva vows...."[83] The *Ten Teaching Sūtra* (*Daśa-dharmaka-sūtra*) mentions[84] *śrāvaka*s within the context of generating the spirit of enlightenment after others have exhorted some persons to adopt it. This is said in reference to persons being exhorted by others to adopt the spirit of enlightenment after *śrāvaka*s have encouraged them and created in them a sense of disenchantment with cyclic existence. The *śrāvaka*s do not perform the ritual.

2′ **The persons who adopt the spirit of enlightenment**

In general, as Jetāri said,[85] the persons who adopt the spirit of enlightenment are "sons or daughters of good lineage who are sound in body and mind." Thus all deities, *nāgas*, etc., who are mentally and physically fit for arousing the aspirational spirit of enlightenment are suitable persons for adopting the spirit of enlightenment. Nevertheless, as the *Commentary on the Difficult Points of the "Lamp for the Path to Enlightenment"* (*Bodhi-mārga-pradīpa-pañjikā*) says at this point,[86] "They [the persons who adopt the spirit of enlightenment] are disgusted with cyclic existence, mindful of death, and have great wisdom and compassion." So the persons who adopt the spirit of enlightenment have trained their minds in the stages of the path explained earlier[87] and have thereby gained some transformative experience with respect to the spirit of enlightenment. **[321]**

3′ How to take part in the ritual of adopting the spirit of enlightenment

The explanation of how to take part in the ritual of adopting the spirit of enlightenment has three parts:

1. The preparation for the ritual
2. Actual ritual
3. The conclusion of the ritual

a″ The preparation for the ritual

The preparation for the ritual has three sections:

1. Performing the special practice of going for refuge
2. Amassing the collection of merit
3. Purifying your attitude

1″ Performing the special practice of going for refuge

Performing the special practice of going for refuge has three parts:

1. After decorating the place of the ritual and setting up representations of the three jewels, arranging the offerings
2. Supplications and going for refuge
3. Stating the precepts of refuge

(a) After decorating the place of the ritual and setting up representations of the three jewels, arranging the offerings

Make neat and purify a place in an area devoid of sinful beings, and there spread about and anoint the area with the five cow products [urine, dung, butter, milk, and yogurt] as well as with marvelous scented waters of sandalwood, etc., and scatter about fragrant cut flowers. Arrange on high thrones, small thrones, or platforms representations of the three jewels that have been cast in metal or made with other materials, volumes of scripture and the like, and images of bodhisattvas. Prepare as well as you are able objects of offering such as canopies and the like, as well as flowers and so forth, and also make ready musical instruments, food, and ornaments, etc. Then, prepare a throne for the teacher and decorate it with flowers.

Former teachers say that you should first accumulate merit by venerating and serving the community and by giving offering cakes to the spirits. As it says in the *Sūtra of the Auspicious Eon* (*Bhadrakalpika-sūtra*),[88] if you have no offerings, you can accomplish this even through offering just the fringe of some cloth. But if you have the resources, you must seek offerings earnestly and without deceit and arrange them in such a way that your friends will be astounded. When some Tibetan teachers asked the Great Elder to confer the ritual for generating the spirit of enlightenment at Samye (bSam-yas) and Mang-yul, he said that they would not generate it because they had made inferior offerings. He further said that with respect to representations you definitely must have a consecrated image of Śākyamūni Buddha, the founder of the teaching; and with respect to volumes of scripture you should have a Perfection of Wisdom sūtra as big or bigger than the *Verse Summary of the Perfection of Wisdom in Eight Thousand Lines* (*Ratna-guṇa-saṃcaya-gāthā*). After you have done this, as he explains in his *Stages of the Activities of the Guru*,[89] you invite the assembly of noble beings, recite three times the "Clouds of Offerings Formula" (*Dharma-megha-dhāraṇī*),[90] and praise them. **[322]**

Next, the students wash, put on good clothes, and sit with hands joined respectfully. The guru encourages the students to wholeheartedly generate clear faith in the good qualities of the field for accumulating the collections of merit and sublime wisdom, has them imagine that they are seated in front of each of the buddhas and bodhisattvas, and then enjoins them to slowly perform the seven branches of worship.[91]

Most earlier Tibetan scholars[92] said that when you adopt the spirit of enlightenment according to the lineage transmitted through Nāgārjuna and Śāntideva, you practice the seven branches of worship, and that when you adopt it according to the lineage from Maitreya and Asaṅga, you practice only two—obeisance and offerings. What is more, in the latter case they say, "If you were to practice the confession of sins, you would need to feel regret, and thus you would be unhappy; the spirit of enlightenment must be generated in one whose mind has joy and delight."

This position is incorrect. With respect to the rituals of the spirit of enlightenment and the vows, the Great Elder stated,[93] "obeisance, offering ritual, and so forth," including the other five branches of worship with the phrase "and so forth." He clearly says in his *Stages of the Activities of the Guru*[94] that you should practice the seven branches before you generate the spirit of enlightenment. Further, if you do accept the reasoning [regarding regret] in the position given above, then you must conclude that the spirit of enlightenment is not generated in the system of Nāgārjuna and Śāntideva.

(b) **Supplications and going for refuge**

Since it is said[95] that you should have the idea that your guru is the Teacher [Buddha], bow down to your guru while believing that he or she is the Buddha, and then offer a maṇḍala and other material offerings. With your right knee bent to the ground, join your hands respectfully and make a supplication for the spirit of enlightenment, reciting the following three times:[96]

> Just as the former perfect buddhas, who are *tathāgatas* and arhats, and the great bodhisattvas on the high levels initially generated the spirit of unexcelled, perfect enlightenment, please, O master, help me, (say your name at this point), to generate the spirit of unexcelled, perfect enlightenment.

Next, perform a practice of going for refuge that is specific to this context. The objects of this refuge are the *bhagavan* buddhas, the teaching that is the truth of the path which emphasizes the Mahāyāna cessations; and the community of noble bodhisattvas, who are irreversible. [**323**] In general think about them as follows: "From now until I reach the heart of enlightenment, and for the sake of protecting all beings, please, buddhas, be my teachers of refuge; please, teaching, be my actual refuge; and please, community, be the ones who assist me to attain refuge." Then make a special thought: Since the *Lamp for the Path to Enlightenment* (*Bodhi-patha-pradīpa*) says,[97] "With an irreversible thought...," make a strong aspiration, "I will never turn away from such a way of thinking about refuge," and go for refuge with a posture like that explained above [one knee on the ground and hands joined]. Recite the following three times:[98]

> "O master, please listen to me. I, (say your name at this point), from now until I reach the heart of enlightenment go for refuge to the *bhagavan* buddhas, supreme among beings. O master, please listen to me. I, (say your name at this point), from now until I reach the heart of enlightenment, go for refuge to the best of teachings, the teachings of peace free from attachment. O master, please listen to me. I, (say your name at this point), from now until I reach the heart of enlightenment, go for refuge to the best of assemblies, the members of the community of noble bodhisattvas, who are irreversible.

Even though there is a request for consideration at each refuge in each of the three jewels and an unusual wording for going for refuge in the teaching, I have written the ritual exactly as Atisha composed it.

(c) **Stating the precepts of refuge**

The master should give here the precepts already explained[99] in the context of teachings for the person of small capacity.

2" **Amassing the collection of merit**

With respect to the ritual for generating the spirit of enlightenment Atisha explains[100] that at this point also you make obeisance, offering, and so forth. **[324]** Follow the *Commentary on the Difficult Points of the "Lamp for the Path to Enlightenment"* where it says that you should perform the seven branches of worship, bringing to mind all the buddhas, bodhisattvas, and your former and present teachers. Understand that making offerings to the gurus should be done at the time you make the earlier offerings as well.[101] Practice the seven branches of worship by following either the text of the *Prayer of Samantabhadra* (*Samantabhadra-caryā-praṇidhāna*) or *Engaging in the Bodhisattva Deeds*.[102]

3" **Purifying your attitude**

Since in his *Lamp for the Path to Enlightenment* Atisha says[103] that you should first feel love in your heart and then generate the spirit of enlightenment upon seeing suffering living beings, vividly bring to mind the objects and the subjective aspects for love and compassion as explained previously.[104]

b" **Actual ritual**

In front of the master you should either kneel with your right knee on the ground or squat down on the balls of your feet and, after you join your hands respectfully, generate the spirit of enlightenment. In reference to this the *Lamp for the Path to Enlightenment* says:[105]

> Develop the spirit of enlightenment
> That is an irreversible commitment.

And the *Ritual Procedures for the Spirit of Enlightenment and the Bodhisattva Vows* (*Cittotpāda-saṃvara-vidhi-krama*) says,[106] "...until I reach the heart of enlightenment." Therefore, it is not that you generate the spirit of enlightenment thinking only, "I will attain buddhahood for others' sake." Rather, you focus on such a thought and make the commitment, "I will not part from this determination to attain buddhahood for the sake of all beings until I reach enlightenment." So generate the attitude with these two aspects in dependence on the ritual.

Do not generate this attitude in this way if you are incapable of learning the precepts of the aspirational spirit of enlightenment. If one were to generate through the ritual just the thought "I will become a buddha for the sake of all living beings," then it would be proper to give the ritual to anyone, whether capable or incapable of learning the precepts of the aspirational spirit of enlightenment. In the case of the aspirational spirit, these two ways of generating the spirit—for those capable of learning the precepts and with the commitment, and for those incapable of learning the precepts and without the commitment—are suitable, but when it comes to adopting the engaged spirit of enlightenment through the ritual, it is completely wrong to give it to those fully incapable of learning the precepts. Therefore, some people[107] have a great misunderstanding when they assert the distinction that in the lineage of Nāgārjuna it is proper to give the bodhisattva vows in many rituals whereas in the lineage of Asaṅga it is improper to do so. Furthermore, some say that when beginners are practicing, they should repeatedly adopt the engaged spirit of enlightenment through its ritual. However, since these beginners do not know the precepts in general and the fundamental transgressions in particular, they cannot demonstrate the particulars of what should then be done, putting them in a very harmful situation. **[325]**

Kamalaśīla's first *Stages of Meditation*, citing the *Advice to the King Sūtra* (*Rājāvavādaka-sūtra*), says that if you cannot learn the precepts of generosity, etc., you achieve much merit in even a simple generation of the spirit of enlightenment, and then says:[108]

> Even those who cannot completely learn the perfections should generate the spirit of enlightenment in order to be imbued with method, because there is a great result.

So it is very clear that while it is correct to give the ritual for generating the spirit of enlightenment to those who cannot learn the precepts of generosity, etc., it is incorrect to give them the bodhisattva vows.

The ritual for adopting the spirit of enlightenment is as follows. Recite the following three times:[109]

> All buddhas and bodhisattvas who reside in the ten directions, please listen to me. O master, please listen to me. By means of my virtuous roots in the nature of generosity, ethics, or meditation—which I, (say your name at this point), in this and all other lives, cultivated, enjoined others to cultivate, or rejoiced in the cultivation of—I, (say your name), will generate the spirit of great, unexcelled, perfect enlightenment from now until I reach the heart of enlightenment, just as the earlier perfect buddhas, who are arhats and *tathāgata*s, and the great bodhisattvas who reside on the high levels generated the spirit of unexcelled, perfect enlightenment. I will liberate all living beings who are not liberated. I will free all living beings who are not freed. I will relieve those without relief. **[326]** I will cause to reach nirvāṇa those who have not reached it.

Even though it is not made clear that you must repeat this after the master in both this part and the refuge part of the ritual, you must do so.

These instructions are the procedure to be followed when a master is present. With respect to how to proceed without a master, the Great Elder's *Ritual Procedures for the Spirit of Enlightenment and the Bodhisattva Vows* says:[110]

> Although there is no master, there is a ritual for developing the spirit of enlightenment oneself as follows. Imagining the Tathāgata Śākyamuni and all the *tathāgata*s of the ten directions, make obeisance and the ritual offerings, etc., and then go through the process of going for refuge and so forth as before, eliminating the word "master" and the supplication to the master.

c" The conclusion of the ritual

The master tells the student the precepts of the aspirational spirit of enlightenment.

6

MAINTAINING THE SPIRIT OF ENLIGHTENMENT

b′ Maintaining and not weakening what you have attained
- 1′ The training in the precepts that cause you not to weaken your spirit of enlightenment in this lifetime
  - a″ The training in the precept to recall the benefits of the spirit of enlightenment in order to increase the strength of your enthusiasm for it
  - b″ The training in the precept to generate the spirit of enlightenment six times each day in order to increase the actual spirit of enlightenment
    - 1″ Not giving up your development of the aspirational spirit of enlightenment
    - 2″ The training to increase the aspirational spirit of enlightenment
  - c″ The training in the precept not to mentally abandon the living beings for whose sake you develop the spirit of enlightenment
  - d″ The training in the precept to accumulate the collections of merit and sublime wisdom
- 2′ The training in the precepts that cause you to not separate from your spirit of enlightenment in future lifetimes as well
  - a″ The training in the precept to eliminate the four dark practices which weaken the spirit of enlightenment
  - b″ The training in the precept to adopt the four light practices which keep the spirit of enlightenment from weakening

c′ The method of repairing the spirit of enlightenment if you do weaken it

b′ Maintaining and not weakening what you have attained

You need to know the precepts, so I will explain them. This has two parts:

1. The training in the precepts that cause you not to weaken your spirit of enlightenment in this lifetime
2. The training in the precepts that cause you to not separate from your spirit of enlightenment in future lifetimes as well

1′ The training in the precepts that cause you not to weaken your spirit of enlightenment in this lifetime

The training in the precepts that cause you not to weaken your spirit of enlightenment in this lifetime has four parts:

1. The training in the precept to recall the benefits of the spirit of enlightenment in order to increase the strength of your enthusiasm for it
2. The training in the precept to generate the spirit of enlightenment six times each day in order to increase the actual spirit of enlightenment
3. The training in the precept not to mentally abandon the living beings for whose sake you develop the spirit of enlightenment
4. The training in the precept to accumulate the collections of merit and sublime wisdom

a″ The training in the precept to recall the benefits of the spirit of enlightenment in order to increase the strength of your enthusiasm for it

Think about the benefits of the spirit of enlightenment, after you have either researched them in the sūtras or listened to them from your guru. They are explained in detail in the *Array of Stalks Sūtra,* so look there.[111] As stated above[112] this text says, "the spirit of enlightenment is like the seed of all the buddha qualities," and it also states, "the spirit of enlightenment is like a summary because it includes all the bodhisattva deeds and aspirational prayers." [327] It is a "summary" in the sense that everything is compiled into a brief indication although there are endless, detailed explanations of the parts. Like a summation of these parts, it is said to be a synopsis which brings together the key points of all the bodhisattva paths.

The benefits mentioned in the *Bodhisattva Levels*[113] are those of the aspirational spirit of enlightenment. That text states two benefits for the first stable generation of the spirit of enlightenment: becoming a pure field for accumulating merit and being fully endowed with protective merit.

The first benefit, becoming a pure field for accumulating merit, is as follows. As *Engaging in the Bodhisattva Deeds* states, "And are revered both in the worlds of humans and deities,"[114] you become an object of worship for all living beings immediately after you have developed the spirit of enlightenment. In accordance with the statement that immediately after developing the spirit of enlightenment you surpass all the great arhats in terms of your lineage, you become superior and highest. Even when you perform a small meritorious action it gives forth limitless effects, so you are a field for accumulating merit. "As all the world relies on you, you are like the earth." Thus, you are like a father to all beings.

The second benefit, being fully endowed with protective merit, is as follows. As you are always protected by guardians that are twice as numerous as those of a universal monarch, you cannot be harmed by *yakṣa*s or local spirits even when you are sleeping, drunk, or careless. Secret mantras and knowledge mantras that can cure epidemics, injuries, and infections but are not effective in the hands of living beings become effective when someone with a stable generation of the spirit of enlightenment uses them. Why mention the mantras that *do* work when used by living beings? The *Bodhisattva Levels* teaches that when your spirit of enlightenment is stable, you also easily accomplish the collections of actions—pacifying and so forth.[115] So if you have this you also quickly accomplish ordinary spiritual attainments. Wherever you are staying, there will arise no fear, no causes of fear, no famine, and no harm from non-humans, and you will quell those that have already happened. **[328]** Also, after death you will have little trouble, and you will be naturally healthy in your next life; even if some harm does arise, it will not last long or be severe. When you engage in the welfare of living beings—giving teachings, etc.—your body will not feel tired, you will not be forgetful, nor will your mind degenerate.

If you are one who abides in the bodhisattva lineage, you naturally have few dysfunctional tendencies; once you have developed the spirit of enlightenment, the dysfunctional tendencies of your mind and body are extremely slight. You are patient and gentle, so that if someone harms you, you bear it and do no harm in return. If you see others hurting each other, you are very displeased. You seldom give rise to anger, jealousy, deceitfulness, concealment, and the like; if these do arise, they are not intense, do not last long, and quickly disappear.

It is difficult for you to be reborn in miserable realms; even if you are reborn there, you will quickly get free. Even while there, your suffering will be slight and because of it you will be very disenchanted with cyclic existence and generate compassion for the beings there.

If the merit of the spirit of enlightenment were to take form, it would not even fit into the sky. Nor does the merit of making material offerings to the Buddha equal even a mere portion of it. The *Questions of the Householder Vīradatta Sūtra* (*Vīradatta-gṛha-pati-paripṛcchā-sūtra*) states:[116]

If whatever merit there is
In the spirit of enlightenment had form
It would fill the entire vault of the sky
And then exceed it.

Were someone to fill the buddha-realms
With jewels as numerous as
The grains of sand of the Ganges
And offer this to the Protector of the World,

Far superior is the merit
In the offering of one who, joining his or her hands,
Reverently generates the spirit of enlightenment.
There is no limit to the merit in this.

While the Great Elder was circumambulating the *vajra* seat in Bodh Gayā,[117] he thought, "How can I obtain full enlightenment quickly?" **[329]** Thereupon, he had a vision wherein the smaller statues stood up and asked the larger statues, "What should those who wish to quickly attain buddhahood train in?" The larger ones replied, "They should train in the spirit of enlightenment." Also in the sky above the main temple a young woman asked this question to an older woman, and Atisha heard the same answer as before. Therefore, it is said, he became more certain about the spirit of enlightenment.

Accordingly, understand that the spirit of enlightenment comprises the key points of all the Mahāyāna's personal instructions, is a great treasure of all the spiritual attainments, is the feature that distinguishes the Mahāyāna from the Hīnayāna, and is the excellent basis that spurs you to undertake the greatly effective bodhisattva deeds. Becoming even more fervent about cultivating it, act like a thirsty person hearing talk of water. For, when the conquerors and their children used their marvelous wisdom to examine the paths in great detail for many eons, they saw just this to be the excellent method of becoming a buddha. As *Engaging in the Bodhisattva Deeds* states:[118]

> Reflecting for many eons, the Master of the Sages
> Saw this alone to be beneficial.

b″ The training in the precept to generate the spirit of enlightenment six times each day in order to increase the actual spirit of enlightenment

The training in the precept to generate the spirit of enlightenment six times each day has two parts:

1. Not giving up your development of the aspirational spirit
2. The training to increase the aspirational spirit of enlightenment

1″ Not giving up your development of the aspirational spirit of enlightenment

You have taken as your witness the buddhas, bodhisattvas, and teachers and, in their presence, committed yourself to liberate all beings who are not liberated, and so forth. If you then see that living beings are so numerous and their behavior is mean, or that the time wherein you must strive for many eons is long, or that you must train in the two collections that are limitless and difficult to do, and you take this as a reason to become discouraged and to abandon your responsibility to develop the spirit of enlightenment, it is a sin greater than a cardinal transgression of the vows of individual liberation. **[330]** The *Verse Summary of the Perfection of Wisdom in Eight Thousand Lines* states:[119]

> Though you practice the ten virtuous actions for ten million eons,
> If you then generate the wish to become a *pratyekabuddha* arhat,
> You damage and weaken your ethical discipline as a bodhisattva.
> This breach of the spirit of enlightenment is far more serious than a cardinal transgression.

Thus it says that such a bodhisattva's ethical discipline is faulty. Restraint from *śrāvaka* and *pratyekabuddha* considerations is the bodhisattvas' highest ethical discipline, so were bodhisattvas to weaken this restraint, they would destroy their ethical discipline. For, if bodhisattvas do not cast aside such restraint, then even were they to indulge in sensory pleasures, they would not destroy the attitude of restraint that is unique to the bodhisattva. Again, the *Verse Summary of the Perfection of Wisdom in Eight Thousand Lines* states:[120]

> Though bodhisattvas enjoy the five sensory objects,
> If they take refuge in the Buddha, the teaching, and the community of noble beings,
> And fix their minds on omniscience, thinking, "I will attain buddhahood,"
> Understand that these adepts keep the perfection of ethical discipline.

If they give up their promised intention, they must wander for a long time in miserable rebirths. *Engaging in the Bodhisattva Deeds* says:[121]

> It is said that once people decide
> To give a small amount of a simple thing
> And then do not give it,
> They cause themselves rebirth as a hungry ghost.
>
> So how could you be reborn in a happy realm
> If you deceive all living beings
> After you have sincerely invited them
> To unsurpassed bliss?

Therefore it also says:

> Like a blind person finding a jewel
> In a heap of garbage,
> By chance the spirit of enlightenment
> Has arisen in me.

Think, "How very wonderful that I have attained something like this," and never give it up. Devoting particular attention to this, vow over and over not to give it up for even an instant.

2" The training to increase the aspirational spirit of enlightenment

It is not enough merely not to give up the aspirational spirit of enlightenment; increase it with great effort three times during the day and three times at night. If you can practice the aforementioned extensive ritual, do so. **[331]** If not, visualize the field for accumulating merit and, after you make offerings, refine your love, compassion, and so forth. Then adopt the spirit of enlightenment six times, reciting the following ritual verse three times on each occasion:[122]

I go for refuge until enlightenment
To the Buddha, the teaching and the community;
By the merit of practicing the six perfections
May I achieve buddhahood in order to help living beings.

c″ The training in the precept not to mentally abandon the living beings for whose sake you develop the spirit of enlightenment

Although this precept is not found in the pertinent sections of the *Lamp for the Path to Enlightenment* or *Ritual Procedures for the Spirit of Enlightenment and the Bodhisattva Vows*, in his *Commentary on the Difficult Points of the "Lamp for the Path to Enlightenment,"* Atisha says:[123]

> By caring for and not abandoning living beings you maintain the spirit of enlightenment for the sake of its object, its benefits, the ritual for generating it, its general increase, and not forgetting it.

It is listed in this context and does not contradict the intended meaning of the root text so train in this also.

The measure of mentally abandoning living beings is when you produce the thought, "Now I will never work for this person's welfare," based upon some conditions such as unacceptable actions, etc.

d″ The training in the precept to accumulate the collections of merit and sublime wisdom

After you have adopted the aspirational spirit of enlightenment through its ritual, strive daily to accumulate the collections—making offerings to the three jewels, etc.—in order to increase the spirit of enlightenment. Although I have seen no authoritative source for this being a precept other than former teachers' statements, it is nevertheless very beneficial.

2′ The training in the precepts that cause you to not separate from your spirit of enlightenment in future lifetimes as well

The training in the precepts that cause you to not separate from your spirit of enlightenment in future lifetimes as well has two sections:

1. The training in the precept to eliminate the four dark practices which weaken the spirit of enlightenment
2. The training in the precept to adopt the four light practices which keep the spirit of enlightenment from weakening

a″ The training in the precept to eliminate the four dark practices which weaken the spirit of enlightenment

In the *Kāśyapa Chapter* (*Kāśyapa-parivarta*) of the *Ratna-kūṭa Collection*[124] there are statements that list the four practices with respect to not actualizing or forgetting the spirit of enlightenment in future lifetimes and that list the four practices with respect to actualizing and not forgetting the spirit of enlightenment, not casting it aside until you reach enlightenment. **[332]** They are presented as precepts of the aspirational spirit of enlightenment.

The four dark practices are as follows.

1. *Deceiving abbots, masters, gurus, and those worthy of offerings.* Understand this in terms of two approaches: the objects of your action and what you do to these objects. According to the explanation in Sthiramati's *Commentary on the Kāśyapa Chapter* (*Kāśyapa-parivarta-ṭikā*),[125] the objects are abbots and masters (this is obvious), gurus (those who want to help), and those worthy of offerings (though not included in the rank of the previous two groups, they have good qualities). What might you do to these objects that would be a dark practice? It is a dark practice if you consciously deceive any of them. With respect to how you deceive them, the *Commentary on the Kāśyapa Chapter* says that when they compassionately explain transgressions, and you then confuse them about yourself with lies, it is "dark." It says that whenever you try to mislead your gurus about yourself with an intention to deceive, it is "dark." However, it has to be misleading with lies—the deception which is not lying will be dealt with below. This is because its remedy is the first of the four light practices, and the *Compendium of Trainings*[126] says that eliminating the dark practices is a light practice. Moreover, it is said that incorrigible students deceive their gurus when they say one thing to the guru and secretly say something very different to others, who then say, "Careful, this will come to the teacher's ears."

2. *Making others feel regret about something that is not regrettable.* This is understood through the same two approaches mentioned previously. The object is persons cultivating virtue without regret. What do you do to them? You intentionally make them regret something they should not regret. The *Commentary on the Kāśyapa Chapter* explains that deceitfully misleading fellow practitioners with respect to a training's wording when they are observing the training correctly is "dark."

For these first two dark practices, it is said to make no difference whether or not you are able to deceive or whether or not you are able to cause regret. The *Commentary on the Kāśyapa Chapter* concurs in this regard. The *Commentary*, however, takes the latter to be a case of misleading as well. [333]

3. *Speaking disparagingly, etc., to beings who have correctly entered the Mahāyāna.* Some say that the object is those who have the spirit of enlightenment, having adopted it through its ritual. Others say it is equally those who have previously developed the spirit of enlightenment and do not currently have it. This latter assertion contradicts the sūtras and is wrong. The *Commentary* says simply "a bodhisattva" with no further clarification. Even though in other scriptural contexts there are many statements that those with the bodhisattva vows who are learning the trainings are the ones who have correctly entered the Mahāyāna, I think that here the object has to be understood as any bodhisattva, starting with those who have generated the aspirational spirit of enlightenment.

What is done to these bodhisattvas is to speak disparagingly, with blame, with libel, and so forth. The assertion that what is said has to be motivated by hatred accords with the *Commentary*. But even though the *Commentary* says that the bodhisattvas to whom it is spoken are diligently seeking the teachings, and the words are spoken in order to stop their belief in or wish to practice the Mahāyāna, it seems to be enough if they understand the meaning of what is said. The *Commentary* explains that something disparaging is, for example, saying that he or she "has poor character," wherein you do not mention any specific fault; blame is, for example, saying "He is not celibate," wherein you are specific; and a libel is, for example, saying "In this or that way he engaged in sex," making it more specific. The *Commentary* attaches the term "criticism" to these three.

I have already discussed briefly[127] the danger of this great offense arising in us. Indeed, if bodhisattvas have even a despising thought toward other bodhisattvas, they have to stay in hell for as many eons as the moments of that thought's duration. And the *Sūtra on the Magic of Final Peace* (*Praśānta-viniścaya-prātihārya-sūtra*) says that no other action apart from slandering another bodhisattva can make a bodhisattva fall into the miserable realms. [334] The *Verse Summary of the Perfection of Wisdom in Eight Thousand Lines* says:[128]

> If bodhisattvas who have not received a prediction of their
> enlightenment

> Have an angry dispute with bodhisattvas who have received a prediction,
> They must put on the armor of practice again
> For as many eons as the moments of their coarse, faulty attitude.

Thus it says that they must travel along the path, starting over again, for eons commensurate with their angry attitude; they become very far distant from their enlightenment. For this reason stop your anger on all occasions, and if it arises, immediately confess it and strive to restrain yourself. That same text states:[129]

> Develop mindfulness, thinking, "This state of mind is not constructive,"
> Confess each instance, and restrain yourself from doing it again.
> Do not rejoice in it; train in the teaching of the Buddha.

If you give hatred a chance, the love and compassion you have developed will weaken and it will be hard to develop any new love and compassion, even if you practice for a long time. Thus, you cut the root of the spirit of enlightenment. If you stop hatred—the unfavorable condition for love and compassion—and cultivate love and compassion according to the previous explanation,[130] they then progressively increase and eventually become limitless. Dharmakīrti's *Commentary on the "Compendium of Valid Cognition" (Pramāṇa-vārttika)* states:[131]

> If unharmed by that with which it is incompatible,
> Love naturally comes into the mind.

And also:

> As you familiarize yourself with
> The attitudes of compassion and the like,
> Which increase from the seeds of prior, similar experiences,
> How could these attitudes remain the same?

4. *In an absence of sincerity, using deceit and misrepresentation to get the service of others.* The object is any living being other than yourself. What is done to this being? You act with deceit and misrepresentation. Sincerity is explained in the *Commentary on the Kāśyapa Chapter*[132] to be your ordinary attitude. Deceit and misrepresentation are cheating while measuring with a scale and so forth. As Gyal-wa-yen-jung (rGyal-ba-ye-'byung) says, it is, for instance, like sending somebody to Dö-lung (sTod-lungs) in order to get them to go to Rag-ma [a place far past Dö-lung], and later asserting that they

might as well go on to Rag-ma. [335] Asaṅga's *Compendium of Knowledge* (*Abhidharma-samuccaya*)[133] says that both deceit and misrepresentation arise because of attachment to goods and services and are similarly included in the category of either attachment or ignorance. He says that deceit is to pretend that you have a good quality that you do not have, and misrepresentation is hiding your fault. Hiding means using some method to conceal a fault.

b″ **The training in the precept to adopt the four light practices which keep the spirit of enlightenment from weakening**

1. *Forsaking consciously lying to any living being whatsoever even in jest or even for the sake of your life.*[134] The object of the first of the four light practices is any living being. What you do is forsake consciously lying even for the sake of your life or even in jest. In this way, you do not deceive special objects of your actions—your abbot, master, etc.—with lies.

2. *Not deceiving but remaining sincere to all living beings.* The object of the second of the four light practices is all living beings. What you do is not deceive them but maintain your sincerity; that is, remain honest. This is the remedy for the fourth dark practice.

3. *Developing the idea that all bodhisattvas are the Teacher.* The object of the third light practice is all bodhisattvas. What you do is develop the idea that they are similar to the Teacher, and voice in the four directions praise of their character. We cultivate some small likeness of virtue, but find that it has no signs of increasing and has many signs of decreasing; this is simply the outcome of our hating, despising, or reviling bodhisattvas and friends. Therefore, it is said that if you are capable of eliminating the first two faults as well as the reviling of bodhisattvas, all the harm related to persons mentioned in the *Compendium of Trainings* will be averted. This is based on the consideration that you do not know who is a bodhisattva, so, as stated in the *Kāśyapa Chapter*,[135] you should train in the pure perception of all living beings that comes from developing the idea that all beings are the Teacher. You should praise bodhisattvas when there are listeners on hand, but you incur no fault if you do not go out into the four directions praising them. This is the remedy for the third dark practice.

4. *Causing the living beings that you are helping to mature to not want the modest vehicle but to adhere to perfect enlightenment.* The object of the fourth light practice is the living beings that you are helping to mature. What you do to them is cause them to not want the modest

vehicle [Hīnayāna] but to adhere to perfect enlightenment. [**336**] Moreover, from your perspective it is necessary for them to connect to the Mahāyāna path, but if your disciples do not develop the intention for it, you incur no fault, because you were simply unable to accomplish it. This light practice eliminates the second dark practice [making others feel regret about something that is not regrettable], because if you want from the depths of your heart for others to set forth toward the culmination of all happiness, you will not do something that brings about unhappiness in others so as to make them feel some regret about their virtuous activity. The *Sūtra Requested by a Lion* (*Siṃha-paripṛcchā-sūtra*) also says:[136]

> If you cultivate the spirit of enlightenment in all lives
> And do not abandon it even in dreams,
> What is the point of mentioning
> Not abandoning it when you are not sleeping?
>
> The Buddha said: "Cause to enter into enlightenment
> The beings in villages and cities
> Or in any other place they may dwell.
> Then you will not relinquish the spirit of enlightenment."

Furthermore, the *Array of Qualities in Mañjuśrī's Buddha-realm* says that if you have these four—destruction of pride, elimination of jealousy, elimination of stinginess, and joy when you see the prosperity of others—you do not relinquish your aspirational prayer [aspirational spirit of enlightenment]. Once you cultivate the spirit of enlightenment, you will not be separated from this precious attitude even in future lives. This is stated clearly in the *Cloud of Jewels Sūtra (Ratna-megha-sūtra)* of the *Ratna-kūṭa Collection:*[137]

> If you train in the spirit of enlightenment in all activities and if you preface any cultivation of virtue with the spirit of enlightenment...

and in the *King of Concentrations Sūtra:*

> As much as people frequently examine
> So much will their minds engage
> Whatever they are thinking over.

and in other sūtras as well.

c′ The method of repairing the spirit of enlightenment if you do weaken it

Many scholars state the following view: "You relinquish the aspirational spirit of enlightenment if a certain period passes and there are the four dark practices, together with a fifth—mentally abandoning living beings—or a sixth, casting aside the spirit of enlightenment by thinking, 'I cannot accomplish buddhahood.' However, if within a period of time you regret these six, they weaken the aspirational spirit of enlightenment but do not cause you to abandon it. And if you fail to adopt the spirit of enlightenment six times each day and allow your training in the two collections to degenerate, it only weakens the spirit of enlightenment. If a cause of relinquishing it occurs, you must repeat the ritual for adopting the aspirational spirit of enlightenment, but for a mere weakening, you do not have to repeat it; making a confession suffices." **[337]**

With respect to this, if you should think, "I cannot accomplish buddhahood," you immediately abandon the spirit of enlightenment; it is never necessary to rely on the passage of a certain period of time, so such an assertion is absolutely incorrect. The four dark practices are not the cause of relinquishing the spirit of enlightenment in this life, but are causes for not manifesting the spirit of enlightenment in future lives, so we should stop them in this life. The *Lamp for the Path to Enlightenment* says:[138]

> In order to remember the spirit of enlightenment even in future lives,
> Maintain the trainings that have been explained.

The "that have been explained" means as explained in the *Kāśyapa Chapter*. This is what the sūtra means because it clearly says this in the context of the four light practices:[139]

> Kāśyapa, the bodhisattvas who possess the four practices will manifest the spirit of enlightenment in all lives immediately after being born and will not cast it aside or forget it until they reach the heart of enlightenment.

So, although it is not stated clearly in the context of the four dark practices whether they affect this life or future lives, understand that it is the latter. (Still, if you resort to the dark practices in this life, your spirit of enlightenment will weaken.) Otherwise, if bodhisattvas who are keeping their vows just lie a bit as a joke, deceive others and misrepresent themselves to them in a trifling way, say something slightly bad about bodhisattvas out of anger, or just engender slight regret in others with respect to their cultivation of a virtuous root, and if they pass a period of time without feeling regret, then they would lose their bodhisattva vows. They would lose them because they would have lost the aspirational spirit of enlightenment, and, according to both the *Bodhisattva Levels* and the *Compendium of Trainings,*[140] when you lose the aspirational spirit you lose the vows as well. If you make the assertion that they do lose their vows, then you have to posit these dark practices as fundamental transgressions, yet this is not said anywhere and is incorrect. [**338**] Furthermore, reckoning a period of time is based upon the period explained in the *Questions of Upāli Sūtra* (*Upāli-paripṛcchā-sūtra*), but since I have proven at length in my *Basic Path to Awakening* (*Byang chub gzhug lam*)[141]—an explanation of the chapter on ethical discipline of the *Bodhisattva Levels*—that this is not the meaning of the sūtra, I will not explain it again here.

To mentally abandon living beings means that when considering them in general you think, "I am not able to work for the welfare of this many beings." When you abandon them with this thought, it is clear that you abandon the aspirational spirit of enlightenment. And when considering a particular living being, if you have the thought, "I will never work for the welfare of this one," then, like destroying a whole collection by destroying just a piece of it, you destroy the spirit of enlightenment, which is developed for the sake of *all* beings. Were it otherwise, you could cast aside many beings—a second, third, fourth, and so forth, develop the spirit of enlightenment for the sake of the remaining beings, and would necessarily have thereby generated a completely perfect spirit of enlightenment. But this is not the case.

The *Commentary on the Difficult Points of the "Lamp for the Path to Enlightenment"* says[142] of these precepts of the spirit of enlightenment that there are the different systems of King Indrabhūti, Nāgārjuna, Asaṅga, Āryaśūra, Śāntideva, Candragomin, Śāntarakṣita, etc. It says that some assert that the precepts of the spirit of enlightenment are "all the precepts for both the initial generation of the spirit of enlightenment and for engaging in the bodhisattva deeds." Others, it says, assert that "you have to observe every precept stated in the sūtras," while still others say that they are "all precepts for a person on the path of accumulation." Some do not assert that they are "a specific training like this or that," and yet others state that "in addition to the precepts of refuge you observe the eight practices of not abandoning the intention to take up the four light practices and forgetting the intention that leads to the four dark practices." The *Commentary* explains, "My guru said that since the systems of these masters are each based on sūtra, you should uphold whatever system your guru gives you.'" It claims that all of these are the meaning of the sūtras. **[339]**

In general, the great teachers of the lineage descended from Geshe Drom-dön-ba do not recognize this *Commentary on the Difficult Points of the "Lamp for the Path to Enlightenment"* to be a commentary by the Great Elder, but the lineages from Nag-tso (Nag-tsho) accept this as the Great Elder's composition and also accept it as a teaching hidden by Nag-tso. Still, it was well known to earlier scholars that Atisha composed a short commentary while in Burang (Pu-rangs). It is said that when he thereafter arrived in Samye, a translator asked him if he could add to it, and the translator subsequently expanded it. Therefore the Great Elder did compose a short commentary. This is supplemented by a number of explanations which are based on various gurus' sayings. There are some obvious mistakes, and there are also many good explanations of the meaning of the scriptures. So I have cited it in this *Stages of the Path* (*Lam rim*) and elsewhere in explanation of the points on which it is not mistaken.

The aforementioned precepts of this *Commentary on the Difficult Points of the "Lamp for the Path to Enlightenment"* are not reliable. The statement that the precepts of the spirit of enlightenment are "all the precepts for both the initial generation of the spirit of enlightenment and for engaging in the bodhisattva deeds" is wrong, because if you take the precepts of the "generation of the spirit of enlightenment" to be the precepts for the engaged spirit of enlightenment, it cannot possibly be sufficient for them to be just avoiding the four dark practices and taking up the four light practices in addition to the precepts of refuge. If you take "generation of the spirit of enlightenment" to be only referring to the aspirational spirit of enlightenment, then when it comes to the precepts of the aspirational spirit, it is not necessary to train in every precept stated in the sūtras, nor in the precepts for everyone up to and including those who are engaged in the bodhisattva deeds. Otherwise, the precepts of the aspirational spirit of enlightenment would be the same as the precepts that come with the bodhisattva vows.

All the aforementioned precepts (except for the two precepts on the light and dark practices, which follow the *Kāśyapa Chapter*) follow the *Lamp for the Path to Enlightenment* and the *Ritual Procedures for the Spirit of Enlightenment and the Bodhisattva Vows*. There is a statement that says to train in the precepts in the *Seven Dharmas Sūtra* (*Chos bdun po'i mdo*), but since it says, "One who wants to quickly attain the superknowledges should observe the precepts," these precepts are not specific to the spirit of enlightenment, so I have not written about them here.

Thus, my own position is that, with the exception of the precepts not to relinquish the aspirational spirit of enlightenment and not to mentally abandon living beings, breaking the precepts does not constitute a transgression relative to the spirit of enlightenment until you receive the bodhisattva vows. Nevertheless, if you break the precepts, you break the precept that comes with your commitment to virtue in the interim before you take the bodhisattva vows; you therefore commit a misdeed, and you should make a confession with the four powers.[143] After you receive the bodhisattva vows, breaking these precepts is a transgression that now breaks the precepts which come with these vows. **[340]** Since it is a transgression, it is sufficient that you repair it in the manner in which you have been instructed, a procedure that is included in the precepts for the engaged spirit of enlightenment, and not anywhere else. However, generating the spirit of enlightenment six times a day is the one precept specific to the aspirational spirit of enlightenment.

7

An Introduction to the Six Perfections

c) How to learn the bodhisattva deeds after developing the spirit of enlightenment
i) The reason why you must learn the trainings after developing the spirit of enlightenment
ii) Demonstrating that you will not become a buddha by learning either method or wisdom separately

c) How to learn the bodhisattva deeds after developing the spirit of enlightenment

How to learn the bodhisattva deeds after developing the spirit of enlightenment has three parts:

1. The reason why you must learn the trainings after developing the spirit of enlightenment
2. Demonstrating that you will not become a buddha by learning either method or wisdom separately
3. Explanation of the process of learning the precepts (Chapters 8 and on)

i) The reason why you must learn the trainings after developing the spirit of enlightenment

It is indeed the case that great benefit comes from mere development of the aspirational spirit of enlightenment without learning the trainings of generosity and so forth. Consider in this regard the passage from the *Life of Maitreya* cited earlier.[144] However, you still have to practice the bodhisattva trainings. If you do not emphasize this practice, you will never become a buddha. So learn the bodhisattva deeds. Thus the *Foremost of Gayā* says:[145]

> Enlightenment is for great bodhisattvas who take practice to heart, but not for those who take a wrong practice to heart.

And the *King of Concentrations Sūtra* also says:[146]

> Therefore take practice to heart. Why? O Prince, because when you take practice to heart, perfect enlightenment is not hard to attain.

"Practice" means the method of achieving buddhahood, i.e., learning the bodhisattva trainings. The first *Stages of Meditation* also says:[147]

> The bodhisattvas, who have thus developed the spirit of enlightenment, understand that without disciplining themselves they cannot discipline others and so involve themselves in the practice of generosity and so forth; without practice they will not attain enlightenment.

And Dharmakīrti's *Commentary on the "Compendium of Valid Cognition"* says:[148]

> In order to destroy suffering, the compassionate
> Work at actualizing the methods; **[341]**
> It is hard for them to explain the methods and their results
> When these remain hidden to them.

Those who have great compassion for others feel the need to relieve others' suffering. To relieve it, the kind thought, "May they be free of their suffering," is not enough; they must engage in the methods that will bring it about. Now, if they do not first engage in those methods themselves, they will be unable to free others. Therefore, if you want to work for others' welfare, you must first discipline yourself. In reference to this the *King of Concentrations Sūtra* says that you should "take practice to heart." Practice is said to be learning the training in the precepts associated with the bodhisattva vows after you have taken them. Therefore, it is very important that you are not mistaken about just what is entailed in taking practice to heart.

ii) **Demonstrating that you will not become a buddha by learning either method or wisdom separately**

It is not enough just to want to attain buddhahood; you must engage in the method of achieving it. This method has to be unmistaken because no matter how much you strive on a mistaken path, you will not obtain the result—like milking a horn in the hope of getting milk. Even if the method is unmistaken, if it is not complete in all particulars, striving will not bring the result, just as the absence of a seed, water, earth, or the like will preclude the production of a sprout. Thus the second *Stages of Meditation* says:[149]

> If you earnestly strive at a mistaken cause, even a tremendous amount of time will not bring you the desired result, like milking a horn. A result does not come from an incomplete causal complex, just as an effect like the production of a sprout does not happen when something like a seed is missing. Therefore, someone who wants the result must depend upon an unmistaken and complete set of causes and conditions.

What, then, is the unmistaken and complete set of causes and conditions? *Vairocana's Great Enlightenment Discourse* (*Mahāvairocanābhisaṃbodhi-dharma-paryāya*) says:[150]

> Lord of Secrets, the sublime wisdom of omniscience comes from compassion as its root. It comes from the spirit of enlightenment as its cause. It is brought to completion by method. **[342]**

In regard to this, I have already explained compassion.[151] The great trailblazer Kamalaśīla explains that the "spirit of enlightenment" is both the conventional and ultimate spirits of enlightenment, and that "method" is all virtues such as generosity and so forth.

Opponents' position: Some persons like the Chinese Ha-shang (Hva-shang), who have a mistaken idea about the path of the two types of spirit of enlightenment, say that any thought—nonvirtuous thoughts, of course, but even virtuous ones—binds us to cyclic existence, so its results do not transcend cyclic existence. It is like being tied up with a golden rope or with an ordinary rope, like white or dark clouds covering the sky, or like the pain from being bitten by a white or a black dog. Therefore, just setting your mind in a state that lacks any thought is the path to future buddhahood. Such virtues as generosity and ethical discipline are taught for foolish people incapable of such meditation on the definitive [emptiness]. To engage in those deeds after you have found the definitive would be like a king descending to a common status or like finding an elephant and then searching for its footprints. Ha-shang attempts to prove this position by citing, from the sūtras, eighty passages which extol this state of mind that lacks any thought.

Reply: Ha-shang's saying, "Everything to do with method is not an actual path to buddhahood," is a tremendous denial of the conventional. And, since he refutes analyzing with discerning wisdom the selfless reality that is at the heart of the Conqueror's teaching, he banishes the system of the ultimate to the far distance. The great bodhisattva Kamalaśīla excellently refuted with a mass of scriptural citation and stainless reasoning this epitome of wrong views in which it is maintained that the sublime path consists of stabilizing the mind in a state that lacks any thought. Such stabilizing of the mind is a practice properly subsumed under the mere category of meditative serenity, no matter how superior it may be. Kamalaśīla then wrote at length on the good path pleasing to the conquerors. **[343]**

Nevertheless, there are still some who continue to do just what Ha-shang did, because the total decline of the Buddha's teaching is drawing near, because the excellent persons who ascertain with total certainty through scriptures of definitive meaning and stainless reasoning all the key points of the path in their entirety are no more, because the merit of living beings is so minimal, and because there are so many who have little faith in the teaching and feeble intelligence. Some belittle the deeds that are part of the path—the vows which are to be kept and the like—rejecting them and so forth when they cultivate the path; others do not accept Ha-shang's mistaken denial of the factor of method, but assert that his way of understanding the philosophical view is excellent; and still others cast aside discerning wisdom and claim that Ha-shang's meditation of not thinking is best.

The path of these persons is indeed not at all in the direction or vicinity of a meditation on emptiness. But even if you were to allow that it is a meditation on emptiness, you would not then go on to say that those with the knowledge that comes from their cultivation of a faultless method of meditation, after they have found the unmistaken meaning of emptiness, should meditate on emptiness alone and "not cultivate conventional states of mind pertaining to deeds," or, alternatively, "do not have to strive at those conventional states of mind in a variety of ways, upholding them as the core practice." To say such things contradicts all the scriptures and completely flies in the face of reason, for the goal for practitioners of the Mahāyāna is a non-abiding nirvāṇa. For this you have to achieve non-abiding in cyclic existence via the wisdom that knows reality, the stages of the path contingent on the ultimate, the "profound path," the collection of sublime wisdom, the so-called "factor of wisdom." You also have to achieve a non-abiding in the peace that is nirvāṇa via the wisdom that understands the diversity of phenomena, the stages of the path contingent on conventional truths, the vast path, the collection of merit, the so-called "factor of method." **[344]** The *Sūtra of Showing the Tathāgata's Inconceivable Secret* (*Tathāgatācintya-guhya-nirdeśa-sūtra*) thus says:[152]

> The collection of sublime wisdom eliminates all afflictions. The collection of merit nurtures all living beings. Bhagavan, since this is the case, *mahāsattva* bodhisattvas should strive for the collections of sublime wisdom and merit.

The *Questions of Sky Treasure Sūtra* (*Gagana-gañja-paripṛcchā-sūtra*) says:[153]

> With the knowledge of wisdom, you completely eliminate all afflictions. With the knowledge of method, you include all living beings.

The *Sūtra Unravelling the Intended Meaning* (*Saṃdhi-nirmocana-sūtra*) says:[154]

> Utterly turning away from the welfare of all living beings and utterly turning away from all participation in motivated action—I have not taught these to be unsurpassed, perfect enlightenment.

The *Teaching of Vimalakīrti* (*Vimalakīrti-nirdeśa-sūtra*) states at length:[155]

> What is bondage for the bodhisattvas and what is their liberation? Attachment to wandering through cyclic existence without method is bondage for a bodhisattva; proceeding through cyclic existence with method is liberation. Attachment to wandering through cyclic existence without wisdom is bondage for a bodhisattva; proceeding through cyclic existence with wisdom is liberation. Wisdom that is not imbued with method is bondage; wisdom imbued with method is liberation. Method not imbued with wisdom is bondage; method imbued with wisdom is liberation.

Therefore, when you are on the path—right from the time of wanting the goal of buddhahood—you must depend on both method and wisdom; you will not attain it by either one alone. The *Foremost of Gayā* says:[156]

> If you summarize the paths for bodhisattvas, there are these two. Which two? Method and wisdom. **[345]**

The *Glorious First and Foremost Tantra* (*Śrī-paramādya-kalpa-rāja*) states:[157]

> The perfection of wisdom is the mother. Skill-in-means is the father.

And the *Kāśyapa Chapter* also says:[158]

> Kāśyapa, it is like this. Just as kings informed by ministers perform all royal duties, so too the wisdom of bodhisattvas imbued with skill-in-means performs all the deeds of a buddha.

Therefore, meditate on an emptiness that has the supremacy of being associated with all aspects, i.e., an emptiness that is complete in all the facets of method—generosity and so forth. By meditating on emptiness in isolation you will never reach the Mahāyāna path. The *Questions of Crest Jewel Sūtra* (*Ratna-cūḍā-sūtra*) states this at length:[159]

> After you put on the armor of love and station yourself in a state of great compassion, you stabilize your mind in meditation on an actual emptiness that has the supremacy of being associated with all aspects. What is an emptiness that has the supremacy of being associated with all aspects? It is one that is not divorced from generosity, that is not divorced from ethical discipline, that is not divorced from patience, that is not divorced from joyous perseverance, that is not divorced from meditative stabilization, that is not divorced from wisdom, and that is not divorced from method.

The *Sublime Continuum* comments on this passage as follows:[160]

> Generosity, ethical discipline, patience, and so forth—
> These are the painters;
> Emptiness supreme in all aspects
> Is said to be the likeness.

This uses the analogy of assembling a group of artists to paint a king's likeness. One knows how to paint a head but not something else, one knows how to paint a hand but not something else, and so on. If even one artist is missing, the painting will not get finished. The king's likeness is analogous to emptiness and the painters are analogous to generosity and so forth. So if method—generosity and so forth—is incomplete, it would be like a decapitated or amputated likeness. **[346]**

Furthermore, to take emptiness in isolation as what is to be meditated on and say, "There is no need to cultivate anything else," expresses an idea that the Bhagavan set forth as a view to be opposed, and he thereupon refuted it. Were the statement true, then the many eons of a bodhisattva's practice of generosity, observance of ethical discipline, etc. would be an exercise in faulty wisdom that did not comprehend the definitive, as the Bhagavan says in the *Sūtra Gathering All the Threads* (*Sarva-vaidalya-saṃgraha-sūtra*):[161]

> Maitreya, fools intending to repudiate the other perfections will speak thus about the bodhisattvas' correct practice of the six perfections for the sake of perfect enlightenment: "Bodhisattvas should train in perfect wisdom alone, the remaining perfections have no use." Ajita [Maitreya], what do you think? Was he who was the king of Kāśi [Śākyamuni Buddha in a previous life] exercising faulty wisdom when he gave his own flesh to the hawk for the sake of the pigeon?
>
> Maitreya replied, "No, Bhagavan, he was not."
>
> The Bhagavan continued, "Maitreya, when I was performing the deeds of a bodhisattva, did the roots of virtue that I accumulated—the roots of virtue that go with the six perfections—harm me?"
>
> Maitreya replied, "No, Bhagavan, they did not."
>
> The Bhagavan continued, "Ajita, you have so far practiced the perfection of generosity over sixty eons, you have practiced the perfection of ethical discipline over sixty eons, the perfection of patience over sixty eons, the perfection of joyous perseverance over sixty eons, the perfection of meditative stabilization over sixty eons, and the perfection of wisdom over sixty eons, in regard to which these fools will say that enlightenment is only reached through a single way—the way of emptiness. [**347**] Their deeds will be completely impure.

Therefore, to say "It is unnecessary for someone who knows emptiness to strive hard to cultivate method" is a mistaken denial that states, in effect, "The period of Our Teacher's previous holy lifetimes was a time when he had no understanding of the definitive."

Opponents' position: Practicing the deeds of generosity and so forth in a variety of ways is for when you do not have a firm knowledge of emptiness. When you do have this firm knowledge, then this is enough.

Reply: This is a very wrong view. If it were correct, then the children of the conquerors who have ascended to the great levels where they have attained the nonconceptual sublime wisdom that perceives the ultimate truth, and, in particular, the eighth-level bodhisattvas, who have control over nonconceptual wisdom, would not need the bodhisattva deeds. This is incorrect because the *Sūtra on the Ten Levels* (*Daśa-bhūmika-sūtra*) says that even though on each of the ten levels there is an emphasis on one of the deeds—generosity, etc.—it is not the case that they do not perform the other deeds, so it is said that they practice all six or ten perfections on each level. Further, since Ajita [Maitreya], Nāgārjuna, and Asaṅga explain the meaning of these sūtras in this fashion, it is not possible to interpret them otherwise.

In particular, bodhisattvas eliminate all afflictions on the eighth level. Therefore, when they stabilize on the ultimate, wherein they have quelled all elaboration, the buddhas exhort them, explaining that they have to train in the bodhisattva deeds: "With just this knowledge of emptiness you cannot become enlightened because the *śrāvaka*s and *pratyekabuddha*s have also obtained this nonconceptuality. Look at my immeasurable body, immeasurable sublime wisdom, immeasurable realm, and so forth. You also do not have my powers and so on. Joyously persevere for the sake of these attributes. Think about the living beings not at peace, disturbed by various afflictions. But do not discard this forbearance [meditation on emptiness]," and so forth. **[348]** To be satisfied with a certain, trivial meditative concentration and to set aside everything else is something ridiculed by scholars. The *Sūtra on the Ten Levels* says:[162]

> Listen! There are children of the conquerors, bodhisattvas, who abide in this bodhisattva's immovable level [eighth level], who have generated the power of previous aspirational prayers, and who are stabilized in the "stream of entrance to the teaching" meditation [meditation on emptiness]. The *bhagavan* buddhas have them accomplish a *tathāgata*'s sublime wisdom, saying this: "Children of good lineage, very good, very good! This goal—the knowledge of all the buddha qualities—is a forbearance of the ultimate. Nevertheless, you do not have my ten powers, fearlessnesses, and so forth, the buddha qualities in all their richness. Joyously persevere at seeking these perfected qualities of a buddha. Do not throw away this very entrance to forbearance [meditation on emptiness]. Children of good lineage, though you have thus attained peace and liberation, think about the ordinary, childish beings, who are not at peace and are driven by various upsurges of diverse afflictions. Children of good lineage, recollect your earlier aspirational prayers, what you should attain for the welfare of living beings, and the inestimable entrance to sublime wisdom. Also, children of good lineage, this is the reality of phenomena. Whether there are *tathāgata*s or not, the sphere of reality simply remains; it is the emptiness of all phenomena, the non-apprehension of all things. Not by this alone are the *tathāgata*s

> to be distinguished; all *śrāvakas* and *pratyekabuddhas* also attain this nonconceptual real nature. [349] Also, children of good lineage, look at my immeasurable body, my immeasurable sublime wisdom, my immeasurable buddha-realm, my immeasurable actualization of sublime wisdom, my immeasurable halo of light, and the immeasurable pure modulations of my voice—and produce something similar in yourselves."

The *Sūtra on the Ten Levels* also gives the example of a ship sailing out to sea, driven by a favorable wind.[163] The distance it covers in a single day exceeds the distance it goes even in a hundred years after starting from port without a wind and using effort to move it. Likewise, it says, after you have reached the eighth level, without a great effort you cover in just a moment an amount of the path to omniscience not possible before reaching this level, even if you were to strive at the path for one hundred thousand eons. You fool yourself, therefore, by saying "I have a shortcut," and then not learning the bodhisattva deeds.

Opponents' position: I do not assert that generosity and so forth are unnecessary, but rather that they are fully present in the state of mind that lacks any thought, because the absence of adherence to a giver, gift, and recipient makes non-apprehending generosity fully present, and in the same way the remaining perfections are fully present, too. It is also because the sūtras say that you include the practice of all six perfections within the practice of each.

Reply: If they are fully present in a state of mind that lacks thought, then when non-Buddhist meditators are in meditative equipoise even in single-pointed states of serenity, all the perfections would be fully present because they also are not adhering to a giver, gift, and recipient. In particular, when *śrāvakas* and *pratyekabuddhas* nonconceptually perceive the real nature, as in the earlier quotation from the *Sūtra on the Ten Levels*, all bodhisattva deeds would be fully present—so they would, absurdly, be Mahāyāna practitioners. And if you assert that just one practice is sufficient because the sūtras say that all six perfections are included in each, well then, since it also says all six are present even when offering a maṇḍala while reciting the verse beginning, "Giving cow dung together with water...," it would also be enough to do only this. [350]

Deeds imbued with the philosophical view and wisdom imbued with method may be understood by way of an analogy. When a mother stricken with grief at the death of her beloved child engages in conversation and other activities with others, the feelings she expresses do not eliminate the force of her grief. Yet not every feeling she expresses is necessarily grief. Similarly, if the wisdom that knows emptiness is very strong, even though the states of mind associated with giving, making obeisance, circumambulating, or reciting are not cognitions of emptiness, this still does not preclude your being involved in them while endowed with the potency or force of the cognition of emptiness. For instance, at the start of a meditation session, if you first generate a very strong spirit of enlightenment, this spirit of enlightenment is not manifestly there when you then enter meditative equipoise in a concentration on emptiness. Yet this does not preclude this concentration's being imbued with the potency of the spirit of enlightenment.

It is this sort of thing that is referred to by the term "non-apprehending generosity." It is not the complete absence of a generous attitude, wherein giving is not feasible. Understand the remaining perfections in a similar way. Know also that this is how method and wisdom are inseparable.

Furthermore, you should not misconstrue statements that things in cyclic existence such as your body, resources, and a long life span are the result of collections of merit; they are so only in the absence of skill-in-means and wisdom. When collections of merit are imbued with these, it is entirely proper that they are the causes of liberation and omniscience. There are limitless passages in the scriptures which say as much, such as this one from the *Precious Garland*:[164]

> To sum up, the embodiment of form,
> O King, is born from the collection of merit.

Moreover, it looks like you are saying that even all ill deeds and afflictions that cause the miserable realms can sometimes become causes of buddhahood, and that virtue—generosity, ethical discipline, and so forth that lead to high status—causes cyclic existence, but does not become a cause of buddhahood. So compose yourself before you speak. **[351]**

Do not misconstrue the following statements: From the sūtras:[165]

> Adhering to the six perfections—generosity and so forth—is demonic activity.

From the *Three Heaps Sūtra* (*Tri-skandhaka-sūtra*):[166]

> Confess each of these: descending to the level of objective existence and giving gifts, observing ethical discipline because of a belief in the supremacy of ethics, etc.

And from the *Sūtra Requested by Brahmā* (*Brahma-paripṛcchā-sūtra*):[167]

> All analysis is conceptual thought; the nonconceptual is enlightenment.

The meaning of the first passage is that generosity, etc. motivated by a mistaken adherence to the two types of self [the self of persons and the self of objects] is not pure, and, therefore, is stated to be "demonic activity." This passage does not teach that generosity and so forth is demonic activity; otherwise, since it mentions all six perfections, you would also have to assert that the perfections of meditative stabilization and wisdom are demonic activity.

The second scriptural passage means that the perfections are impure because of being motivated by a mistaken adherence and explains that you must confess them. It does not teach that you should not be involved in generosity, etc.; otherwise, the mention of a descent to the level of objective existence in the phrase, "descending to the level of objective existence and giving gifts" would be unnecessary, and it would instead have stated, "confess the giving of gifts in general," which it does not in fact say.

This method of response, formulated in the third *Stages of Meditation*, emphasizes an extremely important point, because Hashang's view misunderstands this passage and asserts that the whole range of deeds is qualified by signs, wherein the deeds are taken to be the apprehension of signs of a self of persons and objects. If every sort of virtuous conceptual thought—such as the generous attitude when thinking, "I shall give this thing," and the attitude of restraint when thinking, "I shall restrain from this wrongdoing"—were an apprehension of a self of objects that misconceives the three spheres [agent, object, and recipient], then it would be right and proper that everyone finding the view of the selflessness of objects should completely reject virtuous conceptual thought just as they reject hostility, pride, etc., and it would be quite wrong for them to purposefully cultivate those virtues. **[352]**

If all conceptual thoughts, which think, "This is this," were conceptions of the self of objects that misconceive the three spheres, then what about contemplating the good qualities of a teacher; contemplating leisure and opportunity, death, and the suffering of the miserable realms; training in the practice of going for refuge; thinking how a certain action gives rise to a certain result; training in love, compassion, and the spirit of enlightenment; and practicing the precepts of the engaged spirit of enlightenment? Since all of these paths require only that you induce certain knowledge by thinking, "This is this," "This comes from that," "This has this good quality or that fault," you would increase your conception of a self of objects commensurate to your certainty about these paths. Conversely, you would become less certain about these paths commensurate to the certain knowledge of the selflessness of objects you could sustain in meditation. The deeds component and view component would thus become mutually exclusive, like hot and cold, and you would then never develop a long-lasting and very forceful certainty about both the view and deeds.

Therefore, just as in the context of the goal there is no contradiction that a buddha's embodiment of truth and a buddha's embodiment of form are both presented as attainments, so on the path you must induce without any contradiction (1) certain knowledge of the total freedom from any elaboration of the conception of signs of true existence in the two kinds of self with respect to even a particle of a mental object and (2) certain knowledge that "This comes from that," and "This has this good quality or that fault." This, in turn, is contingent on how you determine the two truths, the philosophical view of what exists. You are counted "a person who knows the two truths and who has found the Conqueror's intent" if you are convinced that the following two valid cognitions not only do not, of course, harm each other, but rather aid each other: (1) the valid cognition that establishes the ultimate, which is determined through scripture and reasoning to be the absence of even a particle of essential nature in the way of being or ontological status of any phenomenon of cyclic existence or nirvāṇa, and (2) the conventional valid cognition that establishes that causes and effects, in their diverse workings, are certain, without any confusion of even the slightest cause or effect. **[353]** I shall explain this system in the insight section.[168]

As to the third scriptural passage, the one from the *Sūtra Requested by Brahmā*, since the context for this passage in the sūtra is an analysis of production and so forth, in order to teach that generosity, etc. are not absolutely produced, it uses the term "conceptual thought" to indicate that they are mere imputations by conceptual thought. It is not teaching that you should not involve yourself in these deeds and reject them.

Therefore, since there is no time when it is not necessary to practice these deeds—the six perfections, etc.—until you become a buddha, it is incumbent upon you to train in these deeds. If you strive right now from the depths of your heart, you will accomplish with effort what you can achieve. With respect to the practices that you are unable to do for the time being, make an aspiration to do them and, as causes of the ability to practice them, accumulate the collections, clear away the obscurations, and make many aspirational prayers. Once you do this, it will not be long before you put them into practice. Otherwise, if you take the position that you, personally, cannot understand the deeds or cannot do them, and you then say to others, "You do not need to train in them," not only do you ruin yourself and bring ruin on others as well, but it also becomes a condition for the decline of the teaching. So do not do this. As Nāgārjuna's *Compendium of Sūtras* (*Sūtra-samuccaya*) says:[169]

> Discerning even the non-composite and still being disillusioned with composite virtue is demonic activity. Understanding even the path to enlightenment and still not seeking the path of the perfections is demonic activity.

And also:

> A bodhisattva who lacks skill-in-means should not strive for the state of profound reality.

And the *Sūtra of Showing the Tathāgata's Inconceivable Secret* says:[170]

> Children of good lineage, it is like this. Fire, for example, burns from a cause and goes out when this cause ceases to exist. Similarly, mind is activated by an observed object; without this it is inactive. The bodhisattvas with this skill-in-means know, through the purity of their perfection of wisdom, the elimination of a truly existent observed object, and yet they do not eliminate the observation of roots of virtue. **[354]** They do not give rise to the observation of the afflictions and yet set their attention on the observed objects of the perfections. They discern an observation of emptiness, yet still observe and consider all living beings with great compassion.

You must distinguish between explanations of how there is no observed object and explanations of how there is an observed object.

Accordingly, while you must loosen the bonds of the afflictions and the conceptions of signs of true existence, you must be firmly bound by the rope of ethical training, and, while you need to eradicate both kinds of misdeeds [deeds that are wrong by nature and deeds that are wrong by prohibition], you must not eradicate virtuous activities. Being bound by ethical training and being bound by conceiving signs of true existence are not the same, and loosening the safeguarding of vows and loosening the chain of the conception of self are not the same either.

You achieve omniscience from a number of causes, each of which is insufficient by itself. So know that the following sort of person is a teacher of nonvirtue who blocks the door to the two collections: someone who says, "Hundreds of birds are driven out with a single stone from a slingshot," and who attains a fortunate life of leisure and should then take advantage of it in many ways, but rather does not train in anything other than one specific aspect of the path.

Also, the difference between the Hīnayāna or Mahāyāna comes down to whether its practitioners train in the limitless collections at the time of putting the teachings into practice, because the "modest vehicle" and Hīnayāna are synonymous, and the meaning of "modest" is "partial." You must achieve even lesser, current results—food, drink, and the like—through many causes and conditions, so it is quite wrong to hold that something partial is sufficient to achieve a person's highest purpose, buddhahood, for it is the nature of dependent-arising that results are made in accordance with their causes. With this in mind the Buddha said in the *Lotus of Compassion Sūtra* (*Karuṇā-puṇḍarīka-sūtra*) that something partial comes from what is partial, and something total comes from what is total. **[355]** This is explained at length in the *Sūtra on the Coming Forth of the Tathāgatas* (*Tathāgatotpatti-saṃbhava*):[171]

> None of the *tathāgata*s arose from a single cause. Why? O conquerors' children! *Tathāgata*s are established from ten times one hundred thousand immeasurable establishing causes. What are the ten? They are these: the genuine cause of not being satisfied with the immeasurable collections of merit and sublime wisdom....

This is also explained at length in the *Teaching of Vimalakīrti*:[172]

> O friends! The bodies of *tathāgata*s are produced from hundreds of meritorious deeds, from all virtues, from immeasurable virtuous paths....

And the protector Nāgārjuna also says in his *Precious Garland*:[173]

> When the causes of even a buddha's embodiment of form
> Have no measure, as with the world,
> How then could there be a measure
> Of the causes of the embodiment of truth?

This training in method and wisdom comprising the six perfections is, as explained earlier, common to both the mantra and perfection vehicles. For in many of the tantric classics we find repeated mention of the complete path of the perfections—the six perfections, the thirty-seven branches of enlightenment, the sixteen emptinesses, etc.—in the context of explanations that the entire celestial mansion and the array of resident deities are the inner qualities of mind. Therefore, know that all the Perfection of Wisdom literature's explanations about what is to be adopted and what is to be discarded are comprehensively shared with the mantra vehicle, except in the case of the tantric teachings for certain exceptional persons in which they must take the experience of sensory objects as the path, and so forth.

Take the above explanation as a seed and reflect on it well. If you are not then certain about a path that is not just partial but complete in all aspects, you have not comprehended the foundation of the Mahāyāna path in general. Therefore, intelligent ones, generate a solid certainty about this path of method and wisdom and, in many ways, continuously grow in your natural capacity for the supreme vehicle. **[356]**

8

Training in the Mahāyāna: Precepts and Perfections

iii) Explanation of the process of learning the precepts
- a′ How to train in the Mahāyāna in general
  - 1′ Establishing the desire to learn the precepts of the spirit of enlightenment
  - 2′ Taking the vows of the conquerors' children after establishing the desire to learn the precepts
  - 3′ How to train after taking the vows
    - a″ What the precepts are based upon
    - b″ How all the precepts are included in the six perfections
      - 1″ A discussion of the main topic, the fixed number of perfections
        - (a) The fixed number of perfections based on high status
        - (b) The fixed number of perfections based on fulfilling the two aims
        - (c) The fixed number of perfections based on perfecting the complete fulfillment of others' aims
        - (d) The fixed number of perfections based on their subsuming the entire Mahāyāna
        - (e) The fixed number of perfections in terms of the completeness of paths or method
        - (f) The fixed number of perfections based on the three trainings
      - 2″ An ancillary discussion of the fixed order of the perfections
        - (a) The order of arising
        - (b) The order in terms of inferior and superior
        - (c) The order in terms of coarse and subtle

iii) **Explanation of the process of learning the precepts**

The explanation of the process of learning the precepts has two parts:

1. How to train in the Mahāyāna in general (Chapters 8 and on)
2. How to train specifically in the Vajrayāna (Chapter 27 of Volume 3)

a′ **How to train in the Mahāyāna in general**

The explanation of how to train in the Mahāyāna in general has three sections:

1. Establishing the desire to learn the precepts of the spirit of enlightenment
2. Taking the vows of the conquerors' children after establishing the desire to learn the precepts
3. How to train after taking the vows (Chapters 8 and on)

1′ **Establishing the desire to learn the precepts of the spirit of enlightenment**

In the discipline of individual liberation and in tantra it is inappropriate to study the precepts before you have first taken the vows, but these bodhisattva vows are different. First you understand the precepts well and then, after you are trained in them, if you have an enthusiasm for taking them, you are given the vows. In this regard the *Bodhisattva Levels* says:[174]

> For persons wanting to take the ethical discipline vows of a bodhisattva you should make known in advance the fundamental precepts and the sources of fault for bodhisattvas taught here in the "Summary of the Bodhisattva Fundamentals" for the bodhisattvas' scriptural collection of the discourses. If after sincere investigation and intelligent analysis these persons are inspired, and if it is not because of being made to do it by someone else and it is not to compete with others, then know that these are reliable bodhisattvas. These persons should be given the vows of ethical discipline and should receive them in accord with the ritual.

This is a very good method because, if you understand the precepts, bring them to mind, establish a wish to train in them from the depths of your heart, and then take the vows, you will be extremely constant.

[357] To explain the precepts both here and below would make for too great a burden of words, so I shall indicate them below.[175]

2′ Taking the vows of the conquerors' children after establishing the desire to learn the precepts

I have already established in detail in my *Basic Path to Awakening* commentary on the *Bodhisattva Levels'* chapter on ethical discipline[176] first how to take the bodhisattva vows, immediately after that how to guard against fundamental transgressions and transgressions which constitute minor infractions, and then how to repair vows if they degenerate. It is most definitely necessary that you read this before you take the vows, so understand them from there.

3′ How to train after taking the vows

How to train after taking the vows has three parts:

1. What the precepts are based upon
2. How all the precepts are included in the six perfections
3. The process of learning the perfections (Chapters 9 and on)

a″ What the precepts are based upon

There are limitless clear categorizations, but if you arrange the bodhisattva precepts by type, you can include them all within the six perfections. The six perfections are thus the great condensation of all the key points of the bodhisattva path. The four ways to gather disciples [generosity, pleasant speech, working at the aims, and consistency of behavior] are also included within these six perfections as follows. That generosity is included is obvious. Pleasant speech is giving instructions to disciples, taking the six perfections as the point of departure; working at the aims is establishing others in the aims of these instructions; and consistency of behavior is practicing just as the disciple does.

Although it is true that the entire bodhisattva path is also subsumed under other condensations such as the two collections, the three trainings [ethical discipline, meditative concentration, and wisdom], and so forth, these are not able to produce the understanding that the six perfections do, so the six perfections are the best inclusive set.

b″ How all the precepts are included in the six perfections

How all the precepts are included in the six perfections has two parts:

1. A discussion of the main topic, the fixed number of perfections
2. An ancillary discussion of the fixed order of the perfections

1″ A discussion of the main topic, the fixed number of perfections

The Bhagavan formulated a bare outline of the six perfections, and the holy Regent [Maitreya] produced certain knowledge of these by explicating in accord with the Buddha's intended meaning the key points of the rationale for formulating the perfections in that fashion. These explanations show that there is a fixed number of perfections. When you are convinced of this and astonished by it, you will understand the practice of the six perfections as the supreme instruction, so obtain such conviction.

The discussion of the main topic, the fixed number of perfections, has six parts:

1. The fixed number of perfections based on high status
2. The fixed number of perfections based on fulfilling the two aims
3. The fixed number of perfections based on perfecting the complete fulfillment of others' aims
4. The fixed number of perfections based on their subsuming the entire Mahāyāna
5. The fixed number of perfections in terms of the completeness of paths or method
6. The fixed number of perfections based on the three trainings

(a) The fixed number of perfections based on high status

To fully complete the greatly effective bodhisattva deeds you need an immeasurably long succession of lifetimes. [358] Moreover, to attain quick success on the path within these lifetimes you need a life excellent in every aspect. Our present life is not excellent in every aspect but rather has only some of the aspects of full excellence; we do not make progress with it though we practice the teachings. You need a life that has four kinds of excellence: (1) resources to use [the result of the perfection of generosity], (2) a body with which you act [the result of the perfection of ethical discipline], (3) companions together with whom you act [the result of the perfection of patience], and (4) work that you are able to accomplish once undertaken [the result of the perfection of joyous perseverance]. Since in many cases these four kinds of excellence alone may themselves become conditions for afflictions, you must not fall under the control of the afflictions [the result of the perfection of meditative stabilization]. As just the four kinds of excellence are not sufficient, you must also distinguish well, in regard to what to adopt and what to cast aside, precisely what things to do and to stop doing [the result of the perfection of wisdom]. Otherwise, just as a bamboo or plantain tree dies after giving fruit, or a mule dies with pregnancy, you will be destroyed by the four excellences.

The wise understand how these six—the four excellences, control of the afflictions, and knowledge of what to adopt and what to cast aside—are the results of earlier virtuous actions, and they strive again at steadily increasing their causes. The unwise use the results of their earlier accumulations of virtue and exhaust them; as they do not increase them anew, they reach the brink of their future suffering.

When you again produce these six in future lives, their production will not be causeless, or from discordant causes, but rather from concordant causes that are the perfections, fixed as six in number. Therefore in this lifetime you must repeatedly habituate yourself to constant reliance on the six perfections because the superiority of the effects is commensurate to the superiority of the causes. A life with the four excellences constitutes temporary high status, whereas the ultimate high status, which consists of ultimate excellence of body, etc., exists at the buddha level. Thus the *Ornament for the Mahāyāna Sūtras (Mahāyāna-sūtrālaṃkāra)* says:[177]

> High status possessed of excellent resources and body,
> Excellent companions and undertakings,
> Not going under the power of the afflictions,
> And never being mistaken in activities.... **[359]**

(b) **The fixed number of perfections based on fulfilling the two aims**

When someone in such a life of high status learns the bodhisattva deeds, these activities are comprehensively categorized as two: those which fulfill your own aim and those which fulfill the aims of others. Therefore, there is a fixed number of perfections based on fulfilling the two aims.

To fulfill the aims of others you must first help them with material goods. Since no benefit will come from generosity accompanied by harmfulness toward living beings, you need ethical discipline, which has a great purpose for others in that it is the state of desisting from harm to others and the causes of such harm. To bring this to its full development you also need patience that disregards the harm done to you, for, if you are impatient with harm and retaliate a time or two, you will not attain pure ethical discipline. When you do not retaliate because of your patience, you prevent others from accumulating a great amount of sin and bring them to virtue by inspiring them with your patience. So this practice has a great purpose for others.

You attain your own aim, the bliss of liberation, through the power of wisdom. Since you will not attain this with a distracted mind, you must set your mind in meditative equipoise by means of meditative stabilization, obtaining a mental serviceability wherein you intentionally set your attention on any object of meditation. Since a lazy person does not produce this, you need joyous perseverance day and night that never slackens, so this is the basis of the other perfections.

For accomplishing the two aims, then, the number of perfections is fixed as six. The *Ornament for the Mahāyāna Sūtras* says:[178]

> Those who strive for the aims of beings
> Work at giving, non-harm, and patience;
> And completely fulfill their own aims
> With stabilization and liberation, together with their basis.

In these six there is no complete fulfillment of others' aims.[179] The mention of "stabilization and liberation" differentiates between the two as (1) the stabilization of the mind on the object of meditation, this being the imprint of meditative stabilization, and (2) the liberation from cyclic existence, this being the imprint of wisdom. Notice that this does not mistake meditative serenity for insight. **[360]** As this is so, those who assert that the meditation of fixing one's attention in an absence of conceptual thought is meditation on the profound are speaking of a meditation that is a single portion of the meditative stabilization that is one of these six perfections. You must attain certain knowledge of the six perfections in their entirety.

(c) **The fixed number of perfections based on perfecting the complete fulfillment of others' aims**

You first relieve others' poverty by giving away material goods. Then you do no harm to any living being and, in addition, are patient with harm done to you. Without becoming dispirited you joyously persevere at helping those who harm you. You depend on meditative stabilization and inspire them through displaying supernormal powers and so forth. When they become suitable vessels for the teachings, you rely on wisdom and give good explanations, cut through their doubts and thereby bring them to liberation. Because you do all this, the perfections are fixed as six in number. The *Ornament for the Mahāyāna Sūtras* states:[180]

> Through relieving others' poverty, not harming them,
> Being patient with their harm, not being dispirited with what they do,
> Delighting them, and speaking well to them
> You fulfill others' aims, which fulfills your own.

This verse, together with the one above, says that it is not possible to fulfill others' and your own aims without relying on the six perfections. Once you are certain about the way in which you fulfill your own and others' aims through these six perfections, you will have respect for the practice of them.

(d) **The fixed number of perfections based on their subsuming the entire Mahāyāna**

You are indifferent to resources because you are not attached to those you have and do not pursue those you lack. Since you then have the ability to safeguard precepts, you adopt and respect ethical discipline. You are patient with the suffering that comes from living beings and inanimate things and you are enthusiastic about whatever virtue you set out to cultivate, so you do not get dispirited by either of these. You cultivate a non-discursive yoga of meditative serenity and a non-discursive yoga of insight. These six comprise all the Mahāyāna practices through which you advance by the six perfections, for you accomplish these practices in stages by means of the six perfections and you do not need any more than these six perfections. The *Ornament for the Mahāyāna Sūtras* states:[181]

> The entire Mahāyāna is summed up in
> Not delighting in resources,

> Reverence, not being dispirited in two ways,
> And the yogas free of discursiveness. **[361]**

Given this, it is a contradiction to want to enter the Mahāyāna and yet to reject the practice of the six perfections.

(e) **The fixed number of perfections in terms of the completeness of paths or method**

The path—i.e., method—for not being attached to the resources that are your possessions is generosity, because you become free from attachment to your things by becoming habituated to giving them away. The method for restraining yourself from the distraction of trying to possess what you do not possess is ethical discipline, for when you maintain a monk's vows, you do not have all the distractions of making a living. The method for not abandoning living beings is patience, because you do not despair at the suffering caused by the harm others inflict. The method to increase virtues is joyous perseverance, because you increase them when you joyously persevere at what you undertake. The methods for clearing away obscurations are the final two perfections, because meditative stabilization clears away the afflictions and wisdom clears away the cognitive obscurations. Thus the perfections are fixed as six in number. The *Ornament for the Mahāyāna Sūtras* states:[182]

> Non-attachment to objects is a path;
> Another is restraint from the distraction of obtaining them;
> Not abandoning beings, increasing virtues,
> And clearing away the obscurations are others.

The following explanation produces strong conviction about the six perfections. In order to avoid being dominated by the distraction of sensual objects, you need generosity that is free from attachment. To prevent sensory experiences that have not occurred, you need ethical discipline that restrains distraction by things that are pointless [deeds that are wrong by prohibition] or counterproductive [deeds that are wrong by nature]. Given that there are a great number of living beings whose behavior is bad and who you are constantly in danger of meeting, you need a powerful conditioning to patience as a remedy for giving up on their welfare. In order to increase virtue in terms of the great number of actions and its practice over long periods of time, you need joyous perseverance that has the intense and long-term enthusiasm that comes from reflecting on the benefits of virtuous actions, etc. In order to suppress afflictions you need meditative stabilization, and to destroy their seeds and the cognitive obscurations you need wisdom. **[362]**

(f) **The fixed number of perfections based on the three trainings**

The nature of the training in ethical discipline [the first of the three trainings] is the practice of ethical discipline. The precondition of the training in ethical discipline is generosity, because once you have generosity that is indifferent to resources, you can properly adopt an ethical discipline. The aid to the training in ethical discipline is patience, because the patience of not retaliating when scolded, etc. safeguards your properly adopted ethical discipline. Meditative stabilization is the training of mind [the second training, the training of meditative concentration], and wisdom is the training in wisdom [the third training]. As for joyous perseverance, it is included in all three trainings, so the perfections are fixed at six in number. The *Ornament for the Mahāyāna Sūtras* states:[183]

> The Conqueror rightly presented six perfections
> In terms of the three trainings: three are the first,
> Two of the six are connected with the final two,
> One is included in all three.

By a certain kind of excellent life you bring to completion either others' or your own aims; you practice certain kinds of trainings by possessing a diversity of methods, depending on which vehicle you are in. Understand in this way that the six perfections comprise and bring to completion the above perspectives on their fixed number—life, aims, the Mahāyāna, the methods, and the trainings. Reflect until you get a deep conviction about how the six perfections are the summation of all the key points of bodhisattva practice.

Furthermore, there are two causes of not initially transcending or rising above cyclic existence—attachment to resources and attachment to a home. The remedies for these are generosity and ethical discipline, respectively.

You may rise above these attachments once, but still turn back without reaching the end. There are two causes of this—suffering from the wrongdoing of living beings and becoming dispirited at the length of time you have pursued virtue. The remedies for these are patience and joyous perseverance, respectively. Once you understand how to sustain a disregard for all suffering and harm, as well as an enthusiasm which views even an eternity as though it were one day, you must practice them in various ways. **[363]** If you do this, you will produce the patience and joyous perseverance that are capable of functioning as remedies to what causes you to turn back. Thus, they are extremely crucial. Never mind the matter of the bodhisattva deeds, even with regard to present-day cultivation of virtue, there are many who start out but few who do not turn back after a while because (1) their forbearance for the slightest hardship is tiny, and (2) their enthusiasm for the path they cultivate is tepid. This is the result of their not putting into practice the personal instructions associated with patience and joyous perseverance.

There are two causes for letting your virtue go to waste even if you do not turn back after a while—distraction, wherein your attention does not stabilize on a virtuous object of meditation, and faulty wisdom. The remedies for these are meditative stabilization and wisdom, respectively. Meditative stabilization is a remedy because it is said that even virtuous practices such as repetition of mantra and daily recitations are senseless if your attention wanders elsewhere. Wisdom is a remedy because if you fail to develop the wisdom that fully delineates the topics in the collections of Buddhist knowledge, you will be mistaken about what to adopt and what to cast aside, even the obvious, and will then conduct yourself wrongly. This fixes the number of perfections at six in terms of their being remedies that eliminate the class of phenomena that are incompatible with virtue.

The number of perfections is fixed at six based on the fact that they are the foundation for achieving every quality of a buddha. This is because the first four perfections are preconditions for meditative stabilization, so through these four you accomplish meditative stabilization—the perfection of non-distraction. Furthermore, when you cultivate insight based on this, you will know reality.

Fixing the number of perfections at six in terms of their being concordant with helping living beings to mature is similar in meaning to the third one [perfecting the complete fulfillment of others' aims] mentioned earlier.

I have explained here the noble Asaṅga's assertions as presented by the master Haribhadra [in his *Long Explanation of the Perfection of Wisdom Sūtra in Eight Thousand Lines (Abhisamayālaṃkārālokā)*]. It is extremely crucial to gain conviction about the six perfections.

2″ An ancillary discussion of the fixed order of the perfections

This discussion has three parts:

1. The order of arising
2. The order in terms of inferior and superior
3. The order in terms of coarse and subtle

(a) **The order of arising**

When you have a generosity that is disinterested in and unattached to resources, you take up ethical discipline. **[364]** When you have an ethical discipline which restrains you from wrongdoing, you become patient with those who harm you. When you have the patience wherein you do not become dispirited with hardships, the conditions for rejecting virtue are few, so you are able to persevere joyously. Once you joyously persevere day and night, you will produce the meditative concentration that facilitates the application of your attention to virtuous objects of meditation. When your mind is in meditative equipoise, you will know reality exactly.

(b) **The order in terms of inferior and superior**

Each preceding perfection is inferior to the superior one that follows it.

(c) **The order in terms of coarse and subtle**

Each preceding perfection is easier than the subsequent one to engage in and perform, so it is coarser than the subsequent one. Each subsequent perfection is more difficult than the preceding one to engage in and perform, so it is more subtle than the preceding one. The *Ornament for the Mahāyāna Sūtras* says:[184]

> Because the subsequent perfections arise contingent on the
> preceding ones,
> Because they are ranked as inferior and superior,
> And because of their coarseness and subtlety,
> The perfections are taught in order.

9

THE PERFECTION OF GENEROSITY

c″ The process of learning the perfections
  1″ How to train in the bodhisattva deeds in general
    (a) Training in the perfections that mature the qualities you will have when you become a buddha
      (i) How to train in the perfection of generosity
        (a′) What generosity is
        (b′) How to begin the development of generosity
        (c′) The divisions of generosity
          (1′) How everyone should practice it
          (2′) Divisions of generosity relative to particular persons
          (3′) Divisions of actual generosity
            (a″) The gift of the teachings
            (b″) The gift of fearlessness
            (c″) Material gifts
              (1″) The generosity of actually giving material things
                (a)) How to give away material things
                  (1)) Recipients of giving
                  (2)) The motivation for giving
                    (a′)) What kind of motivation is required
                    (b′)) What kind of motivation must be eliminated

c″ The process of learning the perfections

The process of learning the perfections has two parts:

1. How to train in the bodhisattva deeds in general (Chapters 9-15)
2. In particular, how to train in the last two perfections (Volume 3)

1″ How to train in the bodhisattva deeds in general

How to train in the bodhisattva deeds in general has two parts:

1. Training in the perfections that mature the qualities you will have when you become a buddha (Chapters 9-14)
2. Training in the four ways to gather disciples that help others to mature (Chapter 15)

(a) Training in the perfections that mature the qualities you will have when you become a buddha

Training in the perfections that mature the qualities you will have when you become a buddha has six parts:

1. How to train in the perfection of generosity (Chapters 9-10)
2. How to train in the perfection of ethical discipline (Chapter 11)
3. How to train in the perfection of patience (Chapter 12)
4. How to train in the perfection of joyous perseverance (Chapter 13)
5. How to train in the perfection of meditative stabilization (Chapter 14)
6. How to train in the perfection of wisdom (Chapter 14)

(i) How to train in the perfection of generosity

How to train in the perfection of generosity has four sections:

1. What generosity is
2. How to begin the development of generosity
3. The divisions of generosity (Chapters 9-10)
4. A summary (Chapter 10)

(a′) What generosity is

The *Bodhisattva Levels* says:[185]

> What is the nature of generosity? It is the intention accompanying bodhisattvas' disinterested non-attachment to all their possessions and their body, and, motivated by this, the physical and verbal actions of giving the things to be given.

Hence it is the virtue of a generous attitude, and the physical and verbal actions which are motivated by this. **[365]**

Bringing the perfection of generosity to completion is not contingent on removing beings' poverty by giving gifts to others.

Otherwise, since there still remain many destitute living beings, all the earlier conquerors would not have attained perfect generosity. Therefore, the physical and verbal aspects of generosity are not the main thing; the main thing is the mental aspect. This is because you perfect generosity after you destroy your stingy clinging to all that you own—your body, resources, and roots of virtue—and you completely condition your mind to giving them away to living beings from the depths of your heart and, not only that, but also to giving to others the effects of this giving as well. Thus *Engaging in the Bodhisattva Deeds* says:[186]

> If generosity were perfected
> By removing beings' poverty,
> Since beings are still destitute
> How could past saviors have perfected it?
>
> Generosity is perfected, it is said,
> Through the attitude of giving away to all beings
> All your possessions, along with the effects of this.
> Therefore, generosity is a state of mind.

Thus the practice of the perfection of generosity entails generating in various ways the intention to give and steadily increasing this generosity, even though you may not be actually giving away something to others.

(b′) **How to begin the development of generosity**

Simply destroying all stinginess in regard to your body and resources is not the perfection of generosity, for stinginess is included within attachment and so even the two kinds of Hīnayāna arhats have totally eliminated it along with its seeds. What is required, then, is that you not only clear away stinginess's tightfistedness, which prevents giving things away, but also that you develop from the depths of your heart the intention to give away to others all your possessions. For this you have to meditate on the faults of holding on to things and the benefits of giving them away. I shall, therefore, discuss these.

The *Moon Lamp Sūtra* (*Candra-pradīpa-sūtra*) says:[187]

> These childish people are attached
> To this rotting body and to this
> Rushing life-force, both of which lack independence
> And are like a dream or a magician's illusion. **[366]**

> So these unintelligent beings do terrible things,
> Fall under the control of sin,
> And, carried away by the chariot of Death's Lord,
> Proceed to unbearable hells.

This says that you should stop attachment by viewing the body as unclean, life as rushing like a mountain cascade, both body and life as devoid of an independent self because they are under the control of karma, and both as false like a dream or a magician's illusion. Furthermore, if you do not stop attachment, you will become dominated by it, build up great wrongdoing, and proceed to miserable realms.

Consider also the *Formula That Accomplishes Limitless Methods (Ananta-mukha-nirhāra-dhāraṇī)*:[188]

> As to living beings who dispute with others,
> It is tightfistedness that is the root cause.
> So renounce that which you crave.
> After you give up craving, the formula will work.

The *Compendium of Trainings* says:[189]

> My body and mind
> Move on moment by moment.
> If with this impermanent body, dripping with filth,
> I attain enlightenment,
> Which is permanent and pure,
> Will I not have attained what is priceless?

And the *Garland of Birth Stories* (*Jātaka-mālā*) states:[190]

> This body devoid of self, perishing, without substance,
> Suffering, ungrateful, and continually impure
> Is of benefit to others; not to delight in this
> Is not to be intelligent.

Though you make much effort to care for your body, which has no substance, you have to discard it. By sincerely giving it away to others you fulfill many of your own and others' aims. After you think, "I would be a fool not to train my mind to do this," do whatever you can to produce the thought of giving away your body and the like to others. *Engaging in the Bodhisattva Deeds* says:[191]

> By giving everything away, I pass from sorrow,
> So my mind reaches nirvāṇa.
> As I have to give up everything [at death],
> It is best to give it to living beings. **[367]**

And the *Compendium of the Perfections* says:[192]

> If you see the impermanence of resources
> And naturally have great compassion
> You will know with good reason that the gifts
> You have kept in your house belong to others.
>
> There is never fear from what has been given away;
> What is kept at home gives rise to fears
> That it is insufficient, ordinary, or needing constant protection.
> If you give it away, these faults never harm you.
>
> By giving you achieve happiness in future lives;
> Not giving brings suffering even in this life.
> Human wealth is like a shooting star—
> What is not given away will cease to exist.
>
> Wealth not given is transitory and will be gone;
> By giving it away it remains a treasury.
> Wealth of no value comes to have value
> When you strive to help living beings.
>
> The wise praise giving wealth away,
> Childish persons like to hoard it;
> No wealth is kept by holding on to it;
> From giving it away excellence always arises.
>
> By giving things away, you no longer grasp the afflictions;
> Being miserly breeds afflictions on an ignoble path.
> Noble beings say generosity is the best path,
> While its opposite is a bad path.

If you dedicate from the depths of your heart all roots of virtue, however great or small they may be, for the sake of accomplishing both temporarily and ultimately extensive benefit and happiness for all living beings, and then give something, you obtain merit related to each living being. Hence you easily complete the collection of merit. The *Precious Garland* states:[193]

> Were the merit of saying this
> To have physical form
> It would not fit into universes as numerous
> As the grains of the Ganges' sand.
>
> The Bhagavan said this
> And there is a logic to it—
> The expanse of living beings is immeasurable;
> The merit of the wish to help them is the same. **[368]**

Furthermore, do not hold on to companions and belongings that have prevented you from increasing your ability to give things away, that have intensified your stinginess, that have stopped the development of previously absent inclinations to give, or that have weakened your inclinations to give. Do not take on these kinds of companions or accept these kinds of material gifts even if others offer them. The *Compendium of the Perfections* states:[194]

> Bodhisattvas give up all possessions
> That intensify the fault of stinginess
> Or that do not expand generosity,
> The deceivers that become an obstacle.
>
> Bodhisattvas should not accept
> Jewels, wealth, or even a kingdom
> If it would harm their generous attitude and
> Obscure the path to perfect enlightenment.

When you act in this way, stinginess may lead you to feel attached to your goods. If so, become unattached by thinking, "The Sage reached enlightenment after he gave away every possession. Previously, recalling my commitment to emulate him, I gave away my body, every resource, and all my virtue to all living beings. If I am still attached to resources, I am behaving just like an elephant, oppressed by the sun, who goes into the water and bathes and then, back on dry land, rolls in the dirt. Then again, after it sees that it is covered in dirt, it goes back into the water and does the same thing over again." The *Compendium of the Perfections* says:[195]

> Recalling the superior deeds of the sages,
> Strive at them and reflect on your commitment;
> Understand the following excellent thoughts
> In order to clear away your attachment to things:
>
> "I gave away my body to all beings;
> Then I relinquished the virtue of this gift.
> My being attached to external objects
> Is senseless, like an elephant's bathing."

If you are able to generate intense delight as you contemplate the many benefits of giving things away and great fear as you reflect on the faults of tightfistedness, you will naturally produce a generous attitude. **[369]** Accordingly, generate the thought of giving away everything to others at the conclusion of cultivating love and compassion, or at the conclusion of reflecting on the life stories of the Conqueror, his children, and so forth. *Engaging in the Bodhisattva Deeds* states how this is done:[196]

> I will give away without a sense of loss
> My body and my resources
> As well as all my virtue from the past, present, and future
> For the welfare of all living beings.

You focus on three things—your body, your resources, and your roots of virtue—and mentally give them away to all living beings.

If you stop the craving that conceives everything to be your personal property and then repeatedly condition yourself to the attitude of giving it all away to others, you will be called a bodhisattva. The *Compendium of the Perfections* says:[197]

> "All these things are yours;
> I have no pride that they are mine."
>
> Someone who has this amazing thought repeatedly
> And emulates the qualities of the perfect Buddha
> Is called a bodhisattva—so said
> The inconceivable Buddha, the supreme being.

At present, as your determination has not matured and is weak, you do not actually give away flesh, etc., though you have already mentally given your body to all beings. According to the *Compendium of Trainings*, however, if you do not train in the thought of giving away your body and life, you will not become accustomed to it and so will remain incapable of giving away your body and life. Therefore, from now on cultivate this thought.

If you use food, clothes, shelter and so on that you have sincerely given away to all beings, and you do so with craving for your personal welfare, forgetting the thought, "I will use them for others' welfare," then you commit a major infraction. When you have no craving but forget to apply the idea of focusing on all living beings, or if you use those resources for a particular living being out of attachment, you commit a minor infraction. **[370]**

With regard to the material goods that you have turned over to others, the *Compendium of Trainings* states[198] that when you use them for your own welfare fully cognizant of their being the property of others, you are stealing, and if the total value is enough, you commit a cardinal transgression of the vows of individual liberation. In response to this, some say that since you have turned over your food, etc., to *all* living beings, it is impossible for the total value of any one being's portion to be enough, so you cannot commit a cardinal transgression. Others say this is not correct because you have turned over your belongings as a whole to each being individually. Others argue that even though you have mentally surrendered them to others, they do not take personal possession of them, so there is no cardinal transgression.

The intended meaning behind the *Compendium of Trainings* statement is that you incur a cardinal transgression (given that the total value requirement has been met) when you sincerely turn your food, etc., over to a human being, and this person knows it and takes possession, whereupon you, fully cognizant of their being another's property, appropriate them for your own use. Therefore, the positions stated by the others are wrong.

There is no fault in using some living beings' resources if you think, while using them, "I do this for their welfare." The *Compendium of Trainings* states:[199]

> There is no fault in using things if you think, "I am taking care of my body which is owned by others with these resources that are owned by others." Slaves have no material goods of their own with which to survive.

You may think, "I incur a fault because, after I have turned over these belongings to living beings, I use them without their permission," but there is no fault. The *Compendium of Trainings* says:[200]

> A servant who labors hard on a master's behalf might use the master's belongings without permission when the master's mind is unclear due to illness and so forth, but incurs no fault.

Do not lack faith and think, "Mentally giving everything away to living beings while not actually giving it is tantamount to a lie and, therefore, is without real substance." The *Compendium of Trainings* says:[201]

> Some people who are close to a bodhisattva who practices in this way fail to understand the bodhisattva's practice accurately and lack faith. This is unwarranted because they are well acquainted with someone who has a great and wonderful spirit of generosity. **[371]** It is wrong for them to doubt this method.

(c′) **The divisions of generosity**

The section on the divisions of generosity has three parts:

1. How everyone should practice it
2. Divisions of generosity relative to particular persons
3. Divisions of actual generosity (Chapters 9-10)

(1′) **How everyone should practice it**

Asaṅga's *Mahāyāna Compendium* says that you practice generosity in association with six supremacies. *Supreme basis* means that you practice generosity based on the spirit of enlightenment; i.e., you act after you have been motivated by it. *Supreme things* means that in general you give all objects that can be given, and, even when you are engaged in specific acts of generosity, you do not give up this thought of giving away everything. *Supreme aim* is when you give things away to all living beings for the sake of their immediate happiness and ultimate benefit. *Supreme skill-in-means* is said to be when generosity is imbued with nonconceptual sublime wisdom; beginning bodhisattvas should take this to be the wisdom that knows the lack of intrinsic nature in objects. *Supreme dedication* means that you dedicate the virtue from generosity to complete enlightenment. *Supreme purity* is when you stop both the afflictive and cognitive obscurations.

Haribhadra's *Long Explanation of the Perfection of Wisdom Sūtra in Eight Thousand Lines* says that you practice generosity with the six perfections present. When you are giving the teachings, for instance, it is extremely powerful if you practice all six perfections. You have ethical discipline when you restrain yourself from the considerations of *śrāvakas* and *pratyekabuddhas*; patience when you bear any hardship while you aspire to the qualities of omniscience and when you are patient with abuse from others; joyous perseverance when you yearn for the ever-greater increase of your generosity; meditative stabilization when you dedicate to complete enlightenment the virtue that you cultivate with one-pointed attention unmixed with Hīnayāna considerations; and wisdom when you know that the giver, gift, and recipient are like a magician's illusion.

(2′) **Divisions of generosity relative to particular persons**

In general it is said that lay bodhisattvas make gifts of material things and renunciate bodhisattvas make gifts of the teachings. **[372]** The *Bodhisattva Vows of Liberation* (*Bodhisattva-prātimokṣa*) says:[202]

> Śāriputra, the renunciate bodhisattva who teaches just a single four-line stanza produces much more merit than the lay bodhisattva who makes offerings of buddha-realms filled with jewels, as many in number as the sand grains of the River Ganges, to the *tathāgatas*, the arhats, the perfectly enlightened buddhas. Śāriputra, the Tathāgata does not permit renunciates to make material gifts.

The *Compendium of Trainings* says the Buddha intended here material gifts that would become a hindrance to study and the like. It is said that renunciates are prohibited from making offerings of material goods that they have worked to obtain, but they must give them away if they obtain many things through the force of their previous merit and without hindering their virtuous activities.

Also, Sha-ra-wa (Sha-ra-ba) said:

> I am not talking to you about the benefits of giving; I am talking to you about the faults of tightfistedness.

It is displeasing news when renunciates harm their ethical discipline as they strain to the utmost in their search for wealth to give away.

(3′) **Divisions of actual generosity**

The presentation of the divisions of actual generosity has three parts:

1. The gift of the teachings
2. The gift of fearlessness
3. Material gifts (Chapters 9-10)

(a″) **The gift of the teachings**

The gift of the teachings is teaching the sublime teaching without making mistakes, teaching the arts and the like (worldly occupations which are blameless and proper to learn), and involving others in upholding the fundamental precepts.

(b″) **The gift of fearlessness**

The gift of fearlessness is protecting living beings from fear of humans such as kings and robbers, from fear of non-human beings such as lions, tigers, and crocodiles, and from fear of the elements such as water and fire.

(c″) **Material gifts**

Material gifts are explained in two parts:

1. The generosity of actually giving material things (Chapters 9-10) **[373]**
2. The generosity which is just mental (Chapter 10)

(1″) **The generosity of actually giving material things**

The generosity of actually giving material things has three parts:

1. How to give away material things (Chapters 9-10)

2. What to do if you are unable to give (Chapter 10)
3. Relying on the remedies for the hindrances to generosity (Chapter 10)

(a)) **How to give away material things**

This section has four parts:

1. Recipients of giving
2. The motivation for giving
3. How to give (Chapter 10)
4. Things to give (Chapter 10)

(1)) **Recipients of giving**

There are ten of these: (1) friends and relatives who help you, (2) enemies who harm you, (3) ordinary people who neither harm nor help you, (4) those with good qualities such as ethical discipline, (5) those with flaws such as faulty ethical discipline, (6) those inferior to you, (7) those equal to you, (8) those superior to you, (9) the rich and happy, and (10) the miserable and destitute.

(2)) **The motivation for giving**

The motivation for giving has two sections:

1. What kind of motivation is required
2. What kind of motivation must be eliminated

(a')) **What kind of motivation is required**

Your motivation should have three attributes: (1) a focus on purpose, which thinks, "Based on this I will complete the perfection of generosity, a precondition for unexcelled enlightenment"; (2) a focus on the thing to be given, which thinks, "From the outset a bodhisattva gives away all possessions to living beings, so the material goods that I am giving belong to others, and it is as if they are receiving things kept in trust"; and (3) a focus on the recipient, which thinks, "Since these recipients, whether asking for the gift or not, bring to completion my perfection of generosity, they are my teachers." The *Compendium of the Perfections* states:[203]

> When someone comes to ask for something,
> Bodhisattvas, so as to build up the preconditions for complete enlightenment,
> Consider what they have as belonging to others, give it as from a trust,
> And consider the person their teacher.

With respect to giving away individual things, understand in detail from the *Questions of Subāhu Sūtra* (*Subāhu-paripṛcchā*) and the *Compendium of the Perfections* your motivation's focus on purpose, which is the thought, "I will give this away for this or for that purpose." As to your motivation's focus on the recipient explained above, you should apply it to all situations of generosity, so it is the general motivation. **[374]** Specific motivations would be when you make a gift to those who harm you, once you have established a loving attitude; to those who suffer, once you have established a compassionate attitude; to those who have good qualities, once you have established an attitude of delight; and to those who help you, once you have established an impartial attitude.

Moreover, you must be even-minded toward all recipients, give away to living beings—such as those who ask and so forth—all the virtuous results of giving, and, in particular, be compassionate to those recipients who are suffering. Candrakīrti says:

> Once the giving is free from stinginess,
> The giver must compassionately make gifts
> Which are given equally with an even-mindedness
> To those who are superior or inferior recipients.
>
> The results of such giving
> Go to both self and other at the same time.
> Holy beings praise this giving without stinginess
> To those who seek gifts.

And the *Praise of Infinite Qualities* says:[204]

> Even when some see a hopeful person who is destitute and of low birth
> They do not care and, out of desire for results, seek other recipients who have good qualities.
> They have a base motive; though givers, they are the same as those asking for gifts, you [Buddha] said.
> Hence, you remain committed out of compassion to giving to those who ask.

(b′) **What kind of motivation must be eliminated**

1. *A motivation that believes in the supremacy of bad views*. Lacking this means that you do not give while thinking, "There is no result from generosity," "Harmful blood offerings are religious," "I am giving as I apply myself to what is good and beneficial," or "Through just the completion of generosity alone I will be free of mundane and supramundane attachments."

2. *A motivation that is arrogant.* Lacking this means that you do not despise the person who asks for something, you do not compete with others, and, after you give something, you do not conceitedly think, "I am so generous; no one else can do like this." **[375]**

The *Purification of the Obscurations of Karma Sūtra* (*Karmāvaraṇa-viśuddhi-sūtra*) explains that when ordinary beings make gifts, they lose faith in those who are stingy, on account of which they get angry and are reborn in a hell, so it is said that this obstructs generosity. When these ordinary persons observe ethical discipline, they speak unflatteringly of those whose ethical discipline is faulty, so they lose faith in many living beings and fall into miserable realms on account of their loss of faith; and when these ordinary people maintain patience and the like, they speak disparagingly of those who do the opposite of these, and so obstruct their own ethical discipline and so forth.

Hence you should do as the *Praise of Infinite Qualities* says:[205]

> At the times when you were learned and very intelligent you did not praise yourself;
> You extolled and revered other persons who had few good qualities.
> When you maintained a mass of good qualities, you seized on even a small fault in your own behavior.

3. *A motivation for support.* Lacking this means that you do not give with the hope of getting praise or fame.

4. *A motivation of discouragement.* Lacking this means that when you give after becoming joyful even before the act of giving, you are filled with faith and then have no regret after giving; and even when you hear about a bodhisattva's vast acts of generosity, you are not discouraged but intensify your enthusiasm without belittling yourself.

5. *A motivation in which you turn your back on someone.* Lacking this means that you give out of an even-minded compassion that is impartial toward enemy, friend, and ordinary persons.

6. *A motivation of expecting something in return.* Lacking this means that you do not give to others out of the hope that they will help you, but because you see that these beings are bereft of happiness, burned by the flames of craving, without the power to relieve their sufferings, and naturally miserable.

7. *A motivation of expecting fruition.* Lacking this means that you do not hope for the fruition of an excellent body and resources in future lives, but give because you see that all composite things are

without substance but can contribute to unexcelled enlightenment. This does not stop you from expecting these results in the short term, but stops you from taking the mere body and resources of cyclic existence to be your goal. **[376]**

Besides these, you should give without the motivation of wrong livelihood in which you think, "If I make this gift, the ruler, etc., will recognize me as a generous person, and I will get some respect." Do not give from fear of becoming poor, or with the motivation to deceive someone who asks for something. Give something when you are free from distraction and feelings of dislike or anger. Make gifts when you are not dispirited due to the various wrong actions of the one who asks for something. Even when you see the faults of someone who has deceived you, etc., do not give with the motivation to proclaim these faults to others. Finally, give in the belief, from which others cannot dissuade you, that each individual act of giving will give rise to an individual result.

10

How to Give

(3)) How to give
(a′)) How not to give
(b′)) How to give
(4)) Things to give
(a′)) Brief presentation of the things which are and are not to be given
(b′)) Detailed explanation of the things which are and are not to be given
(1′)) Detailed explanation about inner things which are and are not to be given
(a″)) Inappropriate giving from the viewpoint of time
(b″)) Inappropriate giving from the viewpoint of purpose
(c″)) Inappropriate giving from the viewpoint of the one who asks for something
(2′)) Detailed explanation about outer things which are and are not to be given
(a″)) How not to give outer things
(1″)) Inappropriate giving from the viewpoint of time
(2″)) Inappropriate giving from the viewpoint of the gift
(3″)) Inappropriate giving from the viewpoint of the person
(4″)) Inappropriate giving from the viewpoint of material things
(5″)) Inappropriate giving from the viewpoint of purpose
(b″)) How to give outer things
(b)) What to do if you are unable to give
(c)) Relying on the remedies for the hindrances to generosity
(1)) The hindrance of not being used to generosity
(2)) The hindrance of declining fortune
(3)) The hindrance of attachment
(4)) The hindrance of not seeing the goal
(2″) The generosity which is just mental
(d′) A summary

(3)) **How to give**

This section has two parts:

1. How not to give
2. How to give

(a')) **How not to give**

Cast aside these thirteen ways of giving because they are to be eliminated: (1) not giving right away but only after you have delayed; (2) giving under stress; (3) giving after you have involved yourself in affairs that accord neither with the teachings nor with the ways of the world; (4) making a commitment beforehand that "I will give this much" and later making a gift of reduced quality or amount; (5) giving in return for favors; (6) giving in installments when you could give all at one time; (7) as a ruler, giving away someone else's child or spouse that you have kidnapped; (8) taking through pressure the belongings of your parents, servants, etc. and then giving them to others; (9) making a gift by a method that will hurt someone else; (10) while you remain idle, employing someone else to do the giving; (11) giving while you criticize and have contempt for the one who asks for something, while you are indirectly critical in a way that implies contempt, or while you intimidate the recipient with harsh words; (12) giving while you violate the Buddha's prohibitive precepts; and, (13) not giving resources as you acquire them but giving them after you accumulate them for a long time. **[377]**

Indeed, bodhisattvas see that it is wrong to give resources that you have stored up, whereas it is not wrong to give them away as you acquire them. This is because there is no additional merit in storing them up and then giving them at one time, and because you turn away many requests for your goods while you are storing them up; you come to feel tormented and may give them to someone who has not asked for them. These points stated in the *Bodhisattva Levels* are very important, for you can see that during the period of storing up the goods you produce many afflictions such as stinginess and the like, that the trouble of safeguarding them and so forth becomes a hindrance to many virtuous actions, and that more often than not you lose them at some point and are not able to give them away in the end anyway.

(b')) **How to give**

First of all, smile with a beaming countenance and then give to any recipient, showing respect by speaking honestly. Give with your own hands, at the appropriate time, without hurting anyone else, and bearing the suffering of any hardship. The result of these actions is described in the *Chapter of the Truth Speaker* (*Satyaka-parivarta*):[206]

> By charity out of a sense of service, you will receive service from others such as your relatives; by using your own hands when giving you will obtain people who serve you; by giving when appropriate you will accomplish your aims on time.

And also:

> By charity without hurting anyone else you will obtain stable resources; by giving while bearing unpleasantness you will have intimate companions.

Vasubandhu's *Treasury of Knowledge* (*Abhidharma-kośa*) states that from giving charity with your own hands you get a vast amount of resources. The *Treasury of Knowledge Auto-commentary* (*Abhidharma-kośa-bhāṣya*) explains that "stable resources" means that others do not interfere with them and that fire, etc. does not destroy them. **[378]**

Furthermore, there is a way to help others to be generous. If you have some belongings, go to the homes of stingy people who have no experience of giving gifts even a few times. Joyfully and in a relaxed manner direct them as follows: "I really do own a vast amount of things. I want some people to ask me for things so that I can complete the perfection of generosity, so if you meet some people who ask you for something, rather than turning them away without giving them anything, take from my wealth and give it to them. Or else lead them to me, and then rejoice in my generosity." This does not destroy their wealth, and they do this with pleasure. In this way they plant the seed for the removal of their stinginess. By gradually getting used to doing this they will give away a little of their own wealth and they will reduce their attachment a little. Contingent upon this, they will reach a moderate absence of attachment, and contingent upon that, a great absence of attachment. In like fashion, give belongings to your abbot, master, students, and friends who have a lot of attachment and are incapable of giving, and to those who are not like that but have no belongings, and then cause *them* to make offerings to the three jewels, rather than doing it yourself. By doing this you produce a great deal of personal merit. It pacifies the afflictions of some, fulfills the desire to practice the teachings in others, gathers beings around you, and causes them to mature.

Similarly, if you have no belongings, you may build up wealth through a craft or a job, and then give it away. Or else you may tell others a religious story in which even the poor or miserly wish to give. Alternatively, send those reduced to begging to the houses of rich persons who have faith, and go there yourself to assist in the giving of gifts to the extent that you are able. Also, as you sort through the material goods for charity, give the better first and give away completely all the goods presented for charity. **[379]**

(4)) **Things to give**

The explanation of the things to give has two parts:

1. Brief presentation of the things which are and are not to be given
2. Detailed explanation of the things which are and are not to be given

(a′)) **Brief presentation of the things which are and are not to be given**

In brief, bodhisattvas should give to others those things which immediately produce in the recipients pleasurable feelings that are free from the causes for a miserable rebirth and which ultimately will benefit them, either eliminating their sin or setting them in virtue. Even if these things do not immediately bring happiness, they should give them if they are beneficial in the end. They should not give things which immediately produce pain and ultimately cause harm, or which are immediately pleasant but ultimately harmful.

(b′)) **Detailed explanation of the things which are and are not to be given**

The detailed explanation of the things which are and are not to be given has two sections:

1. Detailed explanation about inner things which are and are not to be given
2. Detailed explanation about outer things which are and are not to be given

(1′)) **Detailed explanation about inner things which are and are not to be given**

Once you understand how not to give inner things, you will know the opposite of that, what you should give. Therefore, I will first explain how not to give. This has three parts:

1. Inappropriate giving from the viewpoint of time
2. Inappropriate giving from the viewpoint of purpose
3. Inappropriate giving from the viewpoint of the one who asks for something

(a")) **Inappropriate giving from the viewpoint of time**

Right from the start, bodhisattvas give away to all living beings their bodies, etc. with complete sincerity. Nevertheless, though you may be asked, do not give away the flesh of your body and so forth until you have developed an attitude of great compassion. Then you will not despair at the hardship of being asked for such things. The *Compendium of Trainings* says:[207]

> What is the joyous perseverance on account of which you become dispirited? It is when one who has little strength undertakes activity that is weighty or that extends over a long period of time; or when those lacking fully mature belief undertake difficult tasks like, for example, giving away their own flesh and so forth. Though these beginning bodhisattvas have given away their own body to all beings, still they turn away from untimely uses of it. Otherwise they would despair about these beings who ask for flesh, and thereby squander huge masses of good results due to wasting the seed of their spirit of enlightenment. **[380]** Therefore, the *Questions of Sky Treasure Sūtra* says: "Untimely wishes are demonic activity."

Engaging in the Bodhisattva Deeds also says:[208]

> Do not give away your body
> While your compassionate attitude is impure.
> In any case, give it away to achieve a great purpose
> In this and future lives.

(b")) **Inappropriate giving from the viewpoint of purpose**

Do not give away your body for some trifling purpose. *Engaging in the Bodhisattva Deeds* states:[209]

> For something trifling do not harm your body,
> Which is for practicing the sublime teachings;
> In this way you will quickly
> Fulfill the aims of living beings.

When from your perspective you are free of the hindrances to generosity—stinginess, etc.—and from others' perspective there is the greater purpose of accomplishing the aims of many living beings if you do not give away your body, then you do not give away your limbs, etc. even if asked. If you are asked for your body, etc. for the purpose of engaging in wrongdoing such as killing and so forth that will harm yourself and others, do not give yourself away to another even temporarily.

(c″)) **Inappropriate giving from the viewpoint of the one who asks for something**

Do not give your limbs, etc. when demonic deities or beings possessed by them ask for them with an intention of inflicting harm, because it will hurt them. Do not give when asked by a mad person or by those whose minds are disturbed because they are not sincerely asking, and their request is not well-considered. Not only is there no transgression in not giving to these beings, if you do give there is a transgression.

On occasions other than these you should give away your body when it is asked for. Furthermore, there are two ways to give away your body: (1) sectioning out your limbs and so forth and then making a permanent gift, and (2) giving yourself over temporarily into someone else's power as a servant, etc. in order to bring about their religious aims.

(2′)) **Detailed explanation about outer things which are and are not to be given**

This section has two parts:

1. How not to give outer things
2. How to give outer things

(a″)) **How not to give outer things**

How not to give outer things has five parts: **[381]**

1. Inappropriate giving from the viewpoint of time
2. Inappropriate giving from the viewpoint of the gift
3. Inappropriate giving from the viewpoint of the person
4. Inappropriate giving from the viewpoint of material things
5. Inappropriate giving from the viewpoint of purpose

(1″)) **Inappropriate giving from the viewpoint of time**

Inappropriate giving from the viewpoint of time is, for instance, giving an afternoon meal to renunciates or those who have taken a one-day vow.

(2″)) **Inappropriate giving from the viewpoint of the gift**

Inappropriate giving from the viewpoint of the gift is, for instance, giving left-over food and drink to one observing vows; giving food and drink contaminated and polluted by feces and urine, spittle and mucus, or vomit and pus; giving garlic, onion, meat, alcohol, or something tainted by these to those who do not eat or drink these things or who have vows for which it is inappropriate to use these things, even though they might want to eat or drink them; giving away a child, servant, and the like—even if you clearly convey the significance of the giving and they are pleased with it—when requested by someone you dislike, a *yakṣa*, a *rākṣasa*, someone overcome by belligerence, someone who is ungrateful, or someone forgetful; when approached by a sick person who asks for food and drink, giving unwholesome food and drink, and even giving wholesome food without moderation; giving tasty food when asked for it by extremely greedy people who are already satiated; and giving scriptures to non-Buddhist philosophers who have commercial interests, are seeking points of criticism, or do not want to learn the meaning of scripture. This is how the *Bodhisattva Levels* presents it.[210] Understand it in more detail from the *Bodhisattva Levels' Compendium of Determinations (Viniścaya-saṃgrahaṇī)*, where it says:[211]

> If you give a fully written Buddhist text to persons of childish intelligence who ask for it, you incur a misdeed. If you ask others for it to give to them, you also incur a misdeed. If you give it totally within thinking that you can cause them to become interested in or to embrace the profound teachings, you do not incur a misdeed. **[382]** If you give a text of spurious teachings or a treatise by non-Buddhist philosophers to beings who have faith in it after you have it set to writing, or you have an already written text in your possession, or you ask for a text from others, you incur a misdeed.
>
> Bodhisattvas erase the written texts of non-Buddhist philosophers that they have in their possession and have the scriptures of the Buddha written down, or they recognize that the texts are without any substance at all and make it known to others as well that it is better to erase them and to have the Buddha's scriptures written down.
>
> If someone asks you, a bodhisattva, for a stack of blank paper prepared for a text, you should inquire, "What are you going to do with it?" If the reply is, "I am going to use it for commercial

purposes," and the stack of blank paper is one that you are preparing for religious purposes, do not give it. If you have the monetary equivalent of the stack of blank paper, give this to the person. If you do not have the monetary equivalent of the paper and can give neither money nor paper, you still do not incur a misdeed.

If you are not preparing the stack of blank paper for a religious purpose, by all means give it away so that it will be joyfully put to use. Similarly you do not incur a misdeed for not giving it when the request derives from a desire to transcribe a really vile book. It is the same case for someone who wants to transcribe a middling kind of book. But be aware that you do incur a misdeed by not meeting a request made by one who wants to transcribe an exalted text.

(3")) **Inappropriate giving from the viewpoint of the person**

Inappropriate giving from the viewpoint of the person is, for instance, giving away a text to someone who asks for it while you have a desire to understand it—you still have not achieved the purpose of the text but are free from the defilement of stinginess about it.

Why this is inappropriate giving is as follows. Generosity such as this giving of the teachings is for the sake of any of three purposes: (1) removal of your stinginess, (2) completion of your vast collection of sublime wisdom, and (3) fulfilling the vast aims of others. Given this, if you do not give the text, the latter two purposes remain available to you, whereas if you do give it, they are not available to you. **[383]** You do not need to accomplish the first purpose, for in this case you do not have the defilement of stinginess, so it is not necessary to remove this affliction. If you do not give it, you will see an increase in your collection of sublime wisdom, whereas if you do give it, you will not have such a large increase. Furthermore, if you do not give the text, you will accomplish the collection of sublime wisdom for the benefit and happiness of all living beings, so you will be able to bring about happiness for this being who asks for the text and for all other living beings as well. If you do give it, however, just the one living being will be happy.

These greater or lesser purposes are spoken of in this manner in the *Bodhisattva Levels*.[212] Also, *Engaging in the Bodhisattva Deeds* says,[213] "Do not give up something exalted for something lesser," so it is not that there is merely no fault in not giving it away.

The way to refuse to give is to avoid using harsh language, such as saying, "I am not giving it to you." Rather, communicate with skill-in-means and then send the person off.

Skill-in-means is as follows. From the first, bodhisattvas turn over with pure intention all their belongings to all the buddhas and bodhisattvas of the ten directions. This is like, for example, the way that fully ordained monks keep religious robes and the like which they have mentally earmarked for their abbot or master. Because the monks have transferred their robes in this way, even though they accumulate belongings, they are called "bodhisattvas living in the noble family"[214] and infinitely increase merit.

The bodhisattvas, then, hold their belongings in trust, as it were, for the buddhas and bodhisattvas. If someone asks for something, and if the belonging is suitable to be given to this person, then bodhisattvas give it, thinking, "I have no belonging that the buddhas and bodhisattvas have not given away to all living beings." If the belonging is not suitable, the bodhisattvas depend on having transferred their things to the buddhas and bodhisattvas in a way similar to the monastic ritual of earmarking belongings, and then let the person know the situation, saying with soothing words, "My good person, this belongs to someone else. It is not something that I can give to you." Or else, the bodhisattvas might give the monetary equivalent of two or three times the price of the book to someone to whom they have refused a text. **[384]** In any case, the person who asks for it will think with regard to the bodhisattva, "It is not craving that keeps this person from giving me the text; it is not in this person's power to give it." This kind of activity is the generosity of the wise.

(4")) **Inappropriate giving from the viewpoint of material things**

Inappropriate giving from the viewpoint of material things is, for example, such gifts as your parents; food and drink that have bugs; a child, wife, servant, etc. whom you have not told or, even if told, does not want to be given away; or a child or wife who are persons of the sort who have become accustomed to comfort. Though it is said that you should not give your child, wife, etc. into servitude, I have included them here among "material things" because the gift of material things is the form of generosity that is emphasized the most.

The *Bodhisattva Levels' Compendium of Determinations* says that even if you do not satisfy a request for your three kinds of religious robes and any extra belongings [robes] other than those which the Buddha has permitted renunciates to own, you incur no fault if you do not have a stingy attitude toward them, and if they are requisite to your cultivation of virtue. Thus it says:[215]

> If renunciate bodhisattvas give away extra belongings—robes other than their three kinds of religious robes—that are permitted by the Buddha, are resources for their bodies, and are conducive to maintaining their comfort, and do so after they have looked carefully at the persons who want them and ask for them, they do not incur a misdeed. Even if they do not give them away, they incur no misdeed at all as long as their not giving is for the purpose of their cultivation of virtue and they do not have attachment to them.

The *Bodhisattva Vows of Liberation* says:[216]

> Śāriputra, if bodhisattvas give away their three kinds of religious robes, treating the one who asks for them as more important than themselves, they are not relying on few desires.

Hence, if renunciate bodhisattvas give away their three kinds of religious robes, they incur a transgression. **[385]**

(5″)) **Inappropriate giving from the viewpoint of purpose**

Inappropriate giving from the viewpoint of purpose is, for instance, when you fulfill a request for poison, weapons, fire, or alcohol which is for harming either yourself or others; when you meet a request for things to play with and enjoy but which are associated with a prohibitive risk of accumulating the causes for taking a miserable rebirth; or when you satisfy a request for, or a request to learn about, pits, traps, and so forth for the sake of hurting living beings. This means that it is inappropriate even to give instructions about these things for the sake of bringing harm to the lives and resources of beings. Other examples are giving land or bodies of water when they are requested for the sake of harming beings that inhabit watery or dry areas; giving political authority over these or other places for the sake of bringing harm to the human inhabitants; or, when asked for such things by somebody whom you dislike, giving them instead to an enemy of this person.

(b″)) **How to give outer things**

You must give outer things if the timing is not prohibited by the Teacher with respect to the recipient, and if giving the gift to this person is appropriate and suitable. Moreover, if you as the giver are a person opposite to that explained above, and are stingy with regard to a text, you must give it to a person who asks for it and who wishes to understand it, even though you may not have finished using it. This is to say, if you have a second copy, you give that, and if you do not, you should give the cost of having it copied out. If you do not have the money, you should definitely give the text away, thinking, "Though by giving this away I may be stupid in this life, it is all right; I will not acquiesce in my stinginess."

As to material things, you should give everything except those things listed above. If you are a ruler, and someone asks for others' children, wives, and so on, it is inappropriate to meet the request by separating each from their families, but you can give them as a whole together with the family dwelling and the like. Likewise, you must meet requests for things to play with that do not become a cause of taking a miserable rebirth; traps, etc. that do not hurt others; dry or wet places inhabited by living beings when no harm will come to the beings; and food and drink which do not have any bugs. **[386]** You should give even poison, weapons, fire, and alcohol if people ask for them in order to benefit themselves or others.

Qualm: What should you do when you are giving material gifts and two persons ask you for something, one of whom is poor and the other of whom is wealthy?

Reply: If you are confronted by both of them right from the first and you are able to fulfill both of their wishes, you should do so. If you are unable to do this, however, you should first think, "I will fulfill the wishes of the poor person," and work to give the gift to this person. So you should let the wealthy one know the situation, saying with soothing words, "My friend, I have already planned from the first to distribute this article to this poor person. Please do not think that I have spurned you," and then fulfill the wishes of the person who has no wealth.

I have written about the ways to learn these kinds of giving because they are extremely important for beginners who are keeping the bodhisattva vows. With the exception of some special cases I have explained all in accordance with the intended meaning of the *Bodhisattva Levels*.[217]

(b)) **What to do if you are unable to give**

If you are overcome with stinginess when someone asks you for something, think as follows: "This material thing and I are definitely going to be parted by death; it will leave me and I will leave it. So

I might as well take pleasure in giving this away and put it to good use, making a separation just as at the time of death. If I give this away, I will not have attachment to my wealth when the time comes for me to die. I will have no regrets and will give rise to feelings of pleasure and joy."

If you are unable to give it away even though you reflect in this way, then inform the person who asks for it by means of the three things that they should know. This is described in the *Questions of Householder Ugra Sūtra* (*Gṛha-pati-ugra-paripṛcchā-sūtra*),[218] which states that you should say, "I am new to the practice of the Mahāyāna and am still a person of small ability whose roots of virtue are not yet ripened. Also, I am under the influence of an ungenerous attitude. Further, I have a strongly grasping view of self and constantly conceive of a self and that which belongs to the self. So, excellent person, please forgive me and do not make it difficult for me. I shall try to do just what satisfies your thoughts and the thoughts of all living beings." **[387]** According to the *Compendium of Trainings*, this is to eliminate the further fault of each losing confidence in the other, but it does not get rid of the fault of stinginess, a fault in bodhisattvas that is looked down upon. Still it seems that doing this prevents the cardinal transgression of not giving the teachings and wealth because of stinginess. Also, the *Compendium of the Perfections* states:[219]

> If you cannot give because your ability is so small
> Though people come and ask you for something,
> So as to not make them feel low,
> Comfort them with gentle speech.
>
> Henceforth when people come to ask for something,
> Do your best not to make them feel low and despairing,
> And clear away the fault of stinginess.
> Earnestly strive to eliminate craving.

(c)) **Relying on the remedies for the hindrances to generosity**

According to what is found in the *Bodhisattva Levels' Compendium of Determinations*, there are four hindrances:

1. The hindrance of not being used to generosity
2. The hindrance of declining fortune
3. The hindrance of attachment
4. The hindrance of not seeing the goal

(1)) **The hindrance of not being used to generosity**

The hindrance of not being used to generosity is when you do not want to give to those who ask for something, even though you have material goods to give. The remedy for this is to avoid succumbing to the shortcoming of not being accustomed to generosity by quickly becoming aware, examining the situation, and reflecting, "This shortcoming is definitely the result of my previously not getting used to generosity," and "Moreover, if I do not make this gift, I will dislike generosity in my future life as well." Then, be generous.

(2)) **The hindrance of declining fortune**

The hindrance of declining fortune is when you do not feel generous because of the sparseness of your resources. The remedy to this is to make a gift after you willingly accept the suffering of poverty, thinking, "During the time that I have been passing through cyclic existence I have not helped others and have experienced many unbearable sufferings such as thirst, hunger, and the like because of being under the control of something else—that is, my former karma. **[388]** So even if I die from the suffering of this lifetime on account of my helping others, it is just better for me to be generous; whereas to turn away the person who asks me for something is not all right. Even in the absence of those resources, I will survive on some sort of wild plant."

(3)) **The hindrance of attachment**

The hindrance of attachment is when you do not feel generous inasmuch as you have become attached to extremely attractive and excellent material goods that are to be given. The remedy for this is to quickly become aware of your shortcoming of attachment, and then to think, "This mistaken notion that thinks 'I am happy' with regard to what is by nature suffering will bring me suffering in the future." Understanding this, eliminate your attachment and give away your material goods.

(4)) **The hindrance of not seeing the goal**

The hindrance of not seeing the goal is when you do not have in view the benefit of reaching perfect enlightenment that is contingent on generosity, but instead consider the benefit of a great amount of resources and then give things away. The remedy for this is to quickly become aware of this shortcoming; then to consider how, in general, all conditioned things perish moment by moment and how, in particular, your resources perish and leave you; and then to fully dedicate the giving of any gift for the sake of great enlightenment.

If you give while merely considering the karmic result of generosity—resources and the like—you will obtain a large amount of resources, but you will not attain liberation, just as business people who give without any hesitation all their goods to others for a price merely get a profit, but do not obtain merit. Āryadeva's *Four Hundred Stanzas* (*Catuḥ-śataka*) says:[220]

> "From making gifts to this person
> I will get a great reward."
> Such getting and giving are looked down on
> As being like wanting profit in business.

(2″) **The generosity which is just mental**

The generosity which is just mental means that after you go to a quiet place and then withdraw your mind inward, with a pure motivation and faith from the depths of your heart, you construct with your thoughts an immeasurably vast quantity of diverse gifts, and you then imagine that you are offering them to all living beings. **[389]** This increases merit immeasurably with little difficulty and, moreover, is the giving of wise bodhisattvas, according to the *Bodhisattva Levels.*[221] Although it says in the *Questions of Subāhu Sūtra*[222] that this is to be done by those who do not have wealth, it is appropriate for those who have wealth to do it as well.

These ways for wise bodhisattvas to give when they have no resources are employed until they attain the first level, the level of pure wholehearted resolve, whereupon poverty in resources no longer occurs. For, the *Bodhisattva Levels* says:[223]

> Thus, this is the giving of gifts for wise bodhisattvas while they have no resources and until they attain pure wholehearted resolve. Just as bodhisattvas of pure wholehearted resolve obtain a state which transcends miserable rebirths, so also they attain inexhaustible resources in all lifetimes.

(d′) **A summary**

After you have taken the bodhisattva vows, make aspirational prayers with respect to how to learn the practice of generosity on the high levels, and then train in these methods. Understand and learn what is permitted and prohibited with respect to the methods of making gifts that you can engage in right away, as explained above.

In particular, you must rely on the remedies to stinginess with respect to your body, resources, and roots of virtue. After you strive to steadily increase your generosity, you must cultivate joy for this practice and generate a feeling of sorrow for not having earlier trained your mind in that way. For, as it says in the *Questions of Subāhu Sūtra*,[224] once you do this, you will be able to complete the perfection of generosity with little difficulty in another lifetime, whereas if you give all this up and set it aside, not only in this life will you be continually tainted by very grave faults, but in other lives as well you will not want to engage in giving, and it will therefore become extremely difficult to enter into the bodhisattva deeds. **[390]**

Furthermore, the *Compendium of the Perfections* states:[225]

> The spirit of enlightenment is the root of such generosity,
> So do not give up this motive to make such gifts.
> The Conqueror said, "In the world the supreme form of giving
> Is the wish to give accompanied by the spirit of enlightenment."

Thus, being mindful of the spirit of enlightenment—the basis of the bodhisattva deeds—cultivating it, aspiring to enlightenment, and making aspirational prayers to become enlightened form the root of all giving and the supreme kind of giving, so work hard at these. This is the excellent key point that sums up the meaning of the *Questions of Subāhu Sūtra*.

11

The Perfection of Ethical Discipline

(ii) **How to train in the perfection of ethical discipline**

How to train in the perfection of ethical discipline has five parts:

1. What ethical discipline is
2. How to begin the cultivation of ethical discipline
3. The divisions of ethical discipline
4. How to practice
5. A summary

(a′) **What ethical discipline is**

Ethical discipline is an attitude of abstention that turns your mind away from harming others and from the sources of such harm. Therefore, you bring about the perfection of ethical discipline by progressively increasing your habituation to this attitude until you reach completion. However, it is not the case that you bring the perfection of ethical discipline to completion in the external world by establishing beings in a state free of all harm. Otherwise, since there are still living beings who are not free from harm, the conquerors who visited in the past would absurdly not have completed the perfection of their ethical discipline and would therefore also not be able to guide these beings to freedom from harm. Hence, whether all living beings in the external world are freed or not freed from harm makes no difference in this context; the practice of ethical discipline is just the habituation within your own mind to the attitude of abstention which turns away from harm to these beings. *Engaging in the Bodhisattva Deeds* says:[226]

> Where can beings such as fish be sent
> Where they will not be killed?
> So it is said that by attaining an attitude of abstention
> You perfect ethical discipline. **[391]**

Although ethical discipline does indeed have three divisions [the ethical discipline of restraint, the ethical discipline of gathering virtue, and the ethical discipline of acting for the welfare of living beings], it is explained in this context as the attitude of abstention in terms of the ethical discipline of restraint, the principal division. Moreover, in terms that include motivation, it is the ten abstentions that eliminate the ten nonvirtues; and in terms of what it really is, it is seven abstentions, which are the nature of the actions of body and speech that abstain from the seven nonvirtues. Candrakīrti's *Explanation of the "Middle Way" Commentary* (*Madhyamakāvatāra-bhāṣya*) says:[227]

> It is called ethical discipline because it does not acquiesce in the afflictions, because it allows no sins to arise, because it is coolness since it quells the fire of regret, or because it is that upon which the excellent rely since it is the cause of happiness. Moreover, it is characterized by seven abstentions. These are motivated by three qualities—non-attachment, non-hostility, and correct view. Therefore, ethical discipline is explained as the ten paths of action in terms that include motivation.

(b′) **How to begin the cultivation of ethical discipline**

As a person who generates the spirit of enlightenment and then promises to train in the bodhisattva deeds, you have promised to endow all living beings with the ornament of the ethical discipline of the perfect buddhas; therefore, you must accomplish the aims of all beings. In this regard you must first develop the strength of your own pure ethical discipline, for, if your own ethical discipline is impure and degenerates, you will fall to a miserable rebirth and will therefore not even achieve your own welfare, never mind the welfare of others. Hence, once you begin working for the welfare of others, value highly your ethical discipline. You need to sharply focus on safeguarding it and restraining your behavior. Do not be lax. The *Compendium of the Perfections* states:[228]

> Those who strive to endow all beings
> With the ornament of the perfect buddhas' ethical discipline
> Initially purify their own ethical discipline;
> With pure ethical discipline they develop powerful strength. **[392]**

And also:

> If you cannot achieve your own welfare with faulty ethical
> discipline,
> Where will you get strength for the welfare of others?
> Therefore, those who strive for others' welfare
> Do not relax their devotion to this.

Moreover, such pure ethical discipline is based on the practice (just as prescribed) of what to adopt and what to cast aside. This, moreover, depends on a strong and stable attitude of wanting to safeguard your ethical discipline. Consequently, develop a desire to safeguard your ethical discipline by meditating for a long time on the grave consequences of not safeguarding it and the benefits of safeguarding it.

With respect to the first, the grave consequences of not safeguarding your ethical discipline, the *Compendium of the Perfections* says:[229]

> Therefore, see the unbearable fright and
> Eliminate even the smallest thing that should be eliminated.

Thus, once you are frightened by the grave consequences of your misdeeds, you strive to abstain from even the small ones. Think as explained earlier about the grave consequences of the ten nonvirtues, the coarsest factors incompatible with ethical discipline.[230]

With respect to the benefits of safeguarding your ethical discipline, they are as explained earlier[231] and as set forth by the glorious Āryaśūra in his *Compendium of the Perfections*:[232]

> The divine substances, the resources of humans in which to
> delight, and
> The supreme bliss and supreme tastes which are the wonders
> of the deities—

Does anything more marvelous come from ethical discipline?
Even the buddhas and the teaching arise from it.

Furthermore, in dependence on ethical discipline your mind-stream progressively develops; your training becomes the same as that of the *mahāsattva* bodhisattvas, who have a compassionate nature; and you attain the pure sublime wisdom that eliminates all the seeds of wrongdoing. When worldly ornaments adorn the very young or very old, they make these persons seem ridiculous and are therefore ugly. But no matter who has the ornament of ethical discipline—old, young, or in-between—it delights everyone; thus, it is the best of ornaments. The pleasant fragrance of ethical discipline's good name spreads in all directions, whereas other pleasant fragrances must follow the direction of the wind and are thus limited. **[393]** A lotion scented of sandalwood, which relieves the torment of heat, is prohibited for renunciates, but a lotion which protects against the torturous heat of the afflictions is not prohibited and is appropriate for them. Someone who copies the outer appearance of being a renunciate but who has the jewel of ethical discipline is superior to others. The *Compendium of the Perfections* says:[233]

Ethical discipline is the path of special attainment,
Achieves equality with those of compassionate nature,
And has the highest nature of pure sublime wisdom.
Free of flaws, it is called the best of ornaments.

It is a pleasant fragrance throughout the three realms,
And a lotion not prohibited for a renunciate.
Even those who copy appropriate attire, if they have ethical discipline,
Will be superior to other human beings.

Furthermore, other benefits arise from ethical discipline: although you do not speak flattering words and do not strive with great effort and hardship, you naturally gather immediately necessary resources; even without threats of force all beings pay homage to you; there is no casual talk about the lineage of your relatives, etc.; people who previously did not know you or help you are naturally kind to you; and deities and humans revere the dust of your footprint and carry away what they can get as an object of worship. The *Compendium of the Perfections* states:[234]

Even without speaking or undertaking hardship
You gather immediate necessities and service.

Without threat all the world pays homage to you;
You obtain power effortlessly and without toil.

You are among those about whom it is improper to talk casually.
Even all persons who you did not know previously,
Who have not helped you or done what you need,
Pay homage to you, a person with ethical discipline.

Excellent beings revere the dust blessed by your feet,
Touching their heads to it; deities and humans bow down to it,
Place it on the crowns of their heads, and carry away what they can get. **[394]**
Therefore, one who has ethical discipline is in the supreme lineage.

The wise who reflect well on these benefits and grave consequences must safeguard their ethical discipline, as the *Compendium of the Perfections* explains:[235]

Due to a craving for their own happiness, bodhisattvas
Will not compromise ethical disciplines, which must be protected.

And also:

Because you control yourself, you experience happiness;
Because you have the ornament praised by the learned, you safeguard ethical discipline;
As you bring to perfection all the trainings,
Rely on ethical discipline completely and without pride.

Moreover, after you have cleared away your mere fear of the miserable realms and your wish for the mere excellences of deities or humans, safeguard your ethical discipline for the sake of establishing all living beings in ethical discipline. The *Compendium of the Perfections* states:[236]

Whoever aspires to establish in pure ethical discipline
Every living being in worlds beyond measure
And relies on ethical discipline to benefit the world
Is said to bring ethical discipline to perfection.

Therefore, clear away fear of the miserable realms
And the wish for the marvels of kingdoms and high status;
Safeguard a flawless ethical discipline, and depend on
Ethical discipline because you are striving for the welfare of the world.

(c′) The divisions of ethical discipline

There are three divisions of ethical discipline:

1. The ethical discipline of restraint
2. The ethical discipline of gathering virtue
3. The ethical discipline of acting for the welfare of living beings

(1′) The ethical discipline of restraint

The *Bodhisattva Levels* says the ethical discipline of restraint is the seven types of vows of individual liberation.[237] Thus, given that there are those who have taken vows of individual liberation and are also keeping the bodhisattva vows, the ethical discipline of restraint is either the actual vows of individual liberation for the group of either laypersons or renunciates, or it is a practice of restraint and abstention that would be associated with those actual vows. **[395]** Also, given that there are those who have taken the bodhisattva vows who are unsuited to be recipients of the vows of individual liberation, the ethical discipline of restraint is the practice of restraint and abstention that gives up any deed that is wrong by nature or any deed that is wrong by prohibition that would be associated with the vows of individual liberation.

(2′) The ethical discipline of gathering virtue

The ethical discipline of gathering virtue means that you focus on virtues such as the six perfections and then develop the virtues that you have not developed in your mind, do not spoil the ones that you have already developed, and increase both of these ever further.

(3′) The ethical discipline of acting for the welfare of living beings

The ethical discipline of acting for the welfare of living beings means that you focus on the welfare of eleven sorts of living beings, and then accomplish their aims in this and future lives in a suitable manner and without wrongdoing.[238] Since I have already detailed these in my *Basic Path to Awakening*,[239] you should definitely read that over and over again.

Therefore, since the rules of the vows of individual liberation are one aspect of the precepts for renunciates who have taken the bodhisattva vows, they are not set off apart from the precepts for bodhisattvas. Also, within the three divisions of ethical discipline, the ethical discipline of restraint—the actual rules of the individual liberation vows or the practice of engaging in what is to be adopted and rejecting what is to be cast aside that would be associated with these vows—is initially very important even for bodhisattvas, so train in this. The *Bodhisattva Levels' Compendium of Determinations* states:[240]

> Among the three aspects of ethical discipline, the ethical discipline of restraint includes and reaches to the other two; when you are bound by it and safeguard it, you will be bound by the other two and safeguard them as well, and when you are neither bound by nor protect it, you will not be bound by the other two nor safeguard them. Consequently, it is said that if bodhisattvas' ethical discipline of restraint degenerates, all their vows degenerate.

If you think that the vows of individual liberation are for *śrāvaka*s, and if you cast aside their prescriptive and proscriptive rules and say, "There are other precepts, bodhisattva precepts, to train in," then you have not grasped the key point of the bodhisattva training in ethical discipline, for it is often said that the ethical discipline of restraint is the basis and source of the next two types of ethical discipline. **[396]**

Furthermore, the principal aspect of the ethical discipline of restraint is abstaining from deeds that are wrong by nature. Moreover, it is taught in all the vehicles, higher and lower, that this abstention from deeds that are wrong by nature is the abstention from the ten nonvirtues, which comprise the crux of the major faults of the deeds that are wrong by nature. You must correctly restrain yourself physically, verbally, and mentally by not allowing a flicker of mere motivation for these nonvirtues. The *Compendium of the Perfections* says:[241]

> Do not let these ten paths of action degenerate;
> They are the path to the joys of high status or liberation.
> By maintaining these you reach your goals, which are
> Special contemplations wherein you think of helping beings.
>
> Correctly restrain your speech, body, and mind;
> The Conqueror said, "This, in brief, is ethical discipline."
> This is the basis that comprises all ethical discipline,
> So train in this restraint.

The master Candrakīrti also explains the practice of the perfection of ethical discipline as abstaining from the ten nonvirtues in the chapter on the perfection of ethical discipline of his *Explanation of the "Middle Way" Commentary*, and such explanations also occur in many sūtras such as the *Sūtra on the Ten Levels*. Therefore, if you initially train your mind in such restraint as presented above, you easily accomplish the remaining two types of ethical discipline.

(d′) **How to practice**

You practice the three types of ethical discipline in association with the six supremacies and the six perfections. When you practice in association with the six perfections, the generosity of ethical discipline is establishing others in ethical discipline after you have stabilized yourself in it. The remaining perfections are as presented before.[242]

(e′) **A summary**

Not to weaken and to increase steadily the spirit of enlightenment—the basis of the bodhisattva deeds—is the root of engaging in deeds of ethical discipline and so forth. It is also the best way to desist from harming any living being. Aspire to practice the ethical discipline of those at high levels and then train your mind in it. **[397]** Sincerely learn right now what to adopt and what to cast aside, starting with the ethical discipline of a beginning bodhisattva. In particular, each day frequently exercise an attitude of restraint with respect to what you know about deeds that are wrong by nature—such as the ten nonvirtues—and deeds that are wrong by prohibition. Among these also strive again and again to apply an attitude of restraint toward the fundamental transgressions of the vow to which you are committed. Once you do this, you will be able to complete the bodhisattva training in another lifetime as a causally concordant behavioral effect, with little difficulty and with little suffering. However, if you neglect these things now, you will be continually tainted by very grave faults and transgressions, and moreover for many lives you will be unable to learn the bodhisattvas' trainings. So from now on strive at these practices.

12

The Perfection of Patience

(iii) How to train in the perfection of patience
- (a′) What patience is
- (b′) How to begin the cultivation of patience
- (c′) The divisions of patience
  - (1′) Developing the patience of disregarding harm done to you
    - (a″) Stopping impatience with those who harm you
      - (1″) Stopping impatience with those who prevent your happiness and with those who cause you to suffer
        - (a)) Showing that anger is unjustified
          - (1)) On analysis of the object, anger is unjustified
            - (a′)) On analysis of whether the object has self-control, anger is unjustified
            - (b′)) On analysis for either adventitiousness or inherency, anger is unjustified
            - (c′)) On analysis of whether the harm is direct or indirect, anger is unjustified
            - (d′)) On analysis of the cause that impels the harmdoers, anger is unjustified
          - (2)) On analysis of the subject, anger is unjustified
          - (3)) On analysis of the basis, anger is unjustified
            - (a′)) Analyzing the causes of harm and where the fault lies
            - (b′)) Analyzing your commitment
        - (b)) Showing that compassion is appropriate
      - (2″) Stopping impatience with those who prevent your praise, fame, or honor, and with those who have contempt for you, or say offensive or unpleasant things to you
        - (a)) Stopping impatience with those who prevent three things—praise, fame, or honor
          - (1)) Reflection on how praise and so forth lack good qualities
          - (2)) Reflection on how praise and so forth have faults
          - (3)) The need to delight in those who prevent praise and so forth

(b)) Stopping impatience with those who do three things to you—have contempt for you, or say offensive or unpleasant things to you
(b″) Stopping both dislike for harmdoers' attainments and delight in their troubles
(2′) Developing the patience of accepting suffering
(a″) The reason you must definitely accept suffering
(b″) The way to develop acceptance
(1″) Rejecting the idea that when suffering occurs it is absolutely unpleasant
(2″) Showing that it is appropriate to accept suffering
(a)) Reflecting on the good qualities of suffering
(b)) Reflecting on the advantages of bearing suffering's hardships
(1)) Reflecting on the crucial benefits such as liberation, etc.
(2)) Reflecting on the benefit of dispelling immeasurable suffering
(c)) How it is not difficult to bear suffering if you gradually grow accustomed to it, starting with the small
(c″) A detailed explanation from the viewpoint of the bases
(3′) Developing the patience of certitude about the teachings
(d′) How to practice
(e′) A summary

(iii) **How to train in the perfection of patience**

The explanation of how to train in the perfection of patience has five parts:

1. What patience is
2. How to begin the cultivation of patience
3. The divisions of patience
4. How to practice
5. A summary

(a′) **What patience is**

Patience is (1) disregarding harm done to you, (2) accepting the suffering arising in your mind-stream, and (3) being certain about the teachings and firmly maintaining belief in them. There are three sets of factors incompatible with these: for the first, hostility; for the second, hostility and loss of courage; and for the third, disbelief and dislike. Perfecting patience means that you simply complete your conditioning to a state of mind wherein you have stopped your anger and the like. It is not contingent upon all living beings becoming free from undisciplined conduct because you would not be able to bring this about, and because you accomplish your purpose just by disciplining your own mind. *Engaging in the Bodhisattva Deeds* states:[243]

> Undisciplined persons are as limitless as space;
> You could never overcome them.
> If you conquer the single mental state of anger
> It is like vanquishing all your enemies. **[398]**
>
> Where could you get enough leather
> To cover the entire surface of the earth?
> Wearing just the leather of your sandals
> Is like covering all the earth.
>
> Similarly, I cannot change
> External things, but when
> I can change my state of mind,
> Why do I need to change anything else?

(b′) **How to begin the cultivation of patience**

Although there are many ways to cultivate patience, to begin I will explain the meditation on the benefits of patience and the faults of not being patient. The benefits are set forth in the *Bodhisattva Levels*:[244]

> Initially, bodhisattvas consider the benefits of patience. They think, "Persons who have patience will not have many enemies later on and will not have many separations from those to whom they are close. They will have much happiness and contentment. They will have no regret at the time of death, and upon the disintegration of their bodies they will also be reborn among the deities in the happy realms of high status." By looking at such benefits, they too are patient. They engage others in upholding patience, and they also praise patience. When they see patient persons, they are delighted and full of joy.

The *Compendium of the Perfections* says:[245]

> It is said, "Patience is the best approach
> For dealing with the inclination to disregard others' welfare";
> Patience against the fault of anger protects
> All that is excellent in this world.
>
> Patience is the best ornament of the powerful,
> The greatest strength for those who practice asceticism,
> And a stream of water on the wildfire of malice.
> Patience clears away much harm in this and future lives.
>
> The arrows of undisciplined people's words
> Are dulled by a superior being's armor of patience;

These unruly people then give pleasant flowers of praise
Which become attractive garlands of fame. **[399]**

And also:

Patience is also the craftsman that creates a buddha's embodiment of form,
Adorned with the beautiful signs of good qualities.

Thus, Āryaśūra praises patience by way of its many benefits: it stops you from turning away from others' welfare on account of living beings' misperceptions; it protects you from anger, the enemy that destroys many roots of virtue; it is a captivating ornament because it endures the harm of those of little power; it is the excellent strength of ascetics who are tormented by the afflictions; it is a stream of water that extinguishes the wildfire of malice; it is armor that cannot be pierced by the arrows of undisciplined persons' misperceptions; it is the skilled artisan who creates a fine form of golden color that captivates the eyes and minds of beings.

Furthermore, *Engaging in the Bodhisattva Deeds* states:[246]

Whoever works hard and overcomes anger
Is happy in this and future lives.

When you rely on patience continually, you do not spoil your joyful attitude, so you are always happy even in this life. Moreover, patience stops miserable rebirths in future lives, gives special rebirths in happy realms, and ultimately bestows certain goodness, so you are utterly happy in this and future lives.

Meditate on these benefits until you gain a strong, firm certainty about the cause-and-effect relationship wherein benefits such as these arise from patience.

With respect to the faults of anger, the invisible faults are as follows. *Engaging in the Bodhisattva Deeds* states:[247]

Any good deeds, such as
Generosity and worshipping the *sugatas*,
You have collected over a thousand eons
Are all destroyed in one moment of anger.

Āryaśūra formulated this exactly as it is presented in *Engaging in the Bodhisattva Deeds*. The *Play of Mañjuśrī Sūtra* (*Mañjuśrī-vikrīḍita-sūtra*) mentions the destruction of virtue accumulated over a hundred eons, and also Candrakīrti's *Commentary on the "Middle Way"* says that virtue accumulated over a hundred eons of conditioning to the perfections of generosity and ethical discipline is destroyed even by the generation of just a momentary angry thought. **[400]**

Concerning who or what the recipient of such destructive anger must be, some say that it must be bodhisattvas, while others assert that it is recipients in general. The former accords with the statement in the *Commentary on the "Middle Way"*:[248]

> Therefore, a moment's anger toward a conquerors' child
> Destroys the virtue arising from generosity and ethical discipline
> Accumulated over a hundred eons.

With respect to the person who gets angry, Candrakīrti's *Explanation of the "Middle Way" Commentary* says that if anger even by bodhisattvas destroys their roots of virtue, it goes without saying that the anger of non-bodhisattvas toward bodhisattvas does. Regardless of whether the recipient of the anger is ascertained to be a bodhisattva or whether the perceived faults that cause the anger are real, the destruction of virtue is said nonetheless to be just as explained above [i.e., the virtue accumulated over a hundred eons is lost].

In general, for there to be destruction of the roots of virtue it is not required that the anger be toward bodhisattvas. The *Compendium of Trainings* states:[249]

> The text of the Ārya-sarvāstivādins also says: The Bhagavan said, "Monks, consider a monk who makes a full prostration to a *stūpa* that contains a buddha's hair and nails and who has an attitude of faith."
>
> "So be it, Revered One."
>
> "Monks, this monk will experience reigns as a universal monarch a thousand times the number of grains of sand eighty-four-thousand leagues under the ground his prostrate body covers—down to the disk of gold that supports the earth."
>
> Then the venerable Upāli, who was located off to the side from where the Bhagavan was seated, bowed with hands joined respectfully and asked, "The Bhagavan has said that this monk's roots of virtue are so great. O Bhagavan, how are those roots of virtue used up, diminished, erased, and extinguished?" **[401]**
>
> "Upāli, when such a sin as malice is done to fellow practitioners, it is like a wound or maiming. I cannot see its full impact. Upāli, this diminishes, erases, and extinguishes those great roots of virtue. Therefore, Upāli, if you would not feel malice toward a burned stump, what need to mention feeling that way toward a body with consciousness?"

Some scholars' position: "The meaning of destroying the roots of virtue is that in destroying the capacity of previous virtues to issue their effects speedily, you delay the issuance of their effects. So anger, for instance, will give its effect first, but it is certainly not the case that the seeds of the roots of virtue will not issue effects when they later meet with the requisite conditions, because, given that no mundane path can eliminate the seeds that are to be eliminated, it is impossible to have an elimination of the seeds of the afflictions."

Reply: This reasoning is unsound because (1) even the purification wherein ordinary beings clear away nonvirtue by means of its remedy, the four powers of confession, is not an elimination of its seeds; nevertheless, though the seeds of this nonvirtue may later meet with the requisite conditions, they cannot issue a fruition; (2) even virtuous and nonvirtuous karma that are spent upon issuing their individual fruitions do not lose their seeds; nevertheless, even when the seeds of such karma meet henceforth with the requisite conditions, it is impossible for fruitions to arise; and (3) when you attain the peak and forbearance levels of the path of preparation [the second and third of four levels], you do not eliminate the seeds of nonvirtue that cause wrong views and miserable rebirths; nevertheless, even though the seeds of this nonvirtue may meet with the requisite conditions, they cannot give rise to wrong views or a miserable rebirth.

Furthermore, the reasoning is unsound because, as the earlier citation [Vasubandhu's *Treasury of Knowledge Auto-commentary*] says:[250]

> As to the actions that give rise to cyclic existence,
> There are those that are weighty, those that are near,
> Those to which you are habituated, and those you did earliest.
> Among these, the former will ripen first.

Any virtuous or nonvirtuous action that comes to fruition does temporarily stop the opportunity for the fruition of another action; however, it is not said nor can it be established that a mere preceding fruition destroys virtue or nonvirtue. Nor is it appropriate for "destroying the roots of virtue" to mean the mere temporary postponement of fruition; otherwise, it would absurdly follow that all powerful nonvirtuous actions must be considered destroyers of the roots of virtue. **[402]**

Therefore, concerning this the master Bhāvaviveka states (as already explained)[251] that in the case of both the purification of nonvirtue by the four powers of confession and the destruction of roots of virtue by wrong views and malice, the seeds of the virtue or nonvirtue cannot give rise to effects even though they may later meet with the requisite conditions, just as spoiled seeds will not give rise to sprouts even though they may meet with the requisite conditions.

Moreover, as already explained,[252] even though you cleanse your accumulation of sins through purification by the four powers, this does not contradict the fact that you are slow to produce higher paths. Accordingly, for some persons anger destroys, for instance, their resources and excellent body—the respective effects of giving gifts and safeguarding ethical discipline—but is unable to destroy their ability to easily produce roots of virtue again through giving gifts and safeguarding ethical discipline by means of the causally concordant behavioral effect of their habituation to generosity and an attitude of abstention. For other persons, anger destroys the continuous occurrence of a similar type of causally concordant virtuous behavior like ethical self-discipline and so on, but does not destroy the occurrence of an excellent body, resources, and so forth. Some [bodhisattvas] realize a path through which they progress to perfection within one eon, for instance, if they do not generate anger toward a bodhisattva who has obtained a prediction of his or her upcoming enlightenment (as explained earlier).[253] If they produce a single angry thought toward such a bodhisattva, this path is not expelled from their mind-stream, but their progress on the path becomes slow for the length of an eon.

In brief, just as in the case of the purification of nonvirtue there is no need to purify every behavioral effect, so with respect to the destruction of virtue there is no need to destroy every behavioral effect. However, as this is important and as it is critical to analyze it using the scriptures of the unique Buddha and the reasoning based on them, you should research the scriptures well and do an analysis.

Thus, the invisible faults of anger are that it projects its own fruitions, which are extremely unpleasant, and that it prevents the arising of the measureless very pleasant fruitions of its opposite [virtue]. **[403]**

The faults of anger visible in this lifetime are that you do not experience a peaceful and good mind; the joy and happiness that you had previously perish, and you cannot regain them; you cannot sleep well; and you weaken the stability wherein your mind stays calm. When you have great hatred, even those for whom you formerly cared forget your kindness and kill you; even friends and relatives will get annoyed and leave you; although you gather others with your generosity, they will not stay; and so on. *Engaging in the Bodhisattva Deeds* states:[254]

> In the grasp of the mental pains of hate,
> Your mind does not experience peace,
> You do not find joy or happiness,
> Sleep does not come, and you become unstable.
>
> Even those who depend on a master
> Who cares for them with wealth and services
> Will overcome and kill
> A master who gets angry.
>
> His anger disheartens friends.
> Though he gathers people with gifts,
> They will not serve him. In brief,
> No angry person is happy.

The *Garland of Birth Stories* also says:[255]

> When your complexion is spoiled by the fire of anger,
> You cannot look good, though adorned with jewelry.
> You may sleep on a good bed, but
> Your mind suffers the sharp pains of anger.
>
> You forget to achieve goals beneficial to yourself;
> Tormented by anger, you take an evil path.
> You ruin the achievement of your aims and your good name.
> Your grandeur fades like the waning moon.
>
> Though your friends love you,
> You fall into an abyss of wrong.
> Weakening your intelligence about what is helpful and what harmful,
> You mostly transgress and your mind becomes confused.
>
> Through anger you are accustomed to sinful acts,
> So you suffer for a hundred years in miserable realms.
> What harm greater than this could be done
> Even by enemies avenging the great harm you have done?
>
> This anger is the inner enemy;
> I know it to be so.
> Who can bear
> Its proliferation? **[404]**

Meditate until you are firmly convinced that grave consequences such as these arise from anger. Thus, *Engaging in the Bodhisattva Deeds* says:[256]

> There is no sin like hatred
> And no fortitude like patience.
> Therefore, earnestly cultivate
> Patience in a variety of ways.

First, understand the benefits and faults, and then strive to cultivate patience in many ways. The reason behind the first line is set forth in Candrakīrti's *Explanation of the "Middle Way" Commentary*:[257]

> You cannot measure the fruitions of anger, just as you cannot measure the water in the ocean with a balance scale. Therefore, for projecting unpleasant effects and damaging virtue, there is no sin greater than a lack of patience.

For, although other sins result in extremely unpleasant fruitions, they are not great sins on that account alone, given that they do not destroy roots of virtue. Still, there are many wrongs other than anger that combine both production of a terrible fruition and destruction of the roots of virtue: wrong views that deny cause and effect; abandoning the sublime teachings; generating pride in relation to bodhisattvas, gurus, and the like and thus terribly belittling them; and so forth. You can know of these from the *Compendium of Trainings*.

(c′) **The divisions of patience**

The section on the divisions of patience has three parts:

1. Developing the patience of disregarding harm done to you
2. Developing the patience of accepting suffering
3. Developing the patience of certitude about the teachings

(1′) **Developing the patience of disregarding harm done to you**

Developing the patience of disregarding harm done to you has two parts:

1. Stopping impatience with those who harm you
2. Stopping both dislike for harmdoers' attainments and delight in their troubles

(a″) **Stopping impatience with those who harm you**

Stopping impatience with those who harm you has two parts:

1. Stopping impatience with those who prevent your happiness and with those who cause you to suffer **[405]**
2. Stopping impatience with those who prevent your praise,

fame, or honor, and with those who have contempt for you, or say offensive or unpleasant things to you

(1″) **Stopping impatience with those who prevent your happiness and with those who cause you to suffer**

Stopping impatience with those who prevent your happiness and with those who cause you to suffer has two parts:

1. Showing that anger is unjustified
2. Showing that compassion is appropriate

(a)) **Showing that anger is unjustified**

Showing that anger is unjustified has three parts:

1. On analysis of the object, anger is unjustified
2. On analysis of the subject, anger is unjustified
3. On analysis of the basis, anger is unjustified

(1)) **On analysis of the object, anger is unjustified**

On analysis of the object, anger is unjustified has four parts:

1. On analysis of whether the object has self-control, anger is unjustified
2. On analysis for either adventitiousness or inherency, anger is unjustified
3. On analysis of whether the harm is direct or indirect, anger is unjustified
4. On analysis of the cause that impels the harmdoers, anger is unjustified

(a′)) **On analysis of whether the object has self-control, anger is unjustified**

Analyze, thinking, "What would be reasonable grounds for anger toward harmdoers?" Whereupon, you might think, "They first had the thought of wanting to harm me, prepared the method, and then either prevented my happiness or inflicted unpleasant physical or mental suffering, so my anger is justified." Are you angry because they inflicted harm while they had the self-control not to harm you, or are you angry because they were utterly without any self-control and hurt you while helplessly impelled by something else? In the former case, your anger is unjustified because those who inflict harm do not have control over themselves, for, when the conditions and causes—seeds left by afflictions to which they were previously habituated, a nearby object, and erroneous conceptions—come together, they give rise to the thought to harm, even though the harmdoers do not think, "I will feel malice"; whereas if those causes and conditions are not complete, they will never produce the thought to harm, even if the harmdoers think, "I will feel malice." These causes and conditions produce the desire to harm; this in turn produces the work of harming; and this produces suffering for someone else, so those harmdoers do not have even the slightest self-control. Moreover, they have become like servants of their afflictions, because they are under the control of others, i.e., their afflictions.

In the latter case—you are angry because the harmdoers are utterly without any self-control and, being helplessly impelled by something else, they hurt you—then your anger is totally unjustified. **[406]** For instance, some people who have been possessed by demons and have come under their control may wish to hurt those who are helping them to get free of their demons and thereupon beat them, etc. However, their helpers think, "They do this because their demons have eliminated their ability to control themselves," and do not have even the slightest anger toward them. They then strive to the best of their ability to free them from their demons. Likewise, when bodhisattvas are hurt by others, they think, "They do this because the demons of the afflictions have eliminated their ability to control themselves." Without being even the slightest bit angry with those persons they then must generate the spirit of enlightenment, thinking, "I will strive at the bodhisattva deeds in order to free them from these afflictions." Accordingly, Āryadeva's *Four Hundred Stanzas* says:[258]

> Just as a doctor does not fight but helps
> Patients who are possessed by spirits, though they get angry,
> So the Sage sees that the afflictions are at fault,
> Not the persons who have the afflictions.

The master Candrakīrti also states:

> "This is not living beings' fault,
> Rather it is the fault of the afflictions."
> So the learned analyze
> And do not fight with others.

Although many reasonings are set forth in *Engaging in the Bodhisattva Deeds*, it is easy to be certain of this one, and it is a very powerful remedy for anger. Also, the *Bodhisattva Levels* has the same meaning where it states that you can bear harm after you meditate on the idea of mere phenomena, so meditate repeatedly on this remedy until you reach certain knowledge of it.

If these beings had self-control, they would not have any suffering, because they would not want suffering and because they could control it. Furthermore, you should stop your anger by also thinking, "When these beings are moved by strong afflictions, they commit suicide, leap from cliffs, harm themselves with thorns, weapons, etc., and stop eating and so forth. **[407]** If they do this to even their greatly cherished and dear selves, of course they will hurt others." *Engaging in the Bodhisattva Deeds* states:[259]

> Thus, everything is dependent on something else,
> And, because that in turn is dependent, it is not autonomous.
> Understanding this, do not be angry
> At anything, all things being like illusions.

And also:

> Therefore, if you see an enemy or friend
> Doing what is wrong, think
> "This arises from certain conditions,"
> And remain happy.
>
> If all beings could achieve results
> According to their wish, then,
> Since no one wants suffering,
> No one would suffer.

And also:

> While under the control of their afflictions,
> Some people will kill even their dear selves.
> So how can you expect them
> Not to harm the bodies of others?

(b′)) **On analysis for either adventitiousness or inherency, anger is unjustified**

The fault of doing harm to others either is or is not in the nature of living beings. If it is in their nature, it is wrong to get angry, just as it is wrong to get angry at fire for being hot and burning. Similarly, if it is adventitious, it is also wrong to be angry, just as when smoke and the like appear in the sky, it is wrong to be angry at the sky on account of these flaws of smoke and so forth. Thinking in this way, stop your anger. *Engaging in the Bodhisattva Deeds* states:[260]

If doing harm to others
Is natural for the childish,
It is wrong to get angry at them,
Just as it is at fire's burning nature.

Still, if the fault is adventitious,
And the nature of beings is good,
My anger is wrong, just as is
Anger at smoke's appearance in the sky.

(c')) **On analysis of whether the harm is direct or indirect, anger is unjustified**

If you are angry at the agent of harm that directly inflicts the harm, you will have to be angry at the stick, etc., just as you are at the person. If you are angry at the harmdoer who indirectly inflicts harm, then, just as the person impels the stick and so forth to do the harm, so hostility impels the person. **[408]** Therefore, get angry at the hostility. *Engaging in the Bodhisattva Deeds* says:[261]

The stick and so forth directly cause the harm.
But if I am angry at the one who throws it,
Then, since hostility impels them,
It is better to get angry at hostility.

If you are not angry at the stick, it is also wrong to be angry at the one who throws it; if you are angry with the one who throws it, it is correct to be angry also at the hostility. Not believing this, your mind has gone down a wrong path. Therefore, become certain about the overall sameness of the logic here and direct your mind toward not being angry at the person in the same way that you are not angry at the stick. Furthermore, use the reasonings taught earlier that negate the idea that anything has self-control in order to understand that you should not differentiate the stick and the one who throws the stick by whether they have a harmful intent.

(d')) **On analysis of the cause that impels the harmdoers, anger is unjustified**

The experience of suffering produced by those who harm does not occur causelessly or from discordant causes, so it occurs from concordant causes; that is to say, from nonvirtuous actions you have done in the past. Therefore, harmdoers are helplessly impelled to do harm by the power of your karma. Consequently, blame yourself, thinking, "This is my fault, and I am wrong to get angry at others," and stop your anger on all occasions. For example, it is similar to the way that beings produce the guardians of hell with their own bad karma, and these guardians then inflict harm on them. *Engaging in the Bodhisattva Deeds* states:[262]

> I, at a former time, inflicted
> Harm such as this on living beings.
> Therefore, it is fitting that I, who hurt others,
> Should receive this harm.

And also:

> The childish do not want suffering,
> Yet crave the causes of suffering.
> So why should I be angry with others
> When it is my own fault that I am hurt?
>
> For example, just like the guardians of hell
> And the Sword-leafed Forest,
> I produce this harm with my own actions. **[409]**
> So at whom should I get angry?
>
> Those who do me harm arise
> Impelled by my own karma.
> If thereby they go to a hell,
> Have I not ruined them?

Also, Sha-bo-ba said, "When you say, 'I am not at fault,' it indicates that you, in fact, have not internalized even a bit of the teaching."

(2)) **On analysis of the subject, anger is unjustified**

If you get angry at a harmdoer through an inability to bear suffering, it is contradictory because, even as you are failing to bear slight suffering in the present, you are aggressively creating the cause of measureless suffering in the miserable realms. Therefore, induce a sense of embarrassment, thinking, "I am very stupid," and work to contain your anger. *Engaging in the Bodhisattva Deeds* states:[263]

> If I cannot endure
> Even the slight suffering of the present,
> Then why do I not stop my anger,
> The cause of suffering in the hells?

The suffering generated by harm is the effect of previous bad karma; by experiencing it, you exhaust this karma. If you bear the suffering, you do not accumulate new sins and you greatly increase your merit. Therefore, you must not consider how harmdoers ruin their virtue, but view them as kind in that it is as though they are engaged in actions for the sake of clearing away your sins. The *Garland of Birth Stories* says:[264]

> I do not think about this person ruining his virtue,
> But that he is as if engaged in actions to clear away my sins;
> If I am not patient even with this person,
> How could I be any more unkind?

And Candrakīrti's *Commentary on the "Middle Way"* says:[265]

> You want to say that you are exhausting
> The effects of nonvirtuous karma done in the past;
> How then can you sow the seeds of further suffering
> By getting angry and harming others?

Therefore, just as you tolerate bleeding or burning as a treatment to cure a severe illness, it is appropriate to bear small sufferings for the sake of preventing great suffering. **[410]**

(3)) **On analysis of the basis, anger is unjustified**

On analysis of the basis, anger is unjustified has two parts:[266]

1. Analyzing the causes of harm and where the fault lies
2. Analyzing your commitment

(a′)) **Analyzing the causes of harm and where the fault lies**

Engaging in the Bodhisattva Deeds says:[267]

> His sword and my body
> Are both causes of suffering.
> He obtained the sword, I obtained the body;
> At which should I be angry?
>
> If, blinded by craving, I have obtained
> This abscess with a human form,
> So painful that it cannot bear to be touched,
> With whom should I be angry when it is hurt?

And also:

> If some people, out of confusion, harm others
> While others in confusion get angry with them,
> Who is blameless
> And who is to blame?

(b′)) **Analyzing your commitment**

Develop the fortitude of patience, thinking, "It is wrong for even *śrāvakas*, who act for their own purposes alone, to be impatient and get angry. So of course it is wrong for me. I committed myself to achieving the benefit and happiness of all living beings when I generated the spirit of enlightenment. I act for others' welfare and care for all beings." Also, Bo-do-wa said:

> The Buddha's teaching is to commit no sin. When you fail to cultivate patience with a slight harm, you make the curse, "May this eradicate the teaching." Thereby you give up your vow, and this eradicates the teaching. We do not have the teaching as a whole; when we break our vows, we dissipate what we do have.

And also:

> When a yak has been saddled up for carrying goods, if the saddle tightens around his tail, he bucks, and the saddle beats against his legs. If the saddle is loosened, the straps drop, and the yak is happy. Similarly, if you do not relax around a harmdoer, the harmdoer matches what you do, and you steadily become more unhappy.

(b)) **Showing that compassion is appropriate**

Contemplate from the depths of your heart, "All living beings have been in cyclic existence since beginningless time, and there is not one who has not been my friend and relative—father, mother, etc. Being impermanent, they lose their lives and are miserable due to the three types of suffering. Crazed by the demon of the afflictions, they destroy their own welfare in this and future lives. **[411]** I must generate compassion for them. How could it be right to get angry or to retaliate for harm?"

(2") **Stopping impatience with those who prevent your praise, fame, or honor, and with those who have contempt for you, or say offensive or unpleasant things to you**

Stopping impatience with those who prevent your praise and so forth, and with those who have contempt for you and so forth has two parts:

1. Stopping impatience with those who prevent three things—praise, fame, or honor
2. Stopping impatience with those who do three things to you—have contempt for you, or say offensive or unpleasant things to you

(a)) **Stopping impatience with those who prevent three things—praise, fame, or honor**

Stopping impatience with those who prevent three things—praise, and so forth—has three parts:

1. Reflection on how praise and so forth lack good qualities
2. Reflection on how praise and so forth have faults
3. The need to delight in those who prevent praise and so forth

(1)) **Reflection on how praise and so forth lack good qualities**

When others praise you and spread your fame, it serves neither of two purposes: for this life it does not bring you long life, health, and the like, and for future lives it does not bring merit and so forth. Therefore, do not get attached to fame and praise, but reproach yourself by thinking, "My displeasure when my praise and fame are ruined is no different from when small children cry upon the collapse of their sand castles, which lack any of the requisites for a dwelling." *Engaging in the Bodhisattva Deeds* states:[268]

> Praise, fame, and honor
> Do not cause merit, nor longevity,
> Nor cause strength, nor health,
> Nor bring physical well-being.
>
> Once I understand my own welfare,
> What meaning is there for me in those?

And also:

> When their sand castles collapse,
> Children cry in great distress.
> Likewise, my mind is childish
> When my praise and fame are ruined.

(2)) **Reflection on how praise and so forth have faults**

Develop disgust for praise and so forth, thinking, "Praise, fame, and honor distract my mind with the meaningless, destroy my disenchantment with cyclic existence, make me jealous of those with good qualities, and spoil my virtuous activities." *Engaging in the Bodhisattva Deeds* states:[269]

> Praise and so forth distract me,
> Destroy my disenchantment,
> Promote my jealousy of those with good qualities,
> And destroy all that is good. **[412]**

(3)) **The need to delight in those who prevent praise and so forth**

Stop your anger and feel delight from the depths of your heart, thinking, "In that case, damage to my praise, fame, gain, and honor protects me from going to miserable realms, cuts the bonds of my attachment, and, like the Buddha's blessing, blocks the door through which I am about to enter into suffering." Thinking like this, you should from the depths of your heart stop anger and feel happy. *Engaging in the Bodhisattva Deeds* states:[270]

> Therefore, are not those involved in destroying
> Praise of me and the like
> Engaged in protecting me
> From falling into miserable realms?
>
> I diligently seek freedom
> And do not need the bonds of gain and honor;
> How could I get angry
> With those who free me from bondage?
>
> I am about to descend into suffering,
> But, like the Buddha's blessing, they are
> Giving me an opportunity to avoid it.
> How could I be angry with them?

(b)) **Stopping impatience with those who do three things to you—have contempt for you, or say offensive or unpleasant things to you**

Prevent your unhappiness, thinking, "Since the mind is not material, it cannot be directly harmed by others. While the mind is indirectly harmed by directly harming the body, the body cannot be harmed by contempt, offensive speech, and unpleasant words. These harm neither body nor mind, so I should be delighted." When you prevent your unhappiness, you do not give rise to hostility. Thus *Engaging in the Bodhisattva Deeds* says:[271]

> Since the mind is not physical,
> No one can ever destroy it.
> It is strongly attached to the body
> And so it is harmed by physical suffering.
>
> Contempt, offensive speech,
> And unpleasant words
> Do not harm the body,
> Then why, mind, are you so angry?

Sha-ra-wa said:

> No matter what the three geshes Kam-lung-ba, Neu-sur-ba (sNe'u-zur-pa) and Drap-ba (Grab-pa) heard, it was no different from speaking to dirt and rocks, so they remained happy. Since everyone nowadays reacts quickly to what is said, they become unhappy.

When somebody whispered to Shen-dön (gShen-ston), "He said this and then that," Shen-dön replied, "People also say things behind the king's back. You have committed divisive speech, so confess it." **[413]**

When someone said to the yogi Shay-rap-dor-jay (Shes-rab-rdo-rje), "People are talking about us and saying that our attendants are too lax," he replied, "Well, the talk of the people will be about people; what else would they talk about?" Thereafter that person completely stopped the spread of his divisive speech.

Objection: When someone has contempt for me, etc., other people will not like me, so this is why I am unhappy about it.

Reply: This would have some truth if others' dislike were to harm you. However, since their dislike does nothing to you, give up your unhappiness about others' contempt. *Engaging in the Bodhisattva Deeds* says:[272]

Others' dislike for me
Does not devour me
In this or other lives.
Why am I averse to it?

Objection: Indeed I am not harmed by their dislike, but in dependence on it I may be hindered in acquiring things from them, so I will get angry at those who have contempt for me, scorn me, or say unpleasant words to me.

Reply: Even if you acquire things, you must leave them here, whereas the sin of your anger at them will follow you. Hence, of the two choices—dying quickly in destitution or living for a long time improperly—the former is better.

Even if you acquire things and live for a long time, you must die since you are not liberated from death. At the time of death, it is the same whether you have enjoyed pleasure for the previous hundred years or enjoyed it for merely one year, for both alternatives are nothing more than mere objects of memory; and at that time it makes no difference at all for your happiness or suffering. It is analogous to how in a dream the experience of pleasure for one hundred years and the experience of a mere moment's pleasure have no difference at all with respect to your happiness or unhappiness at the time of waking.

When you contemplate in this way and turn away from attachment to gain and honor, you will not become unhappy with unpleasant words and contempt. You have no interest in being special in the eyes of others, so you do not lose your contentment. Thus, *Engaging in the Bodhisattva Deeds* states:[273]

> While I do not like contempt and so forth
> Because they interfere with my prosperity,
> I leave my acquisitions here
> But firmly keep my sins. **[414]**
>
> Better that I die today
> Than live a long, improper life.
> Those like me might live a long time,
> But then there is only the suffering of death.
>
> Someone might wake from a dream
> After experiencing happiness for one hundred years;
> Another might wake from a dream
> After experiencing happiness for a mere moment.
>
> For both persons once they awaken
> Happiness does not return;
> It is like this at the time of death
> Whether your life was long or short.
>
> After acquiring many things,
> I may enjoy pleasure for a long time,
> But just like one robbed by a thief
> I will leave naked and empty-handed.

(b″) **Stopping both dislike for harmdoers' attainments and delight in their troubles**

Contemplate as follows, "After I have generated the spirit of enlightenment for the sake of accomplishing all living beings' benefit and happiness, I get angry at harmdoers when they obtain happiness on their own. After I have said that I want all beings to become buddhas, I get unhappy when harmdoers get even minimal prosperity or honor. This is extremely contradictory." You must eliminate your jealousy regarding any sort of attainment by other persons and delight in it from the depths of your heart. Otherwise your spirit of enlightenment and the achievement of the welfare and happiness of beings are nothing but words. *Engaging in the Bodhisattva Deeds* says:[274]

> Since you want all beings to be happy,
> You have generated the spirit of enlightenment.
> Then, when beings find happiness themselves,
> Why do you get angry with them?

If you wish to attain for living beings' welfare
Buddhahood, which is worshipped in the three worlds,
Why are you tormented when you see
Their most paltry gain or honor?

When a relative finds sustenance
For those whom you should nurture—
Objects of your care and generosity—
Instead of being pleased, are you angry again?

If you do not wish even that for beings,
How can you wish them enlightenment?
Where is the spirit of enlightenment
In someone who gets angry at others' attainments? **[415]**

Whether your enemy gets something from someone
Or it remains in the benefactor's house
It is never yours, so why be angry—
Whether it is given or not?

Even your mere malicious thoughts that delight in your enemies' troubles or that wish for their destruction do not harm your enemy; they lead only to your own suffering. Yet, if such malice were to harm them, you should stop it completely, reflecting on the drawback that this would bring ruin to yourself and others. *Engaging in the Bodhisattva Deeds* states:[275]

When my enemies are unhappy,
What am I pleased about?
My wishes alone
Will cause them no harm.

Even if I should effect their suffering with my wish,
What could I be pleased about?
If I say I will be satisfied,
What could be more ruinous?

Once I am caught by the terrible, sharp hook
Cast by the fishermen, the afflictions,
I will surely be cooked by the hell-guardians
In a kettle for the beings of hell.

You will be unhappy if you view as absolutely undesirable the obstacles to what you and your friends want, movement in directions you do not want, and the prosperity of your enemies. If this unhappiness increases, you become hostile. If you stop your absolute dislike of these three things, you prevent unhappiness. Once you do this, you will not feel hostile. Thus, dispel your absolute dislike of these by using the reasonings previously taught. Take many approaches to stop your anger, because it is a very great fault.

These instructions—the lines of reasoning of the conquerors and their children presented above—provide the techniques for defeating your greatest enemy, anger. They involve arguing with your own afflictions and looking within yourself. When you analyze well with discerning wisdom and stop anger with many lines of reasoning, you prevent many different types of anger, and you become patient in many ways. **[416]** Since this is an experience engendered by penetrating understanding that uses flawless reasoning to get at the meaning of correct scriptures, it leaves an extremely stable latent propensity.

Those who reject meditative analysis with discerning wisdom are those who reject the whole of the great undertaking of bodhisattva deeds such as these. Understand that such rejection is the worst hindrance to using a life of leisure for the benefit of yourself and others. Get rid of it as you would poison.

(2′) **Developing the patience of accepting suffering**

Developing the patience of accepting suffering has three parts:

1. The reason you must definitely accept suffering
2. The way to develop acceptance
3. A detailed explanation from the viewpoint of the bases

(a″) **The reason you must definitely accept suffering**

Engaging in the Bodhisattva Deeds states:[276]

> The causes of happiness sometimes occur,
> Whereas the causes of suffering occur frequently.

As you continually experience whatever suffering is appropriate to you, you absolutely must know how to bring it into the path. Otherwise, as the *Compendium of Trainings* says, you either generate hostility or you become discouraged about cultivating the path, either circumstance interfering with applying yourself to virtue.

Moreover, some sufferings will be caused by others, and some will be produced by your former karma, whether or not you strive at the path. Some, as will be explained below, occur when you engage in virtuous activity but do not occur when you are not so engaged. For the time being, you cannot dispel the sufferings definitely produced by the power of former karma and immediate conditions. You must accept them when they arise, because (1) if you do not do this, in addition to the basic suffering, you have the suffering of worry that is produced by your own thoughts, and then the suffering becomes very difficult for you to bear; (2) if you accept the suffering, you let the basic suffering be and do not stop it, but you never have the suffering of worry that creates discontentment when you focus on the basic suffering; and (3) since you are using a method to bring even basic sufferings into the path, you greatly lessen your suffering, so you can bear it. Therefore, it is very crucial that you generate the patience that accepts suffering. **[417]**

(b″) **The way to develop acceptance**

The way to develop acceptance has two parts:

1. Rejecting the idea that when suffering occurs it is absolutely unpleasant
2. Showing that it is appropriate to accept suffering

(1″) **Rejecting the idea that when suffering occurs it is absolutely unpleasant**

If you can remedy a situation wherein suffering occurs, you do not need to feel that it is unpleasant. If you cannot remedy it, it is not helpful to find it unpleasant, so there is no need for, or effectiveness to, your displeasure; there is even a disadvantage. If you are very impatient, a slight suffering is extremely difficult to bear, whereas if you minimize your impatience, you can endure great suffering. *Engaging in the Bodhisattva Deeds* says:[277]

> If there is a remedy,
> Why be displeased?
> If there is no remedy,
> What is the use of being displeased?

And also:

> I shall not be impatient with
> Heat, cold, wind, and rain,
> Illness, bondage, beatings, and so on;
> If I am, the harm increases.

(2″) **Showing that it is appropriate to accept suffering**

Showing that it is appropriate to accept suffering has three parts:

1. Reflecting on the good qualities of suffering
2. Reflecting on the advantages of bearing suffering's hardships

3. How it is not difficult to bear suffering if you gradually grow accustomed to it, starting with the small

(a)) **Reflecting on the good qualities of suffering**

Suffering has five good qualities: (1) *The good quality of spurring you on to liberation*. This is because if you had no suffering, you would not develop the determination to be free of it. (2) *The good quality of dispelling arrogance*. This is because when suffering strikes you, it reduces your sense of superiority. (3) *The good quality of causing you to shun sin*. This is because when you experience very painful feelings, they arise from nonvirtue, so if you do not want these effects, you must avoid their causes. (4) *The good quality of causing you to like cultivating virtue*. This is because when you are tormented with suffering, you desire happiness, and once you want it, you must cultivate the virtue that causes it. **[418]** (5) *The good quality of producing compassion for those who wander in cyclic existence*. This is because after you have assessed your own situation, you think, "Other beings suffer like this." From these five and what they indicate, recognize other good qualities on your own and then repeatedly train your mind to think, "This suffering is a condition that I want." *Engaging in the Bodhisattva Deeds* says:[278]

> Since without suffering there is no determination to be free,
> You, mind, stay fixed!

And also:

> Furthermore, the good qualities of suffering are that you
> Dispel arrogance with disenchantment,
> Develop compassion for the beings of cyclic existence,
> Carefully avoid sin, and delight in virtue.

(b)) **Reflecting on the advantages of bearing suffering's hardships**

Reflecting on the advantages of bearing suffering's hardships has two parts:

1. Reflecting on the crucial benefits such as liberation, etc.
2. Reflecting on the benefit of dispelling immeasurable suffering

(1)) **Reflecting on the crucial benefits such as liberation, etc.**

Repeatedly make your mind steadfast, thinking, "I know that in the past while passing through cyclic existence I suffered for the sake of trifling desires and minor needs, yet I disregarded the many sufferings, undergoing a great deal of purposeless suffering that will in turn cause immeasurable suffering for me in my future lives. Given this, now that I know that I am engaged in virtue that will accomplish immeasurable benefits and happiness for myself and others, it is appropriate that I accept suffering a trillion times more than before—so of course I will accept sufferings smaller than that." *Engaging in the Bodhisattva Deeds* states:[279]

> For the sake of my desires I have experienced
> Being burned, etc., thousands of times in the hells,
> But have not achieved either my own welfare
> Or the welfare of others.
>
> This is not as harmful as that,
> And it achieves great purpose,
> So it is correct here only to delight
> In suffering that clears away all beings' hurt.

Thus, after you reflect on how you have previously created only hardship that did not accomplish any of your own or others' aims, uplift your mind, thinking, "Why am I not now bearing a suffering that achieves great purpose? Although I am suffering, how excellent that I have found something like this to do." **[419]** Moreover, develop a fearless attitude toward hardship, thinking how you were misled by bad teachers to ignoble, purposeless paths whereon you endured ascetic practices such as leaping on a trident, sitting close to five fires, and the like. Also think how for the sake of inferior, mundane purposes you made yourself bear many sufferings in farming, business, and war.

(2)) **Reflecting on the benefit of dispelling immeasurable suffering**

Reflect well on the differences between short-term and long-term suffering, thinking, "A man who is to be executed is overjoyed when he is freed from execution by having merely his finger cut off. How excellent it would be if similarly, by means of this slight suffering of human hardship, I could permanently dispel the suffering of limitless cyclic existence in general and in particular the suffering of miserable rebirths such as the hells, etc." If you do this well, you produce fearless courage with respect to hardship. *Engaging in the Bodhisattva Deeds* says:[280]

> How is it unfortunate if a man who is to be executed
> Is freed from that by having his hand cut off?
> How is it unfortunate if by human suffering
> You are released from hell?

(c)) **How it is not difficult to bear suffering if you gradually grow accustomed to it, starting with the small**

Engaging in the Bodhisattva Deeds states:[281]

> There is nothing whatsoever
> That does not become easier through habituation.
> So by becoming used to small harms
> You will bear great harms as well.

After you have conceived the armor-like thought to accept suffering, you gradually blend it with suffering, starting with small sufferings. When you do this, you steadily increase your capacity to accept suffering. The *Compendium of Trainings* says:[282]

> Once you have first grown used to small sufferings, you will become accustomed to the difficult and the very difficult. For example, just as all living beings have the idea that suffering is happiness through the power of conditioning, so you maintain the idea of joy whenever you experience suffering by becoming used to applying the idea of joy to these experiences. **[420]**

As to how this comes about, the *Questions of Householder Ugra Sūtra* states:[283]

> Free yourself from a mind that is like a piece of cotton.

And the *Array of Stalks Sūtra* says:[284]

> Daughter, in order to destroy all afflictions you should develop a mind that is hard to defeat.

Thus, you need courage that is very firm and stable; you will not be able to accept suffering with a fragile mind.

If you initially develop a significant degree of courage, even great suffering becomes helpful. It is just like the case of warriors entering a battle and using the sight of their own blood to increase their boldness. If right from the start you belittle yourself, saying, "I have never heard of such a thing, and even if I had heard of it, I could never do something like that," then even a small suffering becomes a cause for you to turn back from the path. It is just like the case of cowards who see others' blood and, fainting, fall unconscious. *Engaging in the Bodhisattva Deeds* says:[285]

> Some, seeing their own blood,
> Become more intrepid.
> Some, seeing others' blood,
> Fall unconscious.

This comes from the mind's fortitude
Or from its timidity.

(c″) **A detailed explanation from the viewpoint of the bases**

Question: Given that one must accept the suffering that occurs, from where do these sufferings come and how does one accept them?

Reply: There are eight bases for accepting suffering:

1. *Acceptance of suffering that is based on objects*. Robes, alms, bedding, seat, medicine, and necessities are objects that enhance pure conduct. Without displeasure and disappointment you accept the suffering that arises when these are given to you and you find them to be inferior or too few, or when they are given with disrespect or after a long delay. **[421]**

2. *Acceptance of suffering that is based on worldly concerns*. The nine worldly concerns are: (1) loss; (2) disgrace; (3) blame; (4) pain; (5) disintegration; (6) extinguishment; (7) aging; (8) sickness; and, (9) the death of what is subject to death subsequent to its decay. After you have analyzed the sufferings based on all or each of these, you accept the suffering.

3. *Acceptance of suffering that is based on physical activities*. The four physical activities are moving around, standing, sitting, and lying down. When all day and all night you purify your mind of obstructions by means of the first [moving around] and third [sitting] of these four, you are accepting the sufferings that arise from them; however, you do not relax on a couch, chair, or bed of straw or leaves when it is not the time to do so.

4. *Acceptance of suffering that is based on upholding the teaching*. The teaching is upheld in seven ways: by (1) worshipping and serving the three jewels; (2) worshipping and serving the guru; (3) understanding the teachings; (4) teaching extensively to others what you have understood; (5) reciting its praises in a loud, clear voice; (6) correctly reflecting on it in solitude; and (7) cultivating meditative serenity and insight that is imbued with yogic attention. When you strive at these, you accept the sufferings that arise.

5. *Acceptance of suffering that is based on living by begging*. The seven aspects of living by begging are (1) you experience having an ugly appearance due to shaving off your hair, beard and so forth; (2) you experience wearing cloth that is patched together and is of poor color; (3) you live by restraining yourself from the conduct of worldly persons and act in a way other than they do; (4) you give up farm work, etc., and then live by getting material goods from others, so you live in dependence on others; (5) since you do not

accumulate or employ material gain, you seek things such as robes, etc., from others for as long as you live; (6) since you give up sexual intercourse, you turn away from human desires until you die; and (7) since you give up dancing, laughter, and the like, you turn away from human merriment until you die in order to give up friends, intimate companions, childhood friends, and the like, as well as pleasures and enjoyments. You accept the suffering that comes about based on these. **[422]**

6. *Acceptance of suffering that is based on fatigue due to perseverance.* You accept the suffering that arises from mental and physical fatigue, hardship, and disturbance while you are persevering at cultivating virtues.

7. *Acceptance of suffering that is based on acting for the welfare of living beings.* There are eleven activities for others' welfare; you accept the sufferings that occur because of these.[286]

8. *Acceptance of suffering that is based on current tasks.* You accept the suffering that arises from tasks for a renunciate, such as the work associated with the begging bowl, robes, and so forth, or from the tasks for a householder, such as faultless work on a farm, in business, as a government employee, etc.

Even if you are stricken with any of the sufferings that arise in dependence on these eight bases, you do not give up your joyous perseverance at each. You act for the sake of enlightenment, joyfully, not letting such sufferings become an obstacle that causes you to turn back once you have set forth.

(3′) **Developing the patience of certitude about the teachings**

The patience of certitude about the teachings means generating the forbearance of conviction. It has eight objects:

1. *The object of faith.* This is the good qualities of the three jewels.

2. *The object to be actualized.* This is the reality of the two selflessnesses.

3. *The desired object.* This is the great powers of the buddhas and bodhisattvas, of which there are three—the power of the superknowledges, the power of the six perfections, and the power which is innate.

4. *The object to be adopted.* This is wanting both the cause—good deeds—and the effect of these deeds.

5. *The object to be discarded.* This is wishing to avoid both the cause—misdeeds—and the effect of these deeds.

6. *The object of meditation that is the goal to be achieved.* This is enlightenment.

7. *The object of meditation that is the method for achieving the goal.* This is all the paths of training in the spirit of enlightenment.

8. *The object of subsequent practice through study and reflection.* According to Dro-lung-ba (Gro-lung-pa), this refers to the province of what is to be known, such as impermanence and so forth. **[423]** The *Power-Lineage Chapter (Bala-gotra-parivarta)* of the *Bodhisattva Levels* mentions that the eighth is the sublime teaching—the twelve branches of scripture and so forth—so I think you have to take it as being this.

The way to have conviction is to become certain about these objects just as they are, and then to think about them again and again, apprehending them without conflict.

In accordance with passages in the *Bodhisattva Levels*, I have set forth the set of eight bases with respect to the patience of accepting suffering and eight objects with respect to the patience of certitude about the teachings. In particular, there is extensive coverage there of the patience of certitude about the teachings.

(d′) **How to practice**

When practicing any kind of patience, you practice it in association with the six supremacies and all six perfections. These are the same as in the earlier explanation, except the generosity of patience means to establish others in patience.[287]

(e′) **A summary**

The recollection and cultivation of the spirit of enlightenment—the basis of the bodhisattva deeds—is the root of the wish to establish all beings in a patience wherein they have extinguished the contaminations. After you steadily increase this spirit, aspire to practice the patience of those at high levels and then train your mind in it. Distinguish the trainings for the patience of a beginning bodhisattva, and then learn these properly. If you transgress the boundaries as explained, you must make an effort to amend this. If you neglect these transgressions at the time of practicing these trainings, you will be continually tainted by many great misdeeds, and even in future lifetimes your practice of the marvelous deeds of the bodhisattvas will be extremely difficult. Seeing that the essentials of the path are supreme, practice right now what you can, and inculcate the intention to practice even those you now cannot. If you do this, then, as the *Questions of Subāhu Sūtra* says, you will bring the perfection of patience to completion with little difficulty and minor suffering. **[424]**

13

The Perfection of Joyous Perseverance

(iv) How to train in the perfection of joyous perseverance
- (a′) What joyous perseverance is
- (b′) How to begin the practice of joyous perseverance
- (c′) The divisions of joyous perseverance
  - (1′) The actual divisions
    - (a″) Armor-like joyous perseverance
    - (b″) Joyous perseverance of gathering virtue
    - (c″) Joyous perseverance of acting for the welfare of living beings
  - (2′) The method of developing joyous perseverance
    - (a″) Eliminating unfavorable conditions that prevent joyous perseverance
      - (1″) Identifying factors incompatible with joyous perseverance
      - (2″) Employing the methods to eliminate the incompatible factors
        - (a)) Stopping the laziness of procrastination
        - (b)) Stopping attachment to ignoble activities
        - (c)) Stopping discouragement or self-contempt
          - (1)) Stopping discouragement about the goal
          - (2)) Stopping discouragement about the means to attain the goal
          - (3)) Stopping discouragement because wherever you are is a place to practice
    - (b″) Gathering the forces of the favorable conditions
      - (1″) Developing the power of aspiration
      - (2″) Developing the power of steadfastness
      - (3″) Developing the power of joy
      - (4″) The power of relinquishment
    - (c″) Based on the elimination of unfavorable conditions and the accumulation of favorable conditions, being intent on joyously persevering
    - (d″) How to use joyous perseverance to make the mind and body serviceable
- (d′) How to practice
- (e′) A summary

(iv) **How to train in the perfection of joyous perseverance**

This section has five parts:

1. What joyous perseverance is
2. How to begin the practice of joyous perseverance
3. The divisions of joyous perseverance
4. How to practice
5. A summary

(a′) **What joyous perseverance is**

When you have focused upon something virtuous, joyous perseverance is enthusiasm for it. *Engaging in the Bodhisattva Deeds* says:[288]

> What is joyous perseverance? It is delight in virtue.

The *Bodhisattva Levels* explains it as a flawless state of mind that is enthusiastic about accumulating virtue and working for the welfare of living beings, together with the physical, verbal, and mental activity such a state of mind motivates.

(b′) **How to begin the practice of joyous perseverance**

Frequently reflect upon the benefits of joyously persevering and the faults of not doing so, for you will develop joyous perseverance if you habituate yourself to this reflection. As to its benefits, the *Exhortation to Wholehearted Resolve* (*Adhyāśaya-saṃcodana-sūtra*) says:[289]

> Always rely upon noble joyous perseverance,
> Which clears away all suffering and darkness,
> Which is the basis of freedom from miserable realms,
> And which is praised by all the buddhas.
>
> One who joyously perseveres
> Has no difficulty accomplishing any project
> Whether mundane or supramundane.
> Who among the learned is disheartened by joyous
>   perseverance?
>
> Those who set forth for the buddhas' enlightenment,
> Perceive the faults of lethargy and sleepiness,
> And then continually persevere with enthusiasm.
> So have I advised them.

Also, the *Ornament for the Mahāyāna Sūtras* states:[290]

> Joyous perseverance is supreme among virtues;
> Based on it, you subsequently attain the rest.

> Through it you immediately gain a supreme state of joy,
> As well as the mundane and supramundane attainments.
>
> With joyous perseverance you attain the pleasures desired in life;
> Become possessed of utter purity;
> Are liberated, transcending the view of the perishing aggregates;
> And reach buddhahood, the supreme enlightenment. **[425]**

And also:

> One who has joyous perseverance
> Is not brought down
> By prosperity, afflictions,
> Discouragement, or petty attainments.

The *Bodhisattva Levels* as well says:[291]

> Because joyous perseverance alone, nothing else, is the principal and highest cause for the correct attainment of a bodhisattva's virtuous qualities, the *tathāgatas* have pointed it out, declaring, "Joyous perseverance is what brings about the attainment of unsurpassed, perfect enlightenment."

The *Compendium of the Perfections* also states:[292]

> If you are free of fatigue and have great joyous perseverance,
> There is nothing you cannot attain or accomplish.

And also:

> Even all non-human beings delight in helping you;
> You attain all types of meditative concentrations
>
> And spend all periods of the day and night fruitfully.
> Your collection of good qualities does not decline,
> And your purposes surpassing the affairs of humankind
> Flourish like the blue *utpala* flower.

As to the faults of not joyously persevering, the *Questions of Sāgaramati Sūtra* states:[293]

> The enlightenment of the lazy is exceedingly far off and distant. The lazy lack all perfections from generosity to wisdom. The lazy do not work for others' welfare.

And the *Mindfulness of the Excellent Teaching* (*Sad-dharmānusmṛty-upasthāna*) states as well:[294]

Whoever has laziness—
The single basis of the afflictions—
Whoever feels some laziness
Lacks all good qualities.

Thus, if you lack joyous perseverance, you come under the influence of laziness and become poor in all good qualities, so you lose every temporary and ultimate purpose of being human.

(c′) **The divisions of joyous perseverance**

The section on the divisions of joyous perseverance has two parts:

1. The actual divisions
2. The method of developing joyous perseverance **[426]**

(1′) **The actual divisions**

The section on the actual divisions has three parts:

1. Armor-like joyous perseverance
2. Joyous perseverance of gathering virtue
3. Joyous perseverance of acting for the welfare of living beings

(a″) **Armor-like joyous perseverance**

When bodhisattvas joyously persevere, prior to actively engaging themselves they put on the armor of a preliminary enthusiastic thought such as, "For a trillion sets of three immeasurably great eons each composed of days as long as a thousand great eons, I shall not relinquish my practice of joyous perseverance. For the sake of relieving the suffering of a single living being, I would rejoice at remaining only as a hell-being until I attain buddhahood. As I exert myself in this manner for the sake of complete enlightenment, what need is there to mention my perseverance over a shorter period or in the face of lesser suffering?"

Such is the joyous perseverance that is like armor. A bodhisattva who produces even an aspiration for, or just faith in, such joyous perseverance is steadfast; how much more so one who is endowed with this perseverance, given that he or she develops measureless causes for joyously persevering for the sake of unsurpassed enlightenment. The *Bodhisattva Levels* says that for such a person there is absolutely no action for the sake of others and for enlightenment that is discouraging or entails hardship. When you become conditioned to such a state of mind, it becomes the definite cause of awakening your potential for the Mahāyāna lineage, so train in it.

Concerning armor-like joyous perseverance the *Compendium of the Perfections* says:[295]

> In as many eons as there are drops of water in the ocean,
> Eons in which the years are composed
> Of long, drawn out days and nights equal in duration
> Even to the temporal limits of cyclic existence,
>
> You produce the spirit of supreme enlightenment once.
> Though you likewise have to accomplish every other collection,
> You do not become disheartened because of your compassion,
> And undiscouraged you achieve sublime enlightenment. **[427]**
>
> To generate this immeasurable steadfast armor
> While disregarding your suffering in cyclic existence
> Is declared the first proper undertaking
> For the disciplined hero possessed of compassion.

Furthermore, even if it took you a hundred thousand years to produce the spirit of enlightenment once and to see one buddha, where each year is composed of twelve months, each month of thirty days, and each day as long as the time from beginningless cyclic existence to the present, and even if it took you this length of time multiplied by the number of grains of sand in the Ganges River to know the mind and behavior of one living being, you similarly must come to know the minds and behaviors of all living beings. The *Teachings of Akṣayamati Sūtra* says the armor of being undaunted is the inexhaustible armor; it is armor-like joyous perseverance of the highest caliber.

In short, if you can generate a single attitude such as this, you easily complete limitless accumulations and purify measureless obscurations. This becomes the most excellent cause for never turning back; by just being joyful no matter how long it takes, you quickly become a buddha. Those who want to become a buddha in a short time, but take no joy at all in the limitless deeds and great length of time required, take a very long time to reach buddhahood, because they thereby fail to produce the wonderful courage of the conquerors' children.

After you have put on such armor, you joyously persevere for two purposes: to gather virtue and to act for the welfare of living beings.

(b") **Joyous perseverance of gathering virtue**

The joyous perseverance of gathering virtue is applying yourself to the practice of the six perfections in order to properly accomplish them.

(c″) **Joyous perseverance of acting for the welfare of living beings**

The joyous perseverance of acting for the welfare of living beings is properly applying yourself to the practice of the eleven activities for others' welfare.

(2′) **The method of developing joyous perseverance**

As explained above, since you produce, maintain, and increase all the virtues of the two collections in dependence upon joyous perseverance, the practice that develops it is very crucial. I shall discuss the system of the text of the great scholar and adept Śāntideva, *Engaging in the Bodhisattva Deeds*, noting that it is complete as well as easy to understand and to sustain in practice. **[428]** The method of developing joyous perseverance has four parts:

1. Eliminating unfavorable conditions that prevent joyous perseverance
2. Gathering the forces of the favorable conditions
3. Based on the elimination of unfavorable conditions and the accumulation of favorable conditions, being intent on joyously persevering
4. How to use joyous perseverance to make the mind and body serviceable

(a″) **Eliminating unfavorable conditions that prevent joyous perseverance**

Eliminating unfavorable conditions that prevent joyous perseverance has two parts:

1. Identifying factors incompatible with joyous perseverance
2. Employing the methods to eliminate the incompatible factors

(1″) **Identifying factors incompatible with joyous perseverance**

There are two factors incompatible with entering the path: (1) not entering even though you see that you can do the practice, and (2) not entering because you become discouraged, thinking, "How can I do such a practice?" Indeed there is also not practicing because you are unconcerned with whether you are capable or not, but this is irrelevant here since this explanation is for those pursuing liberation.

Within the first factor, there are two possibilities: (1) you have the laziness of procrastination, thinking, "There is still time"; and

(2) you are not procrastinating but you are overwhelmed by your attachment to inferior and common activities. In this vein *Engaging in the Bodhisattva Deeds* says:[296]

> The factors incompatible with joyous perseverance
> Are said to be laziness, adhering to what is ignoble,
> And self-contempt out of discouragement.

Causes for the production of laziness are indolence, attachment to the taste of inferior pleasures, craving the pleasure of sleep, and a lack of disenchantment with cyclic existence. *Engaging in the Bodhisattva Deeds* states:[297]

> Laziness arises from craving based upon
> Indolence, enjoyment of pleasure, and sleep;
> And from a lack of disenchantment
> With the suffering of cyclic existence.

Some assert that the first two lines indicate the form that laziness takes rather than its causes.

(2″) **Employing the methods to eliminate the incompatible factors**

Employing the methods to eliminate the incompatible factors has three parts:

1. Stopping the laziness of procrastination
2. Stopping attachment to ignoble activities
3. Stopping discouragement or self-contempt

(a)) **Stopping the laziness of procrastination**

This involves the following three meditations: you contemplate that the body you have at present is rapidly disintegrating, that after death you will fall into miserable realms, and that it will be difficult to find an excellent life such as this one again. Meditation on these stops the laziness that holds to the notion that there is plenty of time, thereby generating the conviction in your mind that there is no time to spare. **[429]** These three meditations were explained earlier in the section on the person of small capacity.[298]

(b)) **Stopping attachment to ignoble activities**

You see that the sublime teaching is the source of endless joy in this and future lives, and that you lose its great purpose when you are distracted in idle chatter and amusements which are the source of much pointless suffering later. Meditate on this and stop your attachment. *Engaging in the Bodhisattva Deeds* states:[299]

How could you abandon the source of infinite joy,
The highest of pleasures, the sublime teaching,
And delight in distractions and amusements
That are the causes of suffering?

(c)) **Stopping discouragement or self-contempt**

It is not enough just to delight in the sublime teaching after you have stopped your procrastination and your attachment to ignoble activities; you must train as a Mahāyāna practitioner. Therefore, if you become discouraged, thinking, "Someone like me is unable to practice that," you must eliminate this discouragement. Stopping discouragement or self-contempt has three parts:

1. Stopping discouragement about the goal
2. Stopping discouragement about the means to attain the goal
3. Stopping discouragement because wherever you are is a place to practice

(1)) **Stopping discouragement about the goal**

Qualm: If the goal is buddhahood—the total elimination of all faults and the total completion of all good qualities—then, since it is extremely difficult for me to accomplish even a few good qualities or to remove even a few faults, how could someone like me be capable of attaining such a result?

Reply: If such a sense of discouragement manifests, it is a very great fault because it constitutes giving up the spirit of enlightenment. Even if such a thought does not fully manifest, you must stop it at its incipient stage.

How to stop it? Encourage yourself with this thought: "The Bhagavan—the authoritative person who speaks what is true and correct, never what is false or erroneous—said that even flies, etc. will attain enlightenment. That being so, why should I not attain it—so long as I do not give up persevering—inasmuch as human birth gives me an excellent basis and I have the mental capacity to analyze what to adopt and what to cast aside?" **[430]** *Engaging in the Bodhisattva Deeds* says:[300]

"How could I attain enlightenment?"
I shall not indulge in such discouragement,
For the truth-declaring Tathāgata
Has spoken this truth:

> "Even flies, mosquitoes,
> Bees, and worms will attain
> Unsurpassed enlightenment, so hard to attain,
> Once they generate the power of perseverance."
>
> Why should someone like me—
> Born into the human race, recognizing benefit and harm—
> Not attain enlightenment,
> As long as I do not give up the bodhisattva deeds?

Furthermore, stop your discouragement with this thought: "In the past there were former buddhas, now there are living buddhas, and in the future there will also be those who reach buddhahood. It is not the case that just one person who has already become a buddha accomplishes the path. Rather, those just like myself, gradually progressing upward, have become buddhas and will become buddhas." The *Cloud of Jewels Sūtra* says:[301]

> The bodhisattva thinks as follows: "All the *tathāgatas*, arhats, perfect buddhas who have attained, who are attaining, and who will attain complete enlightenment have, are, and will attain complete enlightenment through this kind of method, this kind of path, this kind of joyous perseverance." Thus, it is not the case that all these *tathāgatas* are just one person who has already become a *tathāgata* attaining complete enlightenment. Rather, I too shall reach total perfection in utterly unsurpassed, perfect, and complete enlightenment. With joyous perseverance in common with all living beings and joyous perseverance focused upon all living beings, I too shall seek and strive for enlightenment. **[431]**

The *Praise of Infinite Qualities* also says:[302]

> "Even some who have earlier obtained the state of a *sugata* previously fell to states much lower than this one." Thinking thus and in order to inspire us, you [Bhagavan] did not disparage yourself even when you fell into a dreadful condition. To disparage oneself is wrong, causing those with well-developed faculties to become discouraged.

As to this discouragement, since a buddha's good qualities are infinite and results follow from causes, you must accomplish good qualities and remove faults through limitless avenues while on the path. After you have understood this well, you may become discouraged when you then take a look at yourself.

However, this particular discouragement will never arise at a time like the present when an erroneous understanding of the path is in operation. Now, when practicing to attain the limitless buddha qualities, you suppose that they are achieved by one-sidedly pursuing just a single, small portion of a quality and intensively working on it. Yet, in this case your not getting discouraged is not a good sign. Rather, it is the result of your not being certain about how to proceed on the path—or, having a rough understanding but not putting it into practice—so you are confused by its apparent ease. For, when you come up against the practice and receive an explanation of a fairly complete outline of the path, roughly arranged from beginning to end, you say, "If that much is needed, who could do it," and thoroughly give it up. Also, Sha-ra-wa said:

> For bodhisattvas who have not engaged in practice all the bodhisattva deeds seem easy, like looking at a target for arrows, and they do not even get discouraged. At present, we lack a complete practice of the teachings, so we have not even reached the level at which we would have discouragement or self-contempt. When we more fully appropriate the teaching, then there is great danger of discouragement and self-contempt.

This is quite true.

(2)) **Stopping discouragement about the means to attain the goal**

Qualm: To accomplish buddhahood you have to give away your feet, hands, etc., but I am not capable of such feats. **[432]**

Reply: You must bear suffering to that extent, for even those who live as they please without engaging in the bodhisattva deeds experience as they pass through cyclic existence unspeakable sufferings such as having their bodies cut open, torn to pieces, stabbed, set on fire, and so forth, but they do not accomplish even their own welfare. The suffering occasioned by undergoing hardships for the sake of enlightenment is not even a fraction of this suffering, and also has the great purpose of accomplishing both your own and others' welfare. *Engaging in the Bodhisattva Deeds* says:[303]

> "But it frightens me that I must
> Give away my feet, hands, and the like."
> Without distinguishing heavy suffering from light,
> Confusion reduces me to fear.
>
> For countless tens of millions of eons
> I will be cut, stabbed,
> Burned, and torn asunder numerous times,
> Without thereby attaining enlightenment.

> This suffering which brings about my enlightenment
> Does have a limit.
> It is like undergoing the pain of an incision
> To excise an injurious internal disease.
>
> All doctors eliminate illness
> Through forms of discomfort which heal it.
> Thus, I will bear a little discomfort
> To destroy numerous sufferings.

With respect to giving away your body, you do not give it in the beginning when you are afraid. But through graduated training in generosity, you end your attachment to your body. Once you have increased the strength of your great compassion, you have no difficulty when you give it away, provided it is for a great purpose. *Engaging in the Bodhisattva Deeds* states:[304]

> The Supreme Physician does not employ
> Ordinary remedies such as those.
> He heals limitless chronic diseases
> With the most gentle treatments.
>
> At the beginning the Guide enjoins you
> To give vegetables and so forth.
> Later, after you are used to this,
> You gradually offer even your flesh.
>
> Once I come to conceive of my body
> As being like a vegetable and so forth,
> What difficulty will there be in giving away
> Such things as my flesh?

Some say that since practitioners of the perfection vehicle must give away their bodies and lives, they undergo torment and are on a path that is very difficult to follow. This text clearly refutes this, because you do not give away your body so long as you perceive it to be a difficult deed, but rather do so once it becomes very easy, like giving a vegetable. **[433]**

(3)) **Stopping discouragement because wherever you are is a place to practice**

Qualm: Reaching buddhahood requires taking limitless rebirths in cyclic existence, so I will be harmed by the suffering therein. I am not capable of such a thing.

Reply: Reflect as follows. Bodhisattvas have eliminated all sin; therefore, sin's effect—the feeling of suffering—will not arise because they have stopped the cause. Through firm knowledge that cyclic existence lacks an intrinsic nature, like a magician's illusion, they also have no mental suffering. Given that their physical and mental bliss increases, they have no reason to become disheartened even though they are still in cyclic existence. *Engaging in the Bodhisattva Deeds* says:[305]

> Since sin is eliminated, there is no suffering.
> Through knowledge, there is no lack of joy.
> Misconceptions and sin
> Harm the mind and body.
>
> Through merit the body is blissful;
> Through knowledge the mind is too.
> Though remaining in cyclic existence for others' welfare,
> Why should the compassionate ones be disheartened?

And also:

> Thus, after mounting the steed of the enlightenment spirit,
> Which dispels all dejection and fatigue,
> You proceed from joy to joy.
> What sensible person would become discouraged?

Likewise, do not become discouraged even by being delayed in cyclic existence for an immeasurable length of time, because a long length of time is not in itself a reason to be disheartened. If suffering is extremely intense, even a brief period of it is disheartening. But if there is no suffering and you are happy, even a long time is not disheartening. Nāgārjuna's *Precious Garland* states:[306]

> When suffering, even a short time is hard to bear;
> What need mention a time that is long?
> But when free of suffering and joyful,
> What harms you over even endless time?
>
> Bodhisattvas have no physical suffering;
> How could they have mental suffering?
> Out of compassion they feel distress for the world;
> Thus they remain for a long time.
>
> So do not be discouraged,
> Thinking, "Buddhahood is far away."
> Always strive at these collections
> So as to eliminate faults and gain good qualities. **[434]**

Also, since the completion of endless collections is not difficult, do not discourage yourself with the thought, "To become a buddha requires completing limitless collections of merit and sublime wisdom. This is so difficult that I could not possibly do it." First, motivate yourself with the desire to attain the goal of limitless buddha qualities for the welfare of the limitless beings you intend to help. Next, focus on remaining in cyclic existence for a measureless period of time and take the bodhisattva vows, thinking: "I shall accomplish limitless collections!" Then, as long as you keep the vows, whether your mind is distracted by other things or not, asleep or awake, you will constantly accumulate merit as vast as space. The *Precious Garland* states:[307]

> Just as in all directions
> Space, earth, water, fire, and wind
> Are limitless, so, we assert,
> Suffering beings are without limit.
>
> With compassion the bodhisattvas
> Extricate these limitless beings
> From suffering and then determine
> To set them in buddhahood.
>
> Those remaining steadfast in this way
> Properly make this commitment,
> And then, whether asleep or awake,
> And even when careless,
>
> They constantly accumulate merit as limitless
> As living beings, for beings are without limit.
> Because of the limitlessness of this, know
> That limitless buddhahood is not hard to gain.
>
> Those who remain for an immeasurable time
> Seek immeasurable enlightenment
> For the sake of immeasurable beings
> And accomplish immeasurable virtue.
>
> Hence, though enlightenment is measureless,
> How could they fail to attain it
> Before long through a combination
> Of these four immeasurable ways?

It is most wonderful to think, "If only I could attain buddhahood in a brief time for the sake of living beings," because you are moved by the very intense power of your love, compassion, and spirit of enlightenment. **[435]** However, when you are not within the sphere of these motivations, and you see the necessity of a very long training in endless deeds and that much hard work is required, you might think, "If this is the case, who could possibly do it?" If you should then claim that you are seeking a quick path, you directly damage the engaged spirit of enlightenment and indirectly damage the aspirational spirit of enlightenment. Your capacity for the Mahāyāna lineage steadily weakens, and your enlightenment fades into the remote distance, for you have utterly contradicted what Nāgārjuna and Asaṅga determined to be the Conqueror's own thought on how to increasingly strengthen the spirit of enlightenment.

Thus, since becoming discouraged and remaining so brings no benefit at all and only leads to further discouragement, understand well the methods for achieving enlightenment and uplift your mind. When you do this, the completion of your aims is as if in your hand. The *Garland of Birth Stories* says:[308]

> Discouragement does not help to free you from misfortune,
> So, rather than torment yourself in sorrow,
> Develop stable proficiency in the required goals.
> Then even the very difficult becomes easy, bringing liberation.
>
> So achieve what must be done by the indicated method
> Without making yourself fearful and unhappy.
> Support yourself with stability that has the brilliance of
>   proficiency,
> Then, the achievement of all aims is in your hand.

Ārya Asaṅga says repeatedly that you have both to know well the methods of training in extensive practice without being discouraged and to not be satisfied with only minimal qualities. At present you think, "I have reached a high level of the path," when you have produced a single approximation of a good quality; even if it is an actual good quality, it is only one aspect of the path. You are content to meditate solely on it. But then those knowledgeable in the key points of the path explain from within the guidelines of scripture and reasoning that it is indeed a fraction of virtue, but with just that alone you have not reached anywhere. When you understand what they have said, you become extremely discouraged. **[436]** Thus, those who do not remain satisfied with just some portion of virtue, who seek higher distinction, and who are not discouraged even with the necessity to learn limitless trainings are extremely rare.

(b″) **Gathering the forces of the favorable conditions**

This section has four parts:

1. Developing the power of aspiration
2. Developing the power of steadfastness
3. Developing the power of joy
4. The power of relinquishment

(1″) **Developing the power of aspiration**

As it is said that yearning acts as the basis for joyous perseverance, aspiration here refers to yearning. The need to generate it is stated in *Engaging in the Bodhisattva Deeds*:[309]

> My present destitution has arisen
> From my not aspiring for the teachings
> Both now and in the past.
> Who would forsake aspiration for the teachings?
>
> The Sage declared aspiration
> The root of all aspects of virtue.

It then states how to develop aspiration:[310]

> Its root, in turn, is constant meditation
> On karma's fruitional effects.

This means that the way to develop aspiration is to meditate on how pleasant and unpleasant effects arise from virtuous and nonvirtuous karma respectively. This is because it is taught that faith acts as the basis for yearning, so that the faith of conviction in the two types of karma and their effects will generate two kinds of desire: to eliminate nonvirtuous karma and to adopt virtuous karma. Furthermore, you consider karma and its effects in general, and in particular, the causality underlying the benefits of the bodhisattva deeds and the faults of violating them. Understand these from the relevant sections of this text.[311]

Once you aspire to the Mahāyāna, you enter its door through a commitment to clear away all faults and achieve all good qualities for yourself and others. You must exhort yourself, thinking, "I will have to meditate for many eons to purify myself of every single fault along with its latent propensity and to develop every single good quality to the fullest extent. Yet since I have not even a fraction of the joyous perseverance needed to clear away faults or accomplish good qualities, I have pointlessly wasted my leisure." **[437]** *Engaging in the Bodhisattva Deeds* states:[312]

> I will destroy the immeasurable
> Faults of myself and others.
> To destroy each fault
> Will take an ocean of eons.
>
> But if I cannot see in myself even a fraction
> Of the effort needed to terminate a fault,
> I am a source of measureless suffering.
> Why does my heart not break?
>
> I will accomplish numerous
> Good qualities for myself and others.
> To cultivate each good quality
> Requires an ocean of eons,
>
> But I have never conditioned myself
> To even a mere fraction of a good quality.
> Somehow I have obtained this life—
> It is appalling to waste it.

(2") Developing the power of steadfastness

Developing the power of steadfastness means that you bring to conclusion, without turning back, anything at which you joyously persevere. First, do not try to do everything; examine the situation carefully. If you see that you can do it, you engage in it; whereas if you cannot do it, you do not engage in it. You should not even start in the first place things you will do for a while and then discard. The reason is that if you become habituated to giving up in the middle what you have committed yourself to do, then through this conditioning you will in other lives again abandon your commitment to the training, etc. Consequently, your sin will increase in that life, and in subsequent lives the suffering that is the effect of this sin will increase. Furthermore, you will not accomplish other virtues because you will be thinking of carrying out your earlier commitment; there will be an inferior result because you turned away from your earlier commitment; and your earlier commitment itself will not be fulfilled because you did not follow through. In sum, committing yourself to do something but leaving it unfinished is a hindrance to your accomplishment of other projects, and the conditioning also destabilizes your commitment to the vows you have taken. In this vein *Engaging in the Bodhisattva Deeds* states:[313]

First I examine the endeavor
And then undertake it or not.
If unable, it is best not to undertake it,
But once begun, I will not turn back.

Otherwise I will be conditioned to this [starting and then stopping] in other lives
And my sin and suffering will increase.
Also, other actions and their results
Will be poor and unaccomplished. **[438]**

Therefore, if you want to complete what you have committed yourself to do, cultivate three types of pride. *Engaging in the Bodhisattva Deeds* states:[314]

You should have pride in three areas:
Action, ability, and afflictions.

Pride about action means that no matter who else may be your companion as you practice the path, you do not count on them but accomplish it yourself alone. *Engaging in the Bodhisattva Deeds* states:[315]

"I alone shall do it."
This is pride about action.

Also Nāgārjuna's *Friendly Letter (Suhṛl-lekha)* says:[316]

Liberation depends on oneself;
It never occurs through the help of others.

The thought, "I alone shall achieve this without having any expectation of others," is similar to pride, so it is given the name "pride about action."

Pride about ability means that you accomplish your own and others' welfare, thinking: "Since living beings are under the power of afflictions, they are unable to achieve even their own welfare, much less the welfare of others. I am able to accomplish the welfare of both myself and others." *Engaging in the Bodhisattva Deeds* says:[317]

The beings of this world, subject to the afflictions,
Cannot achieve their own welfare.
They are not as able as I am,
So I shall do it for them.

Furthermore, practice while thinking, "If these beings strive at lowly activities without interruption, why should I not perform the actions that will achieve the perfect effect?" *Engaging in the Bodhisattva Deeds* says:[318]

> If others perform lowly actions,
> How can I be idle?

However, when you achieve these two prides [about action and ability], you should not do so with self-conceit, out of contempt for others. Rather, regard others with compassion, and do not mix in any pride. *Engaging in the Bodhisattva Deeds* states:[319]

> I do not do it out of pride,
> I should have no pride.

Thinking, "Others are not capable; I am able," again resembles pride, so it is labelled "pride."

Pride about afflictions means that with contempt for the afflictions on all occasions, you think, "I shall be victorious over these; they shall never defeat me." **[439]** It means being steadfast after you have generated the courageous thought to destroy the incompatible factors. *Engaging in the Bodhisattva Deeds* states:[320]

> I shall conquer all;
> Nothing shall defeat me.
> I, a child of the Victorious Lion,
> Shall continue to have this pride.

Otherwise, if you lose courage, even a small incompatible factor will harm you. *Engaging in the Bodhisattva Deeds* says:[321]

> Even a crow acts like a *garuḍa*
> When it finds a dying snake.
> If I am feeble,
> Even a slight shortcoming will harm me.
>
> How can one who gives up, discouraged,
> Find freedom from destitution?

Sha-ra-wa said:

> The happiness of those who cast aside the teaching does not exceed their happiness before doing so. Consider the fact that if you give up the teaching in this lifetime, you must hereafter undergo endless suffering. If you make no effort, the afflictions will not look upon you with compassion. Also, the remedy will not say, "You are unable to cultivate me, so I will complete the task for you." Even the buddhas and bodhisattvas will not be able to protect you.

If you apply the aforementioned three prides, even great incompatible factors cannot block you, so you must generate these three kinds of pride. *Engaging in the Bodhisattva Deeds* states:[322]

> Against one who strives with pride
> Even great obstacles will be in trouble.
>
> So with a steadfast mind
> I will overcome my shortcomings.

Otherwise, if practitioners are defeated by their shortcomings, their desire to conquer the afflictions of the three realms will be an embarrassment among the learned. *Engaging in the Bodhisattva Deeds* says:[323]

> If I am defeated by shortcomings,
> My desire to conquer the three realms is a joke.

It is called "pride about afflictions" because you have contempt for the afflictions and then want to destroy them.

Some commentators to *Engaging in the Bodhisattva Deeds* explain this pride about afflictions differently, but I think the above explanation accords with the text. **[440]**

Thus, stop expecting something from others and put on the armor of doing it alone. That is, be confident and think, "Unlike me, others cannot do it. I can do it." When you practice with this perspective, you are sure that you will defeat the afflictions—that they will never defeat you—and you consider that it would be a mistake to abandon your commitment after a while. Train yourself until your mind is steadfast in the desire to finish everything to which you have committed yourself after you have carefully examined whether you can do it.

(3") **Developing the power of joy**

You develop the power of joy after the power of aspiration, an intense yearning, produces a joyous perseverance not previously present, and you have achieved the power of steadfastness (also called the power of pride) which causes the perseverance that has already developed to be irreversible. The power of joy means that when you first engage in an activity, you do it joyfully, and once you have engaged, you have a sense of being insatiable in that you do not want to discontinue the activity. With respect to how you develop this sense of insatiability, *Engaging in the Bodhisattva Deeds* says:[324]

> Like those who want the pleasure that results from play,
> Bodhisattvas are passionate
> About any activity they have to do.
> Insatiable, they take joy in their work.

So strive with an attitude like that of children who engage in play without being satiated. That is, you must be just as insatiable about what causes pleasurable results as you are about the results themselves. For, if ordinary persons strive even when they are uncertain whether they will obtain a pleasant result, what need is there to speak about activities which are certain to bear pleasurable results? *Engaging in the Bodhisattva Deeds* states:[325]

> Even though they work for the sake of happiness,
> It is uncertain whether happiness will come.
> But as for those whose work itself is happiness,
> How can they be happy unless they work?

This is also the reason why being satiated is wrong. **[441]** *Engaging in the Bodhisattva Deeds* says:[326]

> If I am never satiated by sensual desires,
> Which are like honey on a razor's edge,
> How could I be satiated with merit,
> Whose fruition is happiness and peace?

Develop an attitude of being insatiable, thinking, "Indulging in sensual pleasures is like licking honey off the sharp blade of a razor; it is the source of a little sweetness, but it slices up the tongue. If I cannot get enough of this experience, which gives me great suffering for the sake of just a slight, temporary pleasure, what sense could there be in feeling that I have had enough of the collections of merit and sublime wisdom, which give flawless, infinite happiness, both immediate and long-term?"

Thus, in order to bring to completion the virtuous activities in which you have engaged, enter them as a sun-scorched elephant enters a pleasing lotus pond at noon. Train in this attitude until you produce it. *Engaging in the Bodhisattva Deeds* states:[327]

> Thus, in order to finish the work,
> I shall enter into it just as
> An elephant, scorched by the midday sun,
> Comes upon a pond and plunges in.

(4″) **The power of relinquishment**

If you become physically or mentally fatigued from your perseverance, you must rest for a while. Otherwise, you will become exhausted and very disheartened, thereby later preventing your joyous perseverance. Immediately after you have rested, persevere again, and when you have completely finished your earlier activity, do not let this satisfy you. You must joyously persevere at other, higher activities. *Engaging in the Bodhisattva Deeds* says:[328]

> When my strength declines,
> I shall leave the task so I can do it later.
> When it is really done, I shall set it aside,
> Seeking the next task and the next.

The next task is important, because if you consider each earlier good quality sufficient, this will be a big obstacle to the attainment of many higher attributes.

The above presentation shows how to joyously persevere. Do not overexert yourself. You must avoid both being overly intense and being overly relaxed, so make your effort continuous like a river. **[442]** The glorious Mātṛceṭa's *Praise in One Hundred and Fifty Verses* states:[329]

> In order to make yourself more exalted
> You never overexerted or relaxed too much.
> Thus your good qualities are indistinguishable
> By former and later phases.

Bo-do-wa also said:

> The scouts of Se-mo-dru-wa (Se-mo-dru-ba), for instance, never get there. But the scouts of Chang-wa (Byang-ba) take their time at the start and pursue the robbers until they reach them. Likewise, practice at a measured pace that you can sustain. For example, a louse proceeds at a modest pace but never stops, so it soon arrives; whereas a flea takes great successive leaps and then stops, so it never gets there.

(c″) **Based on the elimination of unfavorable conditions and the accumulation of favorable conditions, being intent on joyously persevering**[330]

After you have thus identified the three conditions unfavorable to joyous perseverance, you attend to their remedies. You generate three powers: the power of aspiration which is the favorable condition for weakening those as-yet unweakened unfavorable conditions, the power of steadfastness which is the cause of not turning back once you have started, and the power of joy which never wants to discontinue the activity once you have engaged in it. Through the power of relinquishment you become adept at how to joyously persevere. At this point you must develop the power of being intent on joyous perseverance, so I will explain this.

As to how you are to act when you joyously persevere at eliminating what is to be eliminated, *Engaging in the Bodhisattva Deeds* states:[331]

> As a seasoned warrior approaches
> A sword-fight with an enemy,
> I shall parry the blows of the afflictions
> And strongly strike the afflictions, my enemies.

For example, when seasoned warriors—the adepts who are accustomed to the activity of fighting battles—enter into a sword fight, etc., with their enemy, they do not put value only on destroying their opponent. Rather, they must accomplish two things—skillfully avoiding the blows of weapons directed at them and destroying their opponent. Likewise, when practitioners battle their afflictions, they must persevere as they become proficient in two things—taking defensive precautions and thus avoiding a wound to their mind, and, on the offensive, destroying the afflictions by applying their remedies. **[443]** For, otherwise, while they may use the remedy to stop the activity of one portion of the afflictions, they are either robbed of some aspect of virtue by other afflictions, or else they develop a great fault in their mind so that the harm of the afflictions and the creation of virtue are equal, in which case it will be hard to make further progress in the virtuous practice of applying the remedy.

To cite an example, some people may think that knowledge is most important for practicing the teaching and make knowledge alone crucial. When they then inquire into the teachings, they dispel by means of study the confusion of ignorance, but meanwhile—because they were not cautious about the other afflictions—their mind-stream is utterly ruined by the stain of wrong behavior. Other people may think that disciplining the mind is much more important than knowledge and thus emphasize meditation. Casting away caution about the enemy, confusion, they neither study nor learn the teachings, so they become greatly confused about engaging in what is to be adopted and rejecting what is to be cast aside under the rules of the vows they have taken and are thus continually overcome by infractions.

If in battle your sword were to fall from your hand, you would without hesitation immediately retrieve it out of fear for your life. Likewise, when you battle the afflictions and lose the weapon of mindfulness (which does not forget the subjective and objective aspects of engaging in what is to be adopted and rejecting what is to be cast aside), you must immediately reapply mindfulness out of fear of falling into miserable realms. *Engaging in the Bodhisattva Deeds* says:[332]

> If you drop your sword in battle,
> Out of fear, you quickly pick it up.
> Likewise, if I lose my weapon of mindfulness,
> In fear of hell, I quickly retrieve it.

The protector Nāgārjuna [in his *Friendly Letter*] also taught the great importance of mindfulness:[333]

> O lord, the Sugata declared mindfulness of the body
> To be the one path to follow.
> Hold fast to it and guard it.
> When mindfulness declines, all virtues perish.

Furthermore, regarding the object to which mindfulness attends, mindfulness apprehends an object that wisdom has fully discerned; mindfulness does not distinguish its object on its own. **[444]**

Question: What does wisdom discern?

Reply: In general wisdom discerns everything to be adopted and everything to be cast aside as explained in scripture; in particular, it discerns what is to be adopted and what is to be cast aside according to the vows that you have taken. Therefore, once you apply mindfulness and vigilance to these, you will complete your practice; you will not be successful by just applying mindfulness and vigilance within the narrow confines of attention to an object of meditation.

What is more, when warriors are in a battle, they strive from the beginning not to lose their sword; when by chance they do drop it, they pick it up immediately. These two actions rest on a fear of being killed that is not mere words. Likewise, those who cultivate the path are afraid to lose the mindfulness that does not forget what is to be adopted and what eliminated; even if they do lose it, they immediately reapply it. These two actions are based on the development in their minds of a real terror of falling into miserable realms as a result of the pollution of infractions and faults that occur when mindfulness lapses. This, in turn, depends on having made karma and its effects central to their practice and then sustaining that approach. Those who fail to develop the awareness that these points are profound instructions sever the root of the good qualities ensuing from the practice that delights the learned, the sacred foundation of the path.

Question: Well, why is it necessary to look with fear upon even minor misbehavior, and not let it continue but immediately stop it?

Reply: Take the example of a poisoned arrow that makes a tiny surface wound. Before long, the poison from this wound will spread throughout the entire body. You must operate on the wound and remove the poison. Similarly, even when wrong behavior does not make anything more than a small wound in the mind, if you ignore it, it will quickly pervade your mind so that it becomes large. Therefore, from the start you must prevent wrongdoing before it takes place and, if it does happen, you must discontinue it immediately. *Engaging in the Bodhisattva Deeds* states:[334]

> Just as poison spreads throughout the body,
> Carried by the blood,
> So a fault pervades the mind
> If it finds an opportunity. **[445]**

Question: Well, how do those who want victory over the afflictions apply mindfulness and vigilance?

Reply: You must concentrate, just as *Engaging in the Bodhisattva Deeds* says:[335]

> A practitioner must be as concentrated
> As someone carrying a pot full of mustard oil
> Who is fearful when a swordsman before him
> Threatens to kill him if he spills a drop.

Understand this from the scriptural statement with respect to the border region in the story of Kātyāyana.[336] While you are concentrating, if in general you should behave wrongly or in particular you should experience the causes of laziness—such as sleepiness, etc.—then you must not assent to them but must confront and avert them. *Engaging in the Bodhisattva Deeds* states:[337]

> Thus, if a snake came onto your lap,
> You would hastily stand up.

Just so, if sleepiness and indolence come,
Quickly avert them.

Furthermore, do not merely discontinue faults, but actively feel displeasure at their having occurred. Contemplate as follows, "Because I proceeded in this way in the past as well, I have been wandering in cyclic existence up to now. In particular, it is especially blameworthy that I have taken the bodhisattva vows and yet continue with things that are incompatible with the vows' precepts." Become inspired to henceforth restrain yourself, thinking, "From now on I shall make sure that this fault never occurs." Frequently employ both these attitudes. *Engaging in the Bodhisattva Deeds* says:[338]

Whenever a fault occurs,
I shall reproach myself and long ponder,
"By all means I will do whatever it takes
So that this shall never happen again."

Strive at any deep causes that give rise to the continuous, powerful mindfulness that is the root of this practice. Rely on such activities as keeping the company of excellent teachers and excellent companions, and broad learning, which are the causes of this powerful mindfulness. In this vein *Engaging in the Bodhisattva Deeds* states:[339]

"In any of these situations
I will practice mindfulness."
With this motive aspire to meet teachers
And engage in appropriate activities. **[446]**

In summary, you must study and discern well what bodhisattva training requires you to adopt and to cast aside, and then joyously persevere at continuously being mindful in all your conduct of what you have understood about what to adopt and what to cast aside. Hence, it is extremely important not to err about that at which you are to persevere.

(d") How to use joyous perseverance to make the mind and body serviceable

The method for using joyous perseverance to make the mind and body serviceable is the power of mastery. Śāntideva sets forth in the chapter on conscientiousness [in his *Engaging in the Bodhisattva Deeds*] the necessity of learning the bodhisattva trainings; the extremely grave consequences if you do not train in these once you have pledged to do so; how to regard the afflictions as the enemy; and the ways to generate the courage that looks upon the hardship of battling the afflictions as an ornament rather than as a burden. Meditate on these before taking up the task of training in the bodhisattva deeds. Thus stopping all the inhibitions that prevent you from using your body and mind for virtuous activity, rise gladly to that task. *Engaging in the Bodhisattva Deeds* says:[340]

> In order to have strength for everything
> Before engaging in any activity
> I will recall the advice on conscientiousness
> And then gladly rise to the task.

Question: What form will the joyous perseverance produced by such efforts take?

Reply: Just as wind drives a piece of cotton to and fro, a joyful energy, enthused for virtue, controls your body and mind. When you act along with this energy, joyous perseverance is well-established. Once you produce this, you will easily achieve all the collections. *Engaging in the Bodhisattva Deeds* states:[341]

> Just like cotton under the power
> Of a wind that blows to and fro
> So I will be driven by enthusiasm;
> In this way I will accomplish all.

Although such tasks are difficult, it is wrong to give them up. Rather, as the glorious Mātṛceṭa's *Praise in One Hundred and Fifty Verses* says, you must make effort:[342]

> "The sublime state, difficult to reach,
> Is not attained without hardship."
> Knowing this, you intensified your joyous perseverance
> Without concern for yourself. [**447**]

(d′) **How to practice**

You must practice any kind of joyous perseverance in association with the six supremacies and all six perfections. The generosity of joyous perseverance is establishing others in joyous perseverance after you have stabilized yourself therein. The remaining perfections are in accord with the earlier explanation.[343]

(e′) **A summary**

The recollection and cultivation of the spirit of enlightenment—the basis of the bodhisattva deeds—inspires you to train in order to set all living beings in joyous perseverance. So steadily increase this spirit, and then aspire to and train in the methods of joyous perseverance for those at high levels. Also, strive as you are able at the methods of learning joyous perseverance for a beginning bodhisattva. In particular, effectively stop the various forms of discouragement, these being uniquely subject to elimination by joyous perseverance. Mentally put on the armor of joyous perseverance that is enthusiastic about the following: the goal of enlightenment, the aim of accomplishing the happiness and eliminating the suffering of all living beings, the very long period of time, the limitless collections, and the immeasurable hardships. Strive at this attitude because, as the *Questions of Subāhu Sūtra* says, just by generating the powerful surge of such a resolve, you accumulate a great wave of merit. If you do not do this, you fail to secure your Mahāyāna lineage, and you are also continually stained by much wrongdoing. Then, in other lives as well, you will find it very difficult to learn the bodhisattva deeds. Also, after you have become aware of such things, even if you do not practice perfectly, motivate yourself in that direction. If you then joyously persevere to the extent that you are able, then, as the *Questions of Subāhu Sūtra* says, you will quickly complete the perfection of joyous perseverance in future lives, without suffering and with little difficulty.

14

The Perfections of Meditative Stabilization and Wisdom

(v) **How to train in the perfection of meditative stabilization**

The explanation of how to train in the perfection of meditative stabilization has five parts:

1. What meditative stabilization is
2. How to begin the cultivation of meditative stabilization [**448**]
3. The divisions of meditative stabilization
4. How to practice
5. A summary

(a′) **What meditative stabilization is**

Meditative stabilization is a virtuous, one-pointed state of mind that stays fixed on its object of meditation without distraction to other things. The *Bodhisattva Levels* says:[344]

> It is the one-pointed state of mind—stabilized on virtue, and either mundane or supramundane—of bodhisattvas who have first studied and reflected on the bodhisattvas' scriptural collections. Whether it is oriented toward meditative serenity, toward insight, or toward both as the path that conjoins them, understand that this one-pointed state of mind is the bodhisattvas' meditative stabilization.

And *Engaging in the Bodhisattva Deeds* also says:[345]

> Having thus generated joyous perseverance,
> Set your mind in meditative concentration....

(b′) **How to begin the cultivation of meditative stabilization**

Think over the benefits of cultivating meditative stabilization and the faults of not cultivating it. I will explain this in the meditative serenity section.[346]

(c′) **The divisions of meditative stabilization**

In line with the above citation [from the *Bodhisattva Levels*], if you subdivide meditative stabilization according to nature, there are two kinds: mundane and supramundane; and if you do so according to orientation, there are three kinds [oriented toward serenity, toward insight, or toward both conjoined]. If you subdivide it according to function, there are three types: meditative stabilization that stabilizes the body and mind in bliss within the present life, meditative stabilization that achieves good qualities, and meditative stabilization that carries out the welfare of living beings. The first, meditative stabilization that stabilizes the body and mind in bliss within the present life, is all meditative stabilizations that generate mental and physical pliancy when you enter them with equipoise. The second, meditative stabilization that achieves good qualities, is all meditative stabilizations which accomplish good qualities shared with *śrāvakas*—the superknowledges, liberations, totalities, masteries, etc. The third, meditative stabilization that carries out the welfare of living beings, is meditative stabilization that accomplishes the eleven activities for others' welfare.

(d′) **How to practice**

Whenever you practice any virtuous meditative stabilization, you do so in association with the six supremacies and all six perfections. The generosity of meditative stabilization is maintaining meditative stabilization yourself and then establishing others in it. **[449]** Understand the other perfections from the earlier explanation.[347]

(e′) **A summary**

The recollection and cultivation of the spirit of enlightenment—the basis of the bodhisattva deeds—is what inspires you to train in order to set all living beings in uncontaminated meditative stabilization. After you have increased the stability of this spirit, aspire to the high meditative stabilizations and train in these. Even if you are unable to fully develop the meditative stabilizations, you must strive to train from time to time in one-pointed concentration to whatever extent you are able. For, if you do not do so, you will be continually stained with the fault of breaking the precepts, and in other lives as well you will find it most difficult to learn the trainings for entering the many doors of the bodhisattvas' meditative stabilizations. Whereas if you never give up your effort, even in this life your mind will become steadily less distracted, making your accumulations of virtue very powerful. In future lives, as the *Questions of Subāhu Sūtra* says, you will have physical and mental bliss and a joyful mind, thereby easily completing the perfection of meditative stabilization.

I will not elaborate further here as I will be explaining this at length in the meditative serenity section.

(vi) **How to train in the perfection of wisdom**

How to train in the perfection of wisdom has five parts:

1. What wisdom is
2. How to begin the generation of wisdom
3. The divisions of wisdom
4. How to practice
5. A summary

(a′) **What wisdom is**

In general, wisdom is what thoroughly discerns the ontological status of the object under analysis, but in this context wisdom refers to proficiency in the five topics of knowledge and the like. The *Bodhisattva Levels* says:[348]

> Know that the bodhisattvas' wisdom is the thorough analysis of phenomena that engages or has engaged all of what is to be known and that operates through focusing on the five topics of knowledge—Buddhist knowledge, grammar, logic, technical arts, and medicine. **[450]**

Here, the wisdom that "engages" refers to wisdom prior to attaining the bodhisattva levels; wisdom that "has engaged" refers to wisdom after attaining such levels.

(b′) **How to begin the generation of wisdom**

The way to begin the generation of wisdom is to contemplate the benefits of generating wisdom and the faults of not generating it. Since I will explain the benefits and faults of having or lacking the wisdom of reality—selflessness—in the insight section, I will not elaborate on it here.[349] But I will discuss the remaining types of wisdom a little.

With respect to indicating wisdom's benefits, wisdom is the root of all good qualities for this and future lives. As the protector Nāgārjuna's *Hundred Verses on Wisdom* (*Prajñā-śataka*) says:[350]

> Wisdom is the root of all good qualities,
> Seen and not yet seen.
> To achieve both of these,
> Embrace wisdom.
>
> The great source for what you seek
> And for liberation is knowledge.
> So, esteeming it from the start,
> Adhere to wisdom, the great mother.

As the *Verse Summary of the Perfection of Wisdom in Eight Thousand Lines* states, wisdom functions like an eye for the other five perfections—generosity, etc.:[351]

> When the other perfections are completed by wisdom,
> They acquire their eye and fulfill their name,
> Just as a painting may be complete except for the eyes,
> But until the eyes are drawn, no wage is obtained.

How wisdom is necessary for other good qualities is illustrated by the example of a special piece of jewelry made of fine gold that becomes even more breathtaking when adorned with a precious emerald. Likewise, if the gold ornament of the five perfections from generosity to meditative stabilization is adorned with wisdom, which is able to distinguish right from wrong, they become more magnificent, because wisdom makes them much purer. It is similar to the way that the mental consciousness, by distinguishing the merits and faults in the objects of the five sensory faculties (the visual faculty, etc.), causes you to engage in what is to be adopted or reject what is to be cast aside. **[451]** This is what the glorious Āryaśūra's *Compendium of the Perfections* says:[352]

> The merits of generosity and so forth
> Are more powerful with wisdom as their lord,
> Just as an array of fine gold jewelry
> Shines more brightly when inset with jewels.
>
> It is this wisdom that renders vast
> The capacity for virtue in the purpose of each one,
> Just as the mind's additional power clearly displays
> The respective objects of the sensory faculties.

Similarly, wisdom is also crucial for other faculties such as faith and so on. When wisdom is present as lord, your generosity, faith, etc. understand well the merit of virtue and the faults of stinginess and so forth, so you become skilled at eliminating the afflictions and increasing good qualities. The *Compendium of the Perfections* states:[353]

> Among the various faculties of faith and so on,
> Wisdom is chief, as the mind is to the sensory faculties.
> With wisdom as lord, you know what is a fault and what merit,
> So you are skilled in the method of eliminating afflictions.

Bodhisattvas depend on wisdom to purify the other five perfections—generosity, etc. Even when they give their flesh to someone who asks for it, they are unaffected by such thoughts as pride, discouragement, etc. It is as though they were taking a cutting from a medicinal plant. This is because their wisdom makes reality manifest. With the wisdom that sees the troubles of both cyclic existence and the peace of nirvāṇa, they accomplish ethical discipline for the sake of others' welfare, so they practice pure ethical discipline. Through wisdom they know the faults of impatience and the merits of patience, and they then discipline their minds so they are not overpowered by suffering and others' misperceptions of them. With wisdom they understand well everything at which they joyously persevere, so their perseverance brings great success on the path. And through wisdom based on reasoning they accomplish the supreme delight and bliss of the meditative stabilization that is fixed upon the meaning of reality. **[452]** The *Compendium of the Perfections* states:[354]

> Once bodhisattvas have opened the clear eye of wisdom,
> Even when they give their own flesh without a thought,
> They never feel high or low about it,
> As if they were cutting a medicinal plant.

And also:

> Intelligent ones do not practice ethical discipline for their own aims;
> They see the flaws in the prison of cyclic existence
> And aspire to release the entire world from it.
> So of course they do not practice it for mundane aims.

And also:

> Injury done to the wise is not harmful
> Because they possess the good quality of patience,
> Like the best of very tame elephants
> Who are patient with many different tasks.
>
> Perseverance by itself ends in exhaustion;
> If aided by its ally, wisdom, it achieves great purposes.

And also:

> How could the supreme delight and bliss of such meditative stabilizations
> Be established in the minds of crude people who rely
> Upon reasoning that has led them to a wrong path
> That is polluted by the great fault of accumulated errors?

Two good qualities which may appear to be mutually exclusive prove to be non-contradictory for those who have wisdom. When bodhisattvas have become universal monarchs with authority over the entire world, they still do not fall under the control of sensory objects. This is the power of having wisdom as a royal minister. Similarly, the bodhisattvas' love that views living beings with affection is intense, but it is not mixed with even a trace of attachment; although they have a long-lasting and very forceful compassion that cannot bear for living beings to suffer, they do not have the laziness of being overcome with distress and thereby lacking enthusiasm for virtue; they have immeasurable joy, but their minds are free of instability which would distract them from their focus; and they are continually possessed of great impartiality, but they do not neglect for even a moment the welfare of all living beings. Wisdom does all this, because it is what removes the impediments to achieving a balanced strength in these good qualities. Thus the *Compendium of the Perfections* states:[355]

> Even bodhisattvas possessed of great kingdoms,
> Who have sensory objects similar to divine substances,
> Remain uncorrupted in their very nature. **[453]**
> This is the power of having the virtue of wisdom as their
> minister.
>
> Their love, inseparable from helping others,
> Is utterly free of stain from attachment.
> Their compassion, unable to bear for others to suffer,
> Never succumbs to laziness due to the burden of distress.
>
> Possessed of supreme joy, they do not waver from the real.
> Their great impartiality never neglects the welfare of beings.
> Great wisdom removes all that would counteract
> These good qualities, and so it beautifies them.

Mātṛceṭa's *Praise in Honor of One Worthy of Honor* (*Varṇārha-varṇa-stotra*) also says:[356]

> Without rejecting the real nature,
> You are also in accord with the conventional.

Thus, you do not have to forsake the real nature that gives great certainty that there is not even an atom of what your cognitive processes apprehend as signs of true existence. And you are also in accord with and do not contradict the conventional that gives deep certainty that effects arise from their respective internal and external causes and conditions. For others these appear to totally exclude each other, but for those who have wisdom, there is compatibility and a lack of contradiction.

The *Praise in Honor of One Worthy of Honor* states:[357]

> Regarding your proscriptions and prohibitions,
> Some of your word is definitive
> While some of it is not,
> But between these, there is no contradiction.

The two facts—that there are many dissimilarities in proscriptions and prohibitions between higher and lower vehicles and between sūtra and tantra, and that these are all the practices of a single person—are contradictory for those who are confused and lack the power of intelligence to seek the intended meaning of the innumerable scriptures. Yet through wisdom the learned know that these are not mutually exclusive.

There are limitless things that the unwise see as contradictory and the wise see as lacking contradiction—the presentations of the two truths and the many prescriptions in one scripture that are prohibitions in others and vice versa. To say that wisdom distinguishes the non-contradictory, intended meaning behind them is the peerless praise of wisdom. **[454]** In short, all good qualities come from wisdom. The *Compendium of the Perfections* says:[358]

> How wondrous that such excellent things come from wisdom
> That is like a mother who loves her child.
>
> The ten powers of the *sugata,* most excellent of strengths;
> All superior activities, without parallel;
> And all other collections of virtues in their entirety
> Arise based on such wisdom as their cause.
>
> The arts and the best treasures in all worlds;
> The variety of sacred learning that is like an eye;
> Protections, awarenesses, mantras, and so on;
> The different attributes of the teachings that set these forth;
>
> The multitude of enumerations; and the doors to liberation;
> All such types of service to the world
> That display the great power of the conqueror's children,
> All arise from the power of wisdom.

The faults of not having wisdom are as follows. Without wisdom, generosity and the other perfections are as if blind. The *Verse Summary of the Perfection of Wisdom in Eight Thousand Lines* states:[359]

> How could billions of blind people without a guide,
> Who do not know the way, enter the city?
> Once these five perfections lack wisdom, they are blind;
> As they lack a guide, they cannot reach enlightenment.

Consequently, generosity and the other perfections do not become pure, and you do not find the correct view. The *Compendium of the Perfections* states:[360]

> If those intent upon the final fruit are without wisdom,
> Their generosity does not purify them. The Buddha said,
> "Giving for others' sake is supreme generosity."
> Other kinds of giving serve only to increase one's wealth.

And also:

> Ethical discipline does not become pure
> Unless wisdom's light dispels the darkness.
> Ethical discipline without wisdom usually
> Becomes sullied by afflictions through faulty understanding.

And also:

> If your mind is muddled by the fault of erring intelligence,
> You have no interest in keeping the virtue of patience,
> You maintain a dislike for weighing merit and fault,
> And are like an unworthy king who becomes famous. **[455]**

And also:

> For adepts, wisdom is lauded as foremost;
> Nothing else is as subtle or profound.
> Without wisdom, you do not head straight for the mental path
> That is unclouded by the defects of desire.

And also:

> Without maintaining joyous perseverance in wisdom's ways,
> Your view will not become pure.

Here, the "king who becomes famous" refers to an unworthy king for whom fame occurs once, but then declines.

You do not repel the darkness of delusion's confusion as long as wisdom's great light does not shine, but when it does, you cast away the darkness, so you must make an effort to generate wisdom with whatever capacity and strength you have. The *Compendium of the Perfections* says:[361]

> Like the dawning of the sun's great light,
> The enormous power of wisdom's light arises
> And the concealing darkness in beings' minds
> Is completely dispelled, only its name left behind.

And also:

> Therefore, with all the power at your disposal,
> Work hard at the methods for producing such wisdom.

What are the causes of confusion? They are relying on bad friends; laziness; indolence; oversleeping; taking no pleasure in analysis and discernment; lack of interest in the vast variety of phenomena; the pride of thinking "I know" when you do not; the major wrong views; and being discouraged and thinking, "Someone like me cannot do this," and thus not taking pleasure in relying upon the learned. The *Compendium of the Perfections* says:[362]

> Laziness, indolence, and reliance upon bad friends,
> Being governed by sleep, no feeling for discernment,
> No interest in the Sage's most sublime wisdom,
> Inquiring under the influence of false pride,
>
> Lacking the faith to rely upon learned persons
> Due to attachment to self from feelings of inadequacy,
> The great poison of false concepts which are wrong views—
> These are the causes of confusion.

Therefore, as the *Compendium of the Perfections* says:[363]

> Serve and venerate a guru worthy of trust,
> And study to achieve wisdom.

Once you rely on a learned person, you must study in accord with your capacity, for if you do not, you will not produce the wisdom that arises from study and the wisdom that arises from reflection, whereupon you will not know what to meditate upon. **[456]** And if you do study, you will produce the wisdom that arises from reflection by thinking over the meaning of what you have studied, and from this you will gain vast wisdom that arises from meditation. Again the glorious Āryaśūra says:[364]

> Little study is like blindness—you do not know how to meditate.
> Without study, what could there be to reflect upon?
> Therefore, from the cause of making an effort to study
> You meditate in accord with reflection and thereby gain vast wisdom.

The venerable Maitreya also says in the *Sublime Continuum:*[365]

> The conceptualizations of the three spheres
> Are asserted to be cognitive obscurations,
> While conceptualizations such as stinginess and the like
> Are asserted to be afflictive obscurations.
>
> Solely wisdom is the cause
> Of their elimination, nothing else,
> So wisdom is supreme. Study is its basis,
> So study is supreme.

And Śāntideva's *Compendium of the Trainings in Verse (Śikṣā-samuccaya-kārikā)* says:[366]

> Be forbearing and then study;
> Stay in a forest, and then
> Persevere at meditative equipoise.

His auto-commentary [*Compendium of Trainings*] to this says:[367]

> With impatience, you become disheartened and cannot forbear, so your perseverance at study, etc., declines. And without study, you do not know the means for either meditative stabilization or for clearing away the afflictions. Therefore, without becoming disheartened, study.

And the *Questions of Nārāyaṇa Formula* (*Nārāyaṇa-paripṛcchā-dhāraṇī*) also says:[368]

> Just so, child of good lineage, if you study, wisdom will come. If you are possessed of wisdom, the afflictions will be stilled. Once you have no afflictions, demons do not have a chance with you.

Scripture and reasoning establish the following: Those who wish to properly practice the teaching need a broad study of the stainless scriptures and their commentaries, the unexcelled cause that gives rise to the wisdom which thoroughly distinguishes phenomena, which is the sacred life-force of the path. **[457]** However, not achieving wisdom while thinking that a broad study is necessary to develop it is simply the fault of your not being convinced that you need the analytical meditation of discerning wisdom when the time comes for practice, and of having the mistaken conviction that thinks that analytical meditation is not necessary. Therefore, those of you who want what is best for yourselves should eliminate such a mistaken conviction as though getting rid of poison. Nal-jor-ba-chen-bo said:

> Jo-wo-pa (Jo-bo-ba), when it comes to accomplishing the state of omniscient enlightenment, whether you show off or conceal that you studied only a handbook, you cannot get anywhere without reading a yak's load of books.

Pu-chung-wa (Phu-chung-ba) placed an opened sacred text beside his pillow and said:

> We must learn the texts, so even though you do not get a chance to read them, make a wish to read them all. If someone said that you should practice the teaching without understanding it, how would you do it?

Bo-do-wa said three times to a monk of Jen-nga-wa (sPyan-snga-ba) who was escorting him a short distance, "You are enjoying yourself too much." He then continued:

> You rely upon my teacher who is like the sky covering the earth, so do not salivate over other teachers. Since you do not have to

> read the root texts and their commentaries and mark their corresponding passages, you do not have a lot of work. You are happy because you do not think about cause and effect, while you work at certain activities by means of certain tantric practices. And you can be satisfied with these many things?

Sha-ra-wa said:

> Until you become a buddha, your studies are not finished. They are finished when you are a buddha.

Ga-ma-pa (Ka-ma-ba) said:

> Some say, "When you practice the teachings, what need is there of knowledge," and they degenerate. This idea is a real danger for those of us who have studied little. Others say, "If you really try you do not need knowledge." This is very dangerous. If you are making a big effort at the teaching, knowledge is required; since it is not completed in this brief lifetime, we must resolve, "I will study continually through many lifetimes without interrupting the succession of lives having leisure and opportunity." Some think that meditators do not need to study, only those who explain the teachings do. But those who explain the teachings and do not study merely run the risk of sinning, while it is precisely the meditator who must study to avoid straying from the path. **[458]**

Thus you must be convinced that wisdom and the study that causes it are indispensable for proper practice. Moreover, unless you reach certainty about the need for analytical meditation when you practice, you will have a very hard time getting anywhere.

Even some well-regarded scholars of the scriptural collections claim, "Understand study to be either a mere preliminary to practice or to be a background support—like mountains at the back of a valley—but not the actual instructions. For this reason, you need practice to quickly attain buddhahood and study to benefit the Buddha's teaching." This is contradictory nonsense. There are just two kinds of teaching: teaching as scripture and teaching that has been put into practice; the former makes known the procedures for practice, and the latter is assimilating the practice after you have understood the procedures. Therefore, doing the practice without error is the best way to uphold the teaching. Moreover, unerringly upholding the teaching in the sense of practice depends upon an unerring understanding of scriptural teaching.

Therefore, it is not right to forget what you have studied at the time of practice, for you must first know many teachings and then put their very meaning into practice when the time comes to do so.

Even if you do not understand the teachings from the outset, do not be discouraged, but strive to study them in accord with your mental capacity, as much as feasible, whether that be a little or a lot. Do not make study and practice into separate things. Rather, the very thing that you practice must be exactly what you first study and reflect upon. Beginning bodhisattvas must depend with certainty on a single procedure of the path—a practice that is not biased toward one side but is complete in all aspects of the path. When their mental capacity is small, they engage in conditioning themselves to just this process of study followed by practice. If their mental capacity is great or, though at first small, has become greater through conditioning, they steadily expand upon the very stage of the path they know, proceeding in connection with all the scriptures and their stainless commentaries. There is no need for them to pursue something else to study besides these. **[459]**

Therefore if instructions are accurate and complete, then, although summarized, all of the key points of the sūtra and tantra paths and the paths of the higher and lower vehicles must be covered; once they have been explained at length, you must be able to go through all the teachings. Until you reach something like this, it is possible to feel delight about just some portion of your practice, but it is impossible to become certain about the key points of practice for the complete corpus of the teachings.

Consequently, rely upon excellent teachers and companions. Make a foundation of pure ethical discipline to which you commit yourself. Listen again and again to the instructions, do four sessions of meditation, and then sustain the object of meditation and its subjective aspects. After you have made fervent supplications to the deities and gurus, strive at all the causes of engaging from many perspectives in accumulating the collections and purifying obscurations. If you do this, you will become profoundly certain that the good qualities in your mind will steadily improve.

As the former excellent beings said:

> Make all the teachings you have previously heard completely clear in your mind. You must reflect upon them again and again, evaluate them, and deliberate on them. When you have let yourself forget the teachings, there is nothing gained by learning to stabilize your attention on one object of meditation. The best meditators are the best teachers. Mediocre meditators become mediocre teachers. You need knowledge of the teaching and commensurate meditation that both proceed to ever greater levels together.

Once you gain a firm certainty from such reflection, you do not pay heed when bad friends say, "All thoughts, virtuous and nonvirtuous, are conceptualizations and are therefore to be eliminated," but rather think, "The teachings do not say this nor do my teachers assert it." Otherwise, if you are a person who possesses a little faith but no wisdom, you are like the leading edge of water running downhill—you go anywhere you are led, taking anything said to be true, wanting to cry when you see others crying, wanting to laugh when you see others laugh.

(c′) **The divisions of wisdom**

The presentation of the divisions of wisdom has three parts:

1. Wisdom that knows the ultimate [**460**]
2. Wisdom that knows the conventional
3. Wisdom that knows how to act for the welfare of living beings

(1′) **Wisdom that knows the ultimate**

Wisdom that knows the ultimate cognizes the reality of selflessness, either by means of a concept or in a direct manner.

(2′) **Wisdom that knows the conventional**

Wisdom that knows the conventional is wisdom that is proficient at the five topics of knowledge. The *Ornament for the Mahāyāna Sūtras* says:[369]

> Without making effort at the five topics of knowledge,
> Even supreme noble beings do not reach omniscience.
> So they must strive for these so as to refute others,
> To care for others, and to know everything.

The topics are distinguished by the different sorts of purposes for pursuing them. To refute those who do not believe in the teaching, you pursue knowledge of grammar and logic. To help those who do believe, you pursue knowledge of the arts and medicine. To achieve knowledge of all for yourself, you pursue Buddhist knowledge. But to attain buddhahood, there are no such distinctions between them; you must pursue all the topics of knowledge.

(3′) **Wisdom that knows how to act for the welfare of living beings**

Wisdom that knows how to act for the welfare of living beings knows the way to accomplish blamelessly the welfare of beings in their present and future lives.

(d′) **How to practice**

When you develop the three types of wisdom, you do so in association with the six supremacies and all six perfections. The generosity of wisdom is establishing others in wisdom after you have stabilized yourself in it. The remaining perfections are as presented before.[370]

(e′) **A summary**

Even if you have the wisdom that perceives emptiness, it does not become a bodhisattva deed without the spirit of enlightenment, so steadily increase the spirit of enlightenment—the basis of the bodhisattva deeds. Next, aspire to the wisdom of those at high levels and then train your mind in it. From this moment you must strive to produce the three types of wisdom—the method for completing the peerless, great collection of sublime wisdom—and you must study. For, if you do not do this, you contradict the principal precept and will then be destroyed by faults and infractions; in future lives as well you will not take pleasure in broad learning. Consequently, you will be unable to learn the bodhisattva trainings. **[461]** Whereas, if in this life you strive at the methods of developing wisdom, you prevent the infraction of not training in the six perfections as promised; then in other lives as well, as the *Questions of Subāhu Sūtra* says, you will easily be able to complete the perfection of wisdom.

Nowadays, from among the six perfections—the center post of both the sūtra and tantra paths—there exist in slight measure the stages of the practice of meditative stabilization, but the stages of the practice of the other five perfections have disappeared. Therefore, I have explained the key points of their practice in abbreviated form and a little of the method for generating certain knowledge of them. Below, I will teach at length two topics that come from the classic texts: the stages of how to practice insight—wisdom that observes the real nature and the diversity of phenomena—and the stages of the practice of meditative serenity, which is meditative stabilization.

All bodhisattvas who will attain buddhahood do so in reliance upon the six perfections. The *Bodhisattva Levels* says this emphatically at the conclusion of its discussions of each of the six perfections. Hence, these six perfections are to be known as the one path traveled by bodhisattvas of the past, present, and future. And because these six are the great ocean of all virtues, they are the perfect summary of the key points of practice. The *Bodhisattva Levels* states:[371]

> Bodhisattvas who attain unsurpassed, perfect enlightenment by these six perfections are called a great river, a great ocean of virtues; generosity and so forth are the most precious causes of all excellent things for all living beings. Accordingly, there is nothing comparable to the perfections' immeasurable completion of the collections of merit and sublime wisdom and their fruit of unsurpassed, perfect enlightenment. **[462]**

15

Helping Others to Mature: The Four Ways to Gather Disciples

(b) Training in the four ways to gather disciples that help others to mature
- (i) What the four ways to gather disciples are
- (ii) The reason they are stipulated as four
- (iii) Their functions
- (iv) The need for those who gather a following to rely on them
- (v) A somewhat elaborate explanation

(b) **Training in the four ways to gather disciples that help others to mature**

Training in the four ways to gather disciples that help others to mature has five parts:

1. What the four ways to gather disciples are
2. The reason they are stipulated as four
3. Their functions
4. The need for those who gather a following to rely on them
5. A somewhat elaborate explanation

(i) **What the four ways to gather disciples are**

(1) *Generosity* is as earlier explained in the section on this perfection.[372] (2) *Pleasant speech* is teaching the perfections to disciples.

(3) *Working at the aims* is setting disciples to work on the aims as they have been taught, or involving them in correctly taking up these aims. (4) *Consistency of behavior* is stabilizing yourself in the very aims in which you have established others, and then training in them. The *Ornament for the Mahāyāna Sūtras* says:[373]

> Generosity is the same as before; teaching the perfections,
> Involving others in taking them up, and involving yourself
> Are asserted to be pleasant speech, working at the aims,
> And consistency of behavior, respectively.

(ii) **The reason they are stipulated as four**

Question: Why are the ways of gathering disciples set as four?

Reply: In order to gather a following of disciples for the sake of establishing them in virtue, they must first be pleased. This, moreover, depends on your giving them material things, providing benefit to their bodies. Thus pleased, they first must know how to connect to the path. That is to say, by using pleasant speech to explain the teaching, you cause them to cast away ignorance and doubt, and then to correctly apprehend the aims. Once they have understood these, you cause them to accomplish virtue by working at these aims. However, if you have not accomplished virtue yourself, when you say to others, "You have to engage in this, you have to reject that," they will say, "Why do you tell others, 'Accomplish this aim,' when you do not accomplish it yourself? You still need somebody else to correct you." They will not listen to what they have to practice. But if you are practicing yourself, they will think, "This person is established in the virtue to which he (or she) is leading us, so we will definitely derive benefit and happiness if we accomplish it." They then either engage in it anew, or (for those who have already engaged in it) do not reject it and become stable in it. **[463]** So for this you have to be consistent in your behavior. The *Ornament for the Mahāyāna Sūtras* says:[374]

> Know the ways to gather disciples to be four:
> A method to give benefit, involving others in
> Comprehending the teachings, involving them in
> Engaging, and likewise involving yourself.

(iii) **Their functions**

Question: What do these four ways to gather disciples do for the disciples?

Reply: Generosity makes them fit vessels to hear the teaching, for it makes them happy with the person who explains it. Pleasant speech makes them take interest in the teaching that is to be given, because it gives them a detailed understanding of the aims and dispels their doubts. Working at the aims makes them practice in accord with what they have been taught. Consistency of behavior makes those who have engaged in the teachings not reject them but practice for a long time. The *Ornament for the Mahāyāna Sūtras* says:[375]

> By the first they become vessels;
> By the second they take interest;
> By the third they practice;
> By the fourth they train.

(iv) **The need for those who gather a following to rely on them**

Because the buddhas have declared these four ways to gather disciples to be what achieves all the aims of all disciples and to be the superb method, those gathering a following must rely on them. The *Ornament for the Mahāyāna Sūtras* states:[376]

> Those involved in gathering a following
> Rely on this means;
> It is praised as the superb method,
> Achieving all aims for all.

(v) **A somewhat elaborate explanation**

There are two types of pleasant speech. The first, pleasant speech associated with worldly customs, means that you first assume a clear expression free of anger, give a smile, and then please living beings in worldly ways, such as inquiring after their health, etc. The second type, pleasant speech associated with presenting the perfect teaching, means that you instruct living beings in the teaching for their benefit and happiness, beginning with teachings on developing faith, ethical discipline, study, generosity, and wisdom.

The avenues of pleasant speech are as follows. To an enemy who would kill you, you say helpful words without a fault in your heart. With the very dull-witted, you willingly rise to the challenge, tirelessly giving talks on the teaching and causing them to adhere to virtue. **[464]** To devious beings who deceive their masters, abbots, etc., and engage in wrongdoing, you speak pleasantly with helpful words and without anger, teaching even the most difficult persons. In order that persons whose minds have not matured may eliminate obscuration and be reborn in happy realms, you give discourses to them on preliminary practices—generosity and ethical discipline. To persons whose minds have matured, who are rid of obscuration and possessed of a joyful frame of mind, you reveal the foremost and perfect teaching of the four noble truths. You encourage householders and renunciates who are careless to be conscientious, and to those who have doubts you speak elaborately and explain the teaching to them to dispel their doubts.

Working at the aims is twofold: bringing the immature to maturity and liberating the matured. It is also presented in three parts as follows. (1) *Involving persons in taking up the aims of this life* is causing them to employ means consistent with the teaching to acquire, to protect, and to increase their resources. (2) *Involving persons in taking up the purpose of future lives* means to establish persons in the life of a renunciate who lives as a mendicant after they have rid themselves of possessions. Although this is certain to bring happiness in future lives, it is not certain to do so in this life. (3) *Involving persons in taking up the aims of both this and future lives* means to cause householders and renunciates to take up freedom from mundane and supramundane attachment, for this generates mental and physical pliancy in the present life, and the attainment of a purified deity and nirvāṇa in the future.

Work at the aims even when it is very difficult. It is difficult to induce those who have not previously accumulated roots of virtue to take up virtue. It is difficult to work at the aims with respect to those who have magnificent resources because they live in a situation where there are so many grounds for being unconscientious. And it is difficult to work at the aims with respect to those who are indoctrinated with the views of non-Buddhist philosophers because they are hostile to the teaching and, because of their foolishness, do not understand reasoning. **[465]**

With respect to the stages of working at the aims, you first cause those with childlike intelligence to follow easy personal instructions. Then, when their understanding has reached a middling level, you have them follow intermediate personal instructions. Finally, when their wisdom has greatly expanded, you have them follow the profound teaching and subtle personal instructions.

Consistency of behavior means that you maintain practices equal to or superior to those in which you establish others. Accordingly, even though in whatever you do you must first focus on the welfare of living beings and not lose your resolve for others' welfare, you must discipline yourself in conjunction with these pursuits. Triratnadāsa's *Praise of Infinite Qualities* says:[377]

> Some who are undisciplined use reasonable words, but
> Contradict these words, so they are called "unable to help others to discipline themselves."
> Knowing this, you placed all living beings in your heart,
> And strove to discipline yourself wherever you had lacked discipline before.

The four ways to gather disciples also comprise two categories: gathering disciples via material things and gathering disciples through the teaching. Giving material things is the first of the four ways to gather disciples. The remaining three of the four ways are included in the second, gathering disciples through the teaching. Furthermore, this latter category includes the teaching of the objects of meditation, the teaching as put into practice, and the teaching of purifying oneself in practicing these two. The *Ornament for the Mahāyāna Sūtras* states:[378]

> The four ways to gather disciples
> Are asserted as two ways of gathering:
> By material things and by the teaching,
> Which means presenting the objects of meditation, etc.

Moreover, these four ways to gather disciples are the way all the bodhisattvas of the three times work for the welfare of others, so it is the single path to travel. The *Ornament for the Mahāyāna Sūtras* states:[379]

> All those who have gathered disciples,
> Are gathering, or will gather them
> Do so in this way; therefore, this is the path
> For the maturation of living beings.

In general, then, though the bodhisattva deeds are limitless, the six perfections and the four ways to gather disciples are their best summation. For, bodhisattvas have just two tasks, the maturation of causal collections for their own buddhahood and the maturation of the mind-streams of living beings; they accomplish both of these through the perfections and the ways to gather disciples. **[466]** Thus the *Bodhisattva Levels* also says:[380]

> The perfections bring to complete maturation the buddha qualities you will have yourself. The ways to gather disciples bring all

> living beings to complete maturation. In sum, know these to be the active expression of a bodhisattva's virtuous qualities.

Therefore, I have set forth in this section these two categories of practice. If you want to know them in more detail, look in the *Bodhisattva Levels*.

With respect to the way these practices are done during and after meditative equipoise, the Great Elder says:[381]

> The deeds of bodhisattvas are
> The magnificent six perfections and so forth.
> The yogi arisen from meditative equipoise
> Resolutely accomplishes the path of accumulation.

Beginning bodhisattvas who have taken the vows of the conquerors' children and are on the path of accumulation practice only the six perfections, whether in meditative equipoise or subsequent to it. They sustain some of the perfections in meditative equipoise and others in the post-equipoise state. Some aspects of meditative serenity (which is meditative stabilization) and some aspects of insight (which is the perfection of wisdom) are cultivated in meditative equipoise, whereas some other aspects of meditative stabilization and wisdom are sustained in the post-equipoise state, along with the first three perfections. Joyous perseverance occurs in both the meditative equipoise and post-equipoise states, while one type of patience—certain aspects of the patience of certitude about the profound teachings—also occurs in meditative equipoise. The Great Elder says:[382]

> During periods after rising from meditative equipoise,
> Cultivate the view that all things
> Are like a magician's illusions, as in the eight similes.[383]
> Thereby emphasize in post-meditative thought
>
> Purification and the training in method.
> During periods of meditative equipoise
> Continually condition yourself to
> Serenity and insight in equal measure.

When bodhisattvas whose minds are untrained in such marvelous but difficult deeds hear of them, they feel distressed. **[467]** Although they are unable to practice such things at first, they come to understand them and then to intimately familiarize themselves with them as objects of aspiration. Later they engage in them spontaneously without any strain. Thus, familiarization is of the greatest importance, for if these bodhisattvas recognized their inability to actually engage in such deeds and then gave up on even the familiarization conducive to training the mind in them, they would greatly delay reaching the pure path. The *Praise of Infinite Qualities* says:[384]

> Deeds that hurt the worldly even to hear about
> And that even you did not undertake for a long time
> You accustomed yourself to, so in time they became spontaneous.
> Thus, it is difficult to develop good qualities without familiarization.

Those who have taken the bodhisattva vows have no choice but to learn the bodhisattva deeds. But even those who have not adopted the engaged spirit of enlightenment through its ritual strive to inculcate a desire to learn the deeds, thus increasing the force of their enthusiasm for learning them. Then, when they take the vows, their vows will be extremely stable, so make an effort to do this.

From among the stages of the path for persons of great capacity, this concludes the explanation of the stages of the path for training in the aspirational spirit of enlightenment and for learning the deeds of the conquerors' children in general.

Appendix 1
Outline of the Text

[Chapter One ***The Stages of the Path for Persons of Great Capacity*** **13]**

3) Training the mind in the stages of the path for persons of great capacity 15
  a) Showing that developing the spirit of enlightenment is the only entrance to the Mahāyāna 16
  b) How to develop the spirit of enlightenment 21
    i) How the spirit of enlightenment depends on certain causes to arise 22
      a′ The development of the spirit through the four conditions 22
      b′ The development of the spirit through the four causes 24
      c′ The development of the spirit through the four strengths 24

[Chapter Two ***Compassion, the Entrance to the Mahāyāna*** **27]**

    ii) The stages of training in the spirit of enlightenment 27
      a′ The training based on the seven cause-and-effect personal instructions in the lineage descended from the Great Elder [Atisha] 28
      1′ Developing certainty about the order of the stages 28
        a″ Showing that the root of the Mahāyāna path is compassion 28
          1″ The importance of compassion in the beginning 28
          2″ The importance of compassion in the middle 29
          3″ The importance of compassion at the end 29
        b″ How the six other personal instructions are either causes or effects of compassion 31
          1″ How the first four personal instructions—recognition of all living beings as your mothers through the development of love—act as causes of compassion 31
          2″ How wholehearted resolve and the spirit of enlightenment are the effects of compassion 32

APPENDIX 2
GLOSSARY

abbot	*mkhan po*
abstention	*spong ba*
acquiesce	*dang du len pa*
adept	*mkhas pa*
adventitious	*glo bur ba*
afflictions	*nyon mongs*
analysis	*dpyod pa*
analytical meditation	*dpyad sgom*
anger	*khong khro*
arhat	*dgra bcom pa*
arrogance	*dregs pa*
arts	*bzo ba*
ascetic practices	*dka' spyad*
aspiration	*mos pa*
aspirational prayers	*smon lam*
aspirational spirit of enlightenment	*smon pa'i byang chub kyi sems*
attachment	*'dod chags, mngon par zhen pa, chags pa*
attitude of abstention	*spong sems*
authoritative source	*khungs dag po*
authoritative	*tshad ma*
basic suffering	*sdug bsngal gnyug ma*
begging	*slong mos 'tshol ba*
belligerence	*drag shul*
belongings, necessities, goods	*yo byad*
bhagavan	*bcom ldan 'das*

bliss	*bde ba*
bodhisattva deeds	*byang chub sems dpa'i spyod pa*
bodhisattva	*byang chub sems dpa'*
bondage	*'ching ba*
buddha	*sangs rgyas*
categorical distinction	*so sor ris su bcad pa*
causally concordant behavioral effect	*byed pa rgyu mthun gyi 'bras bu*
cause-and-effect personal instructions	*rgyu 'bras man ngag*
celestial mansion	*gzhal yas khang*
certain goodness	*nges legs*
certitude	*nges par sems pa*
cessation	*'gogs pa*
channels	*rtsa*
charisma	*brjid bag*
charity	*bstsal pa*
cherish	*gces la phangs pa*
child of good lineage	*rigs kyi bu*
childish person	*byis pa*
circumambulate	*skor ba byed pa*
cognitive obscurations	*shes sgrib*
collections of merit and sublime wisdom	*tshogs gnyis*
commitment	*dam bca' ba, khas blangs pa*
compassion	*snying rje*
complete enlightenment	*rdzogs byang*
concealment	*'chab pa*
concentration	*ting nge 'dzin*
conception of self	*bdag tu 'dzin pa*
conceptual thought	*rtog pa*
concordant causes	*rjes su mthun pa'i rgyu*
conditioned things	*'du byed*
confession	*bshags pa*
confusion	*rmongs pa*
conqueror	*rgyal ba*
conqueror's children	*rgyal ba'i sras*
conscientiousness	*bag yod*
contaminated	*zag bcas*
contamination	*zag pa*
contempt	*brnyas pa*

conventional	*kun rdzob, tha snyad*
conventional truths	*kun rdzob bden pa*
conventional valid cognition	*tha snyad pa'i tshad ma*
conviction	*nges pa*
correct view	*yang dag pa'i lta ba*
courage	*sro*
craving	*sred pa*
cyclic existence	*'khor ba, srid pa*
deceit	*sgyu*
deceitfulness	*g.yo ba*
deceive	*slu ba*
dedicate, transfer, turn over	*sngo ba*
deed that is wrong by nature	*rang bzhin kyi kha na ma tho ba*
deed that is wrong by prohibition	*bcas pa'i kha na ma tho ba*
deeds	*spyod pa*
definitive	*nges don*
degenerate (era)	*snyigs ma*
deity	*lha*
demon	*gdon, bdud*
dependent-arising	*rten 'brel*
determination to be free	*nges 'byung*
determine, decide	*nges pa*
disbelief	*ma mos pa*
discerning wisdom	*so sor rtog pa'i shes rab*
disciples	*gdul bya*
discouragement	*sgyid lug, –pa*
disenchantment	*skyo ba'i sems*
disheartened	*skyo ba*
disparage	*smad, smod*
dispirited	*skyo ba*
disreputable persons	*ma rabs rnams*
diversity of phenomena	*ji snyed pa*
divisive speech	*phra ma*
drops	*thig le*
dysfunctional tendencies	*gnas ngan len*
elaboration	*spros pa*
embarrassment	*khrel pa*
embodiment of form	*gzugs sku*
embodiment of truth	*chos sku*
emptiness	*stong pa nyid*
engaged spirit of enlightenment	*'jug sems*

enlightened activities	*'phrin las*
enlightenment	*byang chub*
enthusiasm	*mngon par spro ba, spro ba*
equanimity	*btang snyoms*
erroneous conception	*tshul bzhin ma yin pa yid la byed pa*
essential nature	*rang bzhin*
ethical discipline	*tshul khrims*
ethical training	*bslab pa* [in context]
even-minded	*sems snyoms, –pa*
excellent being	*dam pa*
factor of method	*thabs kyi cha*
faith	*dad pa*
faith of conviction	*yid ches kyi dad pa*
fame	*grags pa*
fearlessness	*mi 'jigs pa*
five topics of knowledge	*rig pa'i gnas nga bo*
flawless	*phyin ci ma log pa*
forbearance	*bzod pa*
forbearance of conviction	*mos pa'i bzod pa*
fortitude	*bsran*
four dark practices	*nag po'i chos bzhi*
four light practices	*dkar po'i chos bzhi*
four powers	*stobs bzhi*
four ways to gather disciples	*bsdu ba'i dngos po bzhi*
fundamental transgressions	*rtsa ltung*
garuḍa	*mkha' lding*
generosity	*sbyin pa*
generous attitude	*gtong ba'i sems*
gesture	*phyag rgya*
give, give away	*gtong ba*
giving	*sbyin pa, gtong ba*
good qualities	*yon tan*
grammar	*sgra*
great persons	*skyes bu* [in context]
grief	*mya ngan*
guru	*bla ma*
habituation	*goms pa*
hands joined respectfully	*thal mo sbyar ba*
hatred, hostility	*zhe sdang*
hell	*dmyal ba*
high status	*mngon mtho*

Hīnayāna	*theg dman*
honest	*drang po*
hostility	*sdang ba*
hungry ghost	*yi dwags*
ignorance	*ma rig pa, gti mug*
ill deeds	*nyes spyod*
immediate necessities	*nyams su mkho ba*
impartiality	*btang snyoms*
impatient	*bze re*
impermanent	*mi rtag pa*
impure	*ma dag pa*
indolence	*snyom pa*
initiation	*dbang bskur*
insatiability	*mi ngoms pa*
insight	*lhag mthong*
inspire	*yid 'dun pa*
intended meaning	*dgongs pa*
internalize	*gong du chud pa*
irreversible	*mi sdog pa*
jealousy	*phrag dog*
joy	*dga' ba, yid dga' ba*
joyous perseverance	*brtson 'grus*
karma	*las*
kindness	*drin*
laziness	*le lo*
league	*dpag tshad*
leisure	*dal ba*
lethargy	*rmugs pa*
liberation	*thar pa*
lineage	*rigs pa*
living beings	*sems can*
local spirits	*mi ma yin gnyug mar gnas pa*
logic	*gtan tshigs*
Lord of Death	*gshin rje*
love	*byams pa*
lying	*brdzun smra*
Mahāyāna	*theg chen*
major transgression	*nyon mongs can gyi ltung ba*
make effort	*'bad pa*
make gifts	*sbyin pa byed pa*
malice	*gnod sems*

maṇḍala	*dkyil 'khor*
mantra	*sngags*
master	*slob dpon*
masteries	*zil gnon*
material goods/things	*rdzas, zang zing*
mean behavior	*bya ba ngan pa*
medicine	*gso ba*
meditation	*sgom pa*
meditative equipoise	*mnyam bzhag*
meditative stabilization	*bsam gtan*
merit	*bsod nams*
method	*thabs*
mindfulness	*dran pa*
minor transgression	*nyon mongs can ma yin ba'i ltung ba*
misconception	*tshul bzhin ma yin pa'i rnam rtog*
misdeed	*kha na ma tho ba*
miserable realms	*ngan 'gro*
misperception	*log sgrub*
misrepresentation	*g.yo*
modest vehicle	*nyi tshe ba'i theg pa*
monastic ritual of earmarking belongings	*rnam brtag gis cho ga*
monk	*dge slong*
motivation	*kun slong*
nirvāṇa	*mya ngan las 'das pa*
noble being	*'phags pa*
non-abiding nirvāṇa	*mi gnas pa'i mya ngan*
non-attachment	*ma chags pa*
non-Buddhist philosophers	*mu stegs pa*
nonconceptual	*mi rtog pa*
non-discursive yoga	*rnal 'byor mi rtog pa*
non-distraction	*mi g.yeng ba*
non-hostility	*zhe sdang med pa*
obeisance	*phyag tshal*
obscuration, obscurations	*sgrib pa*
observed object	*dmigs pa*
offering	*mchod pa*
offering cakes	*gtor ma*
omniscience	*rnam mkhyen, kun mkhyen*
one-pointed	*rtse gcig pa*
ontological status	*sdod lugs, gnas lugs*

opportunity	*'byor ba*
ordinary person	*tha mal ba*
pacifying	*zhi ba*
passion	*zhen pa*
path of accumulation	*tshog lam*
patience	*bzod pa*
peace	*zhi ba*
perfection	*pha rol tu phyin pa*
perfection vehicle	*pha rol tu phyin pa'i theg pa*
permanent	*rtag pa*
personal instructions	*man ngag*
pliancy	*shin tu sbyangs pa*
possessions	*bdog pa*
poverty	*dbul ba, phongs pa*
praise	*bsngags pa, bstod pa*
pratyekabuddha	*rang sangs rgyas, rang rgyal*
precept	*bslabs bya*
prediction of enlightenment	*lung bstan*
pride	*nga rgyal*
procrastination	*phyi bshol*
prohibitive precepts	*bcas pa'i bslab pa*
prosperity	*'byor ba*
prostration	*phyag 'tshal*
rākṣasa	*srin po*
real nature	*ji lta ba*
reality	*chos nyid, de zhin nyid, de kho na nyid*
recite	*bzlas rjod byed pa*
refuge	*skyabs pa*
regret	*'gyod*
reliable person	*yid ches pa*
religious robes	*chos gos*
relinquishment	*dor ba*
renunciate	*rab tu byung ba*
restraint	*sdom pa*
ritual	*cho ga*
roots of virtue	*dge ba'i rtsa ba*
rule	*bcas pa*
sage	*thup ba, drang srong*
sayings	*gsungs sgros*

scriptural collections	*sde snod*
self-centered	*rang gi kha 'dzin*
self-cherishing	*rang gces pa*
self-contempt	*bdag nyid brnyas pa*
self-control	*rang dbang*
selflessness	*bdag med pa*
sensory objects	*'dod yon*
sensual pleasures	*'dod pa'i bde ba*
serenity	*zhi gnas*
serviceability	*las su rung ba*
shamelessness	*ngo tsha med pa*
signs	*mtshan ma*
sin	*sdig pa*
sincerely	*bsam pa thag pa nas*
sincerity	*lhag pa'i bsam pa*
six supremacies	*dam pa drug*
skill-in-means	*thabs mkhas pa*
sleep	*gnyid pa*
speaking disparagingly	*mi bsngags pa smra ba*
spirit of enlightenment	*sems bskyed, byang chub kyi sems*
śrāvaka	*nyan thos*
steadfastness	*brtan pa*
stealing	*ma byin len*
stinginess	*ser sna*
study	*thos pa*
subjective aspect	*rnam pa*
sublime wisdom	*ye shes*
suffering	*sdug bsngal*
sugata	*bde bar gshegs pa*
superknowledge	*mngon shes*
supernormal powers	*cho 'phrul, rdzu 'phrul*
sūtra	*mdo*
take responsibility	*khur du bzhes pa*
tantra	*gsang sngags*
tantric classics	*sngags kyi gzhungs che ba*
tathāgata	*de bzhin bshegs pa*
tightfistedness	*yongs su 'dzin pa*
totalities	*zad pa*
training	*bslab pa*
transformative experience	*yid 'gyur ba'i myong ba*
transgression	*pham pa*

transgression that is a minor infraction	*nyes byas kyi ltung ba*
ultimate	*don dam pa*
uncontaminated	*zag med*
uncontrived	*bcos ma min pa*
universal monarch	*'khor los sgyur rgyal*
vacuity	*stong pa*
Vajrayāna	*rdo rje'i theg pa*
valid cognition	*tshad ma*
view, philosophical view	*lta ba*
vigilance	*shes bzhin*
virtue	*dge ba*
vow	*sdom pa*
vow of individual liberation	*so so thar pa'i sdom pa*
wealth, possessions	*nor*
what to engage in and what to reject	*'jug ldog*
wholehearted resolve	*lhag pa'i bsam pa*
winds	*rlung*
wisdom	*shes rab*
work for the welfare of	*don byed pa*
yakṣa	*gnod sbyin*
yearning	*'dun pa*

Appendix 3
Emendations to the Tibetan Text

336.12: *dkon brtsegs las/ spyod lam thams cad du byang chub kyi sems sbyong ba dang dge ba ci byed kyi sngon du byang chub kyi sems gtong ba byas na skye ba gzhan du'ang sems rin po che dang mi 'bral ba ni/ ji lta ji ltar mang du mis brtags na/ zhes sogs kyis gsal bar bstan to—skye ba gzhan du'ang sems rin po che dang mi 'bral ba ni/ dkon brtsegs las/ spyod lam thams cad du byang chub kyi sems sbyong ba dang dge ba ci byed kyi sngon du byang chub kyi sems gtong ba byas na zhes dang/ ting nge 'dzin rgyal po las/ ji lta ji ltar mang du mis brtags na/ zhes sogs kyis gsal bar bstan to,* Geshe Yeshe Tapkay following the *Śikṣā-samuccaya,* P5336: 199.3.6-8.

393.18: *dben pa—dpen pa,* Ganden Bar Nying: 197b.1.

382.5: *lags pa kho nar—legs pa kho nar,* Ganden Bar Nying: 191b.6.

407.16: *rang bzhin nges pa—rang bzhin des pa,* Ganden Bar Nying: 204a.2.

434.15: *mi dka' zhes bya—mi dka' shes bya,* Hopkins 1998, v. 218.

434.18: *rnam bzhi yis—rnam bzhi yi,* Hopkins 1998, v. 220.

436.20: *bdag gis ngal ba—bdag gis dal ba,* Ganden Bar Nying: 218a.2.

459.14: *da ltar bsams pas—de ltar bsams pas,* Ganden Bar Nying: 229a.7.

NOTES

The citation reference in the notes first supplies the Sanskrit reference if extant, giving first the chapter and then the verse, or simply the page number(s). This is followed by the Tohoku catalogue (Ui et al. 1934) reference (identified by the abbreviation D), giving the section followed by the page and line numbers. These have all been given following Tsultrim Kelsang Khangkar's critical edition of the Tibetan text (Khangkar 2001). Where the reference was not available in Khangkar, its location in Suzuki (1955-61) has been supplied, giving the page, folio, and line numbers.

Chapter One *The Stages of the Path for Persons of Great Capacity*

1. LRCM begins this section with the title: "From the stages of the path for persons of great capacity, the training in the aspirational spirit of enlightenment and the general way to learn the deeds of the conqueror's children." This is not in the LRCM outline (*sa bcas*). The Ganden Bar Nying (140a) simply has the title: "From the great treatise on the stages of the path to enlightenment, the beginning of the section on the person of great capacity," *byang chub lam rim che ba las/skyes bu chen po'i skabs kyi dbu phyogs.*

2. *Pāramitā-samāsa* (PS): 6.65-66; D3944: Khi 234b6-7. The two lower vehicles are the *śrāvaka* vehicle and the *pratyekabuddha* vehicle.

3. Ibid.: 6.67; D3944: Khi 234b7-235a1.

4. *Śiṣya-lekha:* 100-101; D4183: Nge 52a5-6.

5. Ibid.: 102; D4183: Nge 52a7-b1.

6. PS: 6.69; D3944: Khi 235a2.

7. *Bodhisattva-caryāvatāra* (BCA): 1.9a-c, 3.26cd. Also cited at LRCM: 90.6; *Great Treatise* 1: 134.

8. The citation is from the first *Bhāvanā-krama* (Bk1), Tucci 1958: 501; D3915: Ki 24a5-6. The translation in the *Ārya-maitreya-vimokṣa*, apparently a name for a part of the *Buddhāvataṃsaka-nāma-mahā-vaipulya-sūtra* (*Flower Ornament Sūtra*), D44: A 323a5-b1, differs slightly.

9. *Rāja-parikathā-ratnāvalī* (Rā): 2.73cd-74ab; Hahn 1982: 66.

10. *Vajrapāṇy-abhiṣeka-mahā-tantra,* D496: Da 148b3-4.

11. The *Gaṇḍa-vyūha-sūtra* of the *Buddhāvataṃsaka-sūtra,* D44: Ka 309b1. The citation is found in Bk1, Tucci 1958: 502; D3915: Ki 25a1.

12. *Ratna-gotra-vibhāga-mahāyānottara-tantra-śāstra* (RGV): 1.34ab; D4024: Phi 7a6-7.

13. *Prajñā-pāramitā-stotra,* Pandeya 1994: verse 17; D1127: Ka 76b3-4. The author is given variously as Nāgārjuna, Lakṣā Bhagavatī, and Rahula-bhadra.

14. Rā: 4.90; Hahn 1982: 126-127.

15. *Abhisamayālaṃkāra-prajñā-pāramitopadeśa-śāstra* (AA): 1.10ab; D3786: Ka 2a5.

16. BCA: 1.25, 1.30bcd, 1.36ab, 3.32cd.

17. Cittamātrins are divided into those who assert that the form (*ākāra*) of the blue in the eye-consciousness perceiving blue is real and those who assert it is not. Satyākāravādins are the former. The latter are called Alīkākāravādins. See *Great Treatise* 3, note 535. This means that Atisha's philosophical view was superior to that of his teacher.

18. BCA: 1.6bcd, 1.14ab, 1.21-22, 1.12.

19. AA: 1.18ab; D3786: Ka 2b5.

20. *Yoga-carya-bhūmau-bodhisattva-bhūmi* (Bbh), Wogihara 1971: 16-17; D4037: Wi 10a7-b2.

Chapter Two *Compassion, the Entrance to the Mahāyāna*

21. *Ārya-akṣayamati-nirdeśa-nāma-mahāyāna-sūtra,* D175: Ma 132a5-6. The citation is found in Bk1, Tucci 1958: 497; D3915: Ki 22a6-b1.

22. *Ārya-gayā-śirṣa-nāma-mahāyāna-sūtra,* D109: Ca 286b3-4. The citation is found in Bk1, Tucci 1958: 497; D3915: Ki 22b1.

23. Bk1, Tucci 1958: 497-498; D3915: Ki 22b2-4.

24. *Ārya-śraddhā-balādhānāvatāra-nāma-mahāyāna-sūtra,* D201: Tsha 15a4.

25. Second *Bhāvanā-krama* (Bk2), D3916: Ki 42b-7.

26. *Madhyamakāvatāra* (MAV): 1.2; D3861: Ha 201a2-3.

27. *Ārya-dharma-saṃgīti-nāma-mahāyāna-sutra,* D238: Zha 84a5-b3. The citation is found in Bk1, Tucci 1958: 497; D3915: Ki 22a3-6.

28. *Śata-pañcāśatka-stotra:* 19; D1147: Ka 110b6-7. In the Tibetan translation the author is given as Aśvaghoṣa.

29. Cf. *Ārya-sāgaramati-paripṛcchā-nāma-mahāyāna-sūtra,* D152: Pha 86a3-6.

Chapter Three *The Seven Cause-and-Effect Personal Instructions*

30. In the context of application (a topic of meditative serenity), *btang snyoms* is rendered "equanimity," but in the context of feelings and the four immeasurables it is rendered "impartiality." See *Great Treatise* 3, note 149.

31. Bk2, D3916: Ki 42b7-43a4.

32. *Ārya-candrottama-dārikā-vyākaraṇa-nāma-mahāyāna-sutra,* D191: Tsa 231b4-5.

33. The fault of uncertainty is the first of the six sufferings. See LRCM: 221; *Great Treatise* 3: 281-282.

34. Bk2; D3916: Ki 43a2-3.

35. *Yoga-caryā-bhūmi* (*Sa'i dngos gzhi*), D4034: Tshi 100b6-7. On the use of the term *Sa'i dngos gzhi,* see *Great Treatise* 3, note 45.

36. *Śiṣya-lekha:* 95; D4183: Nge 52a1.

37. Ibid.: 96-97; D4183: Nge 52a1-3.

38. *Guṇāparyanta-stotra,* D1155: Ka 196b3-4.

39. *Madhyamaka-hṛdaya,* D3855: Dza 2b2-3.

40. *Nāga-rāja-bheri-gāthā,* D325: Sa 205b3-4.

41. *Śikṣā-samuccaya,* Vaidya 1961b: 195; D3940: Khi 194a5-6.

42. The citation is from *Śikṣā-samuccaya,* D3940: Khi 171b2-3. Cf. *Samādhi-rāja-sūtra,* Vaidya 1961a: 169; D127: Da 115b6.

43. *Ārya-mañjuśrī-buddha-kṣetra-guṇa-vyūha-nāma-mahāyāna-sutra,* D59: Ga 262b4-263a1.

44. Rā: 5.283-285; Hahn 1982: 88.

45. *Ārya-suvarṇa-prabhāsottama-sūtrendra-rāja-nāma-mahāyāna-sūtra,* D556: Pa 172a1.

46. Bk1, Tucci 1958: 500; D3915: Ki 23b4-7.

47. LRCM: 209-232; *Great Treatise* 1: 268-295.

48. Bbh, P5538: 190.5.1-192.1.1.

49. Bk1, Tucci 1958: 500; D3915: Ki 23b7-24a1.

50. Ibid., D3915: Ki 24a2.

51. *Mahāyāna-saṃgraha,* D4048: Ri 31b1.

52. Ba-so-chos-kyi-rgyal-mtshan (*mChan*: 587.6) says that this refers to LRCM: 308.08, effortlessly generating the spirit of enlightenment.

53. BCA: 3.22-26.

54. AA: 1.19-20, cited here as *Pha rol tu phyin pa'i man ngag gi bstan bcos,* the *Prajñāpāramitopadeśa-śāstra* (*Treatise of Instruction in the Perfection of Wisdom*).

55. Bk2, P5311: 31.2.3-4.

56. *Deśanā-stava,* D1159: Ka 206a5.

57. LRCM: 134-140; *Great Treatise* 1: 181-187.

58. *Ārya-tathāgata-jñāna-mudrā-samādhi-nāma-mahāyāna-sūtra,* D131: Da 240b5-7 cited in Bk1, Tucci 1958: 500; D3915: Ki 24a3-5.

59. LRCM: 291.14.

60. BCA: 1.15; *Gaṇḍa-vyūha-sūtra,* D44: A 308a7-b1.

61. Bk1, Tucci 1958: 503; D3915: Ki 25a3-4.

Chapter Four *Exchanging Self and Other*

62. BCA: 8.120, 8.129-131.

63. BCA: 8.119, 8.112cd.

64. For a presentation of the process of rebirth, see *Great Treatise* 1: 311-313.

65. BCA: 8.111.

66. *Śikṣā-samuccaya,* Vaidya 1961b: 191; D3940: Khi 192a4-5.

67. BCA: 8.99, 101.

68. BCA: 8.154 cd, 8.155, 8.157.

69. BCA: 8.137-138.

70. BCA: 8.169-172.

71. BCA: 8.136d.

72. BCA: 6.113.

73. *Bodhicitta-vivaraṇa:* 77-80, Lindtner 1986: 206-208; D1801: Nya 41a5-b1.

74. Ibid.: 82cd-84, Lindtner 1986: 208; D1801: Nya 41b1-3.

75. Ibid.: 85-87ab, Lindtner 1986: 208-210; D1801: Nya 41b3-4.

76. Ngag-dbang-rab-brtan (*mChan:* 612.3-5) explains that the human strategies are to sustain friends and the horse strategy, to overcome enemies. The eighteen do not need to be enumerated because the cause of the spirit of enlightenment is living beings—our friends—and thus eighteen indicates that they are numerous. The import of the horse strategy is that our enemy is just one—self-cherishing.

77. *Mahāyāna-patha-sādhana-varṇa-saṃgraha* (*Concisely Written Method of Achieving the Mahāyāna Path*), D3954: Khi 300a6-7.

78. This heading is not repeated in the Tibetan text here (LRCM: 320) but has been added for consistency. It was previously given at LRCM: 289.8.

79. LRCM: 308.

Chapter Five *The Ritual for Adopting the Spirit of Enlightenment*

80. *Mahāyāna-patha-sādhana-varṇa-saṃgraha*, D3954: Khi 300a7.

81. The four bases of Brahmā (*tshangs pa'i gnas; brahmā-vihāra)* are the four immeasurables of love, compassion, joy, and impartiality.

82. *Guru-kriyā-krama*, D3977: Gi 256b2.

83. *Bodhicittotpāda-samādāna-vidhi* (*Ritual for Generating the Spirit of Enlightenment*), D3968: Gi 242a1.

84. *Ārya-daśa-dharmaka-nāma-mahāyāna-sūtra*, D53: Kha 168a4-5; cf. Bk1, Tucci 1958: 500; D3915: Ki 24a3-4.

85. *Bodhicittotpāda-samādāna-vidhi*, D3968: Gi 241b7-242a1.

86. *Bodhi-mārga-pradīpa-pañjikā*, D3948: Khi 247a5-6.

87. LRCM: 292-320.

88. *Ārya-bhadra-kalpika-nāma-mahāyāna-sūtra*, D94: Ka 288b7, cited in *Śikṣā-samuccaya*, Vaidya 1961b: 8; D3940: Khi 7b1.

89. *Guru-kriyā-krama*, D3977: Gi 256b3-4.

90. *Oṁ namo bhagavate vajra-sāra-pramardaṇe tathāgatāya, arhatye samyak-saṃbuddhāya, tad-yathā, oṁ vajre vajre, mahā-vajre, mahā-teja-vajre, mahā-vidya-vajre, mahā-bodhi-citta-vajre, mahā-bodhi-maṇḍopa-saṃkramaṇa-vajre sarva-karmāvaraṇa-visodhana-vajre svāha.*

91. 'Jam-dbyangs-bzhad-pa (*mChan:* 617.1) says that the verses for the seven branches of worship are from the *Prayer of Samantabhadra* (*Samantabhadra-caryā-praṇidhāna*). For these verses, see LRCM: 56-59; *Great Treatise* 1: 94-98.

92. For Sakya Pandita's (Sa-skya Paṇḍi-ta) view, see Rhoton 2002: 82-83, 91-92, note 2. Khangkar 2001: 38 cites *bsTan rim chen mo* (Lhasa edition): 205b4-206a3.

93. In *Cittotpāda-saṃvara-vidhi-krama* (*Ritual Procedures for the Spirit of Enlightenment and the Bodhisattva Vows*), D3969: Gi 254a4.

94. *Guru-kriyā-krama*, D3977: Gi 256b3-5.

95. *Daśa-cakra-kṣitigarbha-nāma-mahāyāna-sūtra*, P905: 96.3.6-7, cited at LRCM: 43.18; *Great Treatise* 1: 81.

96. *Cittotpāda-saṃvara-vidhi*, D3969: Gi 245a5-6.

97. *Bodhi-patha-pradīpa*, D3947: Khi 238b4.

98. *Cittotpāda-saṃvara-vidhi*, D3969: Gi 245a7-b2.

99. LRCM: 143-158; *Great Treatise* 1, Chapter Twelve.

100. *Cittotpāda-saṁvara-vidhi*, D3969: Gi 245b2-4.

101. LRCM: 322.2-4.

102. The verses from the *Samantabhadra-caryā-praṇidhāna* (D44: A 358b7-359b2) are at LRCM: 56-59 (*Great Treatise* 1: 94-98); BCA: 2.1-65, 3.1-21.

103. *Bodhi-patha-pradīpa*, D3947: Khi 238b6.

104. LRCM: 304.18-309.20.

105. *Bodhi-patha-pradīpa*, D3947: Khi 238b6.

106. *Cittotpāda-saṃvara-vidhi*, D3969: Gi 245b6. Also cited below.

107. Cf. Rhoton 2002: 82, verse 13.

108. Bk1, Tucci 1958: 500; D3915: Ki 24a7, citing the *Ārya-rājāvavādaka-nāma-mahāyāna-sūtra*, D221.

109. *Cittotpāda-saṃvara-vidhi*, D3969: Gi 245b4-246a1.

110. Ibid.: 246a1-2.

Chapter Six *Maintaining the Spirit of Enlightenment*

111. *Gaṇḍa-vyūha-sūtra*, D44: Ka 309a3-325a3.

112. LRCM: 285.15.

113. Bbh, Wogihara 1971: 19; D4037: Wi 11a7-b1.

114. BCA: 1.9d. The first three lines of this verse occur at LRCM: 284.6.

115. The four kinds of action are pacifying, subduing, increasing, and violent.

116. The *Ārya-vīradatta-gṛha-pati-paripṛcchā-nāma-mahāyāna-sūtra*, D72: Ca 202b6-203a1. The citation is found in Bk1, Tucci 1958: 502; D3915: Ki 24b7-25a1.

117. This and the following stories take place in what is now known as Bodh Gayā, where the Buddha attained enlightenment sitting under the Bodhi Tree. The place where he sat is known as the *vajra* seat, and a large *stūpa* was built next to it. The statues mentioned here are on the sides of the *stūpa*, and the main temple mentioned in the next story is located in the base of the *stūpa*.

118. BCA: 1.7ab.

119. *Ratna-guṇa-saṃcaya-gāthā*: 31.5; D13: Ka 18b3.

120. Ibid.: 31.4; D13: Ka 18b2.

121. BCA: 4.5-6, 3.27.

122. *Bodhisattvādikarmika-mārgāvatāra-deśanā (Teaching About a New Bodhisattva's Entry into the Path)*, D3952: Khi 296b7-297a1.

123. Cf. *Bodhi-mārga-pradīpa-pañjikā*, D3948: Khi 252a1-2.

124. *Ārya-kāśyapa-parivarta-nāma-mahāyāna-sūtra*, D87: Cha 120a6-b6. The full name of the *Ratna-kuṭa Collection*, a collection of forty-nine works (Pagel 1995: Appendix III), is *Ārya-mahā-ratna-kūṭa-dharma-paryāya-śata-sāhasrika-grantha*, P760, vols. 22-24.

125. The section on the four dark and four light practices cited in the following section is found in the *Ārya-mahā-ratna-kuṭa-dharma-paryāya-parivarta-śata-sahāsrikā-kāśyapa-parivarta-ṭīkā*, D4009: Ji 206b3-207a4.

126. *Śikṣā-samuccaya*, Vaidya 1961b: 33; D3940: Khi 35a2-4.

127. LRCM: 178-179; *Great Treatise* 1: 231-233.

128. *Ratna-guṇa-saṃcaya-gāthā*: 24.5; D13: Ka 14b4-5.

129. Ibid.: 24.6b-d; D13: Ka 14b5-6.

130. LRCM: 304.18-309.19.

131. *Pramāṇa-vārttika-kārikā*: 2.129cd, 2.126; Miyasaka 1972: 20-21.

132. *Kāśyapa-parivarta-ṭīkā*, D4009: Ji 207a4.

133. *Abhidharma-samuccaya*, D4049: Ri 50b6-51a1.

134. The names of the four light practices are not listed in the Tibetan but are imbedded in the Tibetan text. They are listed as headings here for the sake of clarity.

135. *Kāśyapa-parivarta*, D87: Cha 120b5. The idea that all beings are the Buddha means to respect all beings just as we respect the Buddha, for both are equal in the sense that both help us to attain buddhahood.

136. The *Ārya-siṃha-paripṛcchā-nāma-mahāyāna-sūtra*, D81: Cha 28b7-29a1. The citation is found in *Śikṣā-samuccaya*, Vaidya 1961b: 33; D3940: Khi 35a6-7.

137. *Śikṣā-samuccaya,* Vaidya 1961b: 33; D3940: Khi 35a7-b2, citing the *Mañjuśrī-buddha-kṣetra-guṇa-vyūha-sutra,* the *Ārya-ratna-megha-nāma-mahāyāna-sūtra,* and the *Samādhi-rāja-sūtra.* Geshe Yeshey Tapkay has reconstructed this section to follow the *Śikṣā-samuccaya,* P5336: 199.3.6-8. He has considered as Tsong-kha-pa's own words the sentence *skye ba gzhan du'ang sems rin po che dang mi 'bral ba ni.* The last two lines of the *Samādhi-rāja* citation—*de la gnas pa'i rnam par rtog pa des/ de lta de ltar de la sems gzhol 'gyur*—were added for clarity.

138. *Bodhi-patha-pradīpa,* D3947: Khi 239a3.

139. *Kāśyapa-parivarta,* D87: Cha 120a3-4.

140. Bbh, Wogihara 1971: 160-161; D4037: Wi 85b7-86a4. *Śikṣā-samuccaya,* Vaidya 1961b: 41; D3940: Khi 43a5-b2.

141. *Byang chub sems dpa'i tshul khrims kyi rnam bshad byang chub gzhung lam,* Tatz 1986: 187-194. The name here is *Tshul khrims le'u rnam bshad.* The *Ārya-upāli-gṛhapati-paripṛcchā-nāma-mahāyāna-sūtra* is D68.

142. *Bodhi-mārga-pradīpa-pañjikā,* D3948: Khi 249b3-250b1.

143. For the four powers of confession, see LRCM: 195-203; *Great Treatise* 1: 251-259.

Chapter Seven *An Introduction to the Six Perfections*

144. *Ārya-maitreya-vimokṣa,* cited at LRCM: 284.10. Khangkar's reference here is to D44: A 324a5-7.

145. *Gayā-śirṣa,* D109: Ca 291b3-4. The citation is found in Bk1, Tucci 1958: 502-503; D3915: Ki 25a6.

146. The citation is from Bk1, Tucci 1958: 502-504; D3915: Ki 25a7-b1. Cf. *Samādhi-rāja-sūtra,* Vaidya 1961a: 54; D127: Da 28b6-7.

147. Bk1, Tucci 1958: 502-503; D3915: Ki 25a5-6.

148. *Pramāṇa-vārttika-kārikā*: 2.132; Miyasaka 1972: 20-21.

149. Bk2, D3916: Ki 42a4-5.

150. *Mahā-vairocanābhisambodhi-vikurvitādhiṣṭhāna-vaipulya-sūtrendra-rāja-nāma-dharma-paryāya,* D494: Tha 153a5. The citation is from Bk1, Tucci 1958: 507; D3915: Ki 27b5-6.

151. See LRCM: 293-298; 306-310.

152. The citation from the *Ārya-tathāgatācintya-guhya-nirdeśa-nāma-mahāyāna-sūtra,* D47, is from the third *Bhāvanā-krama* (Bk3), Tucci 1971: 12; D3917: Ki 61a2-3.

153. *Ārya-gagana-gañja-paripṛcchā-nāma-mahāyāna-sūtra,* D148: Pa 253b6; Bk2, D3916: Ki 53b1-2.

154. *Ārya-saṃdhi-nirmocana-nāma-mahāyāna-sūtra,* D106: Ca 19b6-7; cited in Bk2, D3916: Ki 53b2-3 and Bk3, Tucci 1971: 22; D3917: Ki 64b7-65a1.

155. *Ārya-vimalakīrti-nirdeśa-nāma-mahāyāna-sūtra,* D176: Ma 201a7-b2; cited in Bk1, Tucci 1958: 504; D3915: Ki 25b3; Bk2, D3916: Ki 52b4-5; and Bk3, Tucci 1971: 22; D3917: Ki 65a2-4. The earlier part is a paraphrase.

156. *Gayā-śirṣa*, D109: Ca 288b7-289a1; cited in Bk1, Tucci 1958: 505; D3915: Ki 25a6; Bk2, D3916: Ki 52b3-5.

157. *Śrī-paramādya-nāma-mahāyāna-kalpa-rāja*, D487: Ta 2. The citation is from Bk2, D3916: Ki 52b3-4.

158. *Ārya-kāśyapa-parivarta-nāma-mahāyāna-sūtra*, D87: Cha 129a6; cited in Bk2, D3916: Ki 52a6; Bk3, Tucci 1971: 27; D3917: Ki 67b2-3.

159. *Ārya-ratna-cūḍa-paripṛcchā-nāma-mahāyāna-sūtra*, D91: Cha 120b2-4; cited in Bk2, D3916: Ki 51b1 and *Śikṣā-samuccaya*, Vaidya 1961b: 145; D3940: Khi 150b1-2.

160. RGV: 1.92; P5525: 25.5.2-3. The original metaphor suggests painting a woman's body. Generosity, ethical discipline, patience and so forth are paint-strokes (*lekhakā*) with those forms, and emptiness that has the supremacy of being associated with all aspects is the body (*pratimā*) decorated with body paint.

161. *Ārya-sarva-vaidalya/vaipulya-saṃgraha-nāma-mahāyāna-sūtra*, D227: Dza 183a3-7.

162. *Daśa-bhūmika-sūtra*, D44: Kha 240b3-241a3.

163. Ibid.: 242a1-5.

164. Rā: 3.12; Hahn 1982: 74-75.

165. Cited in *Sūtra-samuccaya*, D3934: Ki 163a6 and Bk3, Tucci 1971: 22-23; D3917: Ki 65a5-7.

166. *Ārya-tri-skandhaka-nāma-mahāyāna-sūtra*, D284: Ya 72b1-2; cited in Bk3, Tucci 1971: 23; D3917: Ki 65b3-4.

167. *Ārya-brahmā-viśesa-cinti-paripṛcchā-sūtra*, D160: Ba 58b5; cited in Bk3, Tucci 1971: 23-24; D3917: Ki 65b5-7.

168. See LRCM: 564-805; *Great Treatise* 3: 107-359.

169. *Sūtra-samuccaya*, D3934: Ki 164a2-4; cited in Bk3, Tucci 1971: 22; D3917: Ki 65a4-5.

170. The citation from the *Tathāgatācintya-guhya-nirdeśa-sūtra* is from Bk3, Tucci 1971: 27-28; D3917: Ki 67b4-6.

171. The *Tathāgatotpatti-saṃbhava* is chapter 43 of the *Buddhāvataṃsaka-sūtra*, D44: Ga 80a4-b1; cited in Bk3, Tucci 1971: 12; D3917: Ki 61a3-5.

172. *Vimalakīrti-nirdeśa-sūtra*, D176: Ma 183b3-184a1; cited in Bk3, Tucci 1971: 13; D3917: Ki 61a5-6.

173. Rā: 3.10; Hahn 1982: 73.

Chapter Eight *Training in the Mahāyāna: Precepts and Perfections*

174. Bbh, Wogihara 1971:155; D4037: Wi 85a4-6. Ngag-dbang-rab-brtan (*mChan* 671.3-4) comments that the "Summary of the Bodhisattva Fundamentals" refers to both the Bbh chapter on ethical discipline and the Bbh itself.

175. LRCM: 364.10. The entire section of the outline under the heading "c" The process of learning the perfections," which starts at Chapter 9.

176. The name here is *Tshul khrims le'u 'grel pa*.

177. *Mahāyāna-sūtrālaṃkāra-kārikā* (MSA): 16.2; D4020: Phi 21a6-7.

178. MSA: 16.3; D4020: Phi 21a7.

179. Geshe Yeshe Tapkay says that Tsong-kha-pa seems to be making the general statement that one needs more than just the six perfections to completely fulfill others' aims—such things as the exchange of self and other and the spirit of enlightenment.

180. MSA: 16.4; D4020: Phi 21a7-b1.

181. MSA: 16.5; D4020: Phi 21b1.

182. MSA: 16.6; D4020: Phi 21b1-2.

183. MSA: 16.7; D4020: Phi 21b2-3.

184. MSA: 16.14; D4020: Phi 21b4-5.

Chapter Nine *The Perfection of Generosity*

185. Bbh, Wogihara 1971: 114; D4037: Wi 61b4-5.

186. BCA: 5.9-10.

187. *Candra-pradīpa-sūtra* (another name for the *Samādhi-rāja-sūtra*), D127: Da 73b4-6; cited in *Śikṣā-samuccaya*, Vaidya 1961b: 14; D3940: Khi 13b5-6.

188. The citation of the *Āryānanta-mukha-nirhāra-dhāraṇī* / *Āryānanta-mukha-sādhaka-nāma-dhāraṇī*, D525 (cf. Jñānagarbha's *Āryānanta-mukha-nirhāra-dhāraṇī-ṭīkā*, D2696), is from *Śikṣā-samuccaya*, Vaidya 1961b: 194; D3940: Khi 13b6-7.

189. *Śikṣā-samuccaya*, D3940: Khi 193b3.

190. *Jātaka-mālā* 22; D4150: Hu 3b4-5.

191. BCA: 3.11.

192. PS: 1.49-54; D3944: Khi 221a3-4.

193. Rā: 5.86-87; Hahn 1982: 162-163.

194. PS: 1.3-4; D3944: Khi 218b7-219a1.

195. PS: 1.5-6; D3944: Khi 219a1-3.

196. BCA: 3.10.

197. PS: 1.11cd-12; D3944: Khi 219a6.

198. *Śikṣā-samuccaya*, Vaidya 1961b: 79; D3940: Khi 80b3-4.

199. Ibid.: Khi 80b4-5.

200. Ibid.: Khi 80b5-6.

201. Ibid.: Khi 80b6-7.

202. The citation of the *Bodhisattva-prātimokṣa-catuṣka-nirhāra-nāma-mahāyāna-sūtra*, D248, is from *Śikṣā-samuccaya*, Vaidya 1961b: 80; D3940: Khi 81a7-b2.

203. PS: 1.55; D3944: Khi 221a7-b1.

204. *Guṇāparyanta-stotra*, D1155: Ka 197a4-5.

205. Ibid.: Ka 197b3.

Chapter Ten *How to Give*

206. *Satyaka-parivarta* (the fourth chapter of the *Ārya-bodhisattva-gocaropāya-viṣaya-vikurvāṇa-nirdeśa-nāma-mahāyāna-sūtra*), D146: Pa 112b2-3.

207. *Śikṣā-samuccaya*, Vaidya 1961b: 79; D3940: Khi 34a2-3.

208. BCA: 5.87.

209. BCA: 5.86.

210. Bbh, Wogihara 1971: 126; D4037: Wi 68b4-5.

211. *Viniścaya-saṃgrahaṇī*, D4038: Zi 39a3-b2.

212. Bbh, Wogihara 1971: 126-127; D4037: Wi 68b6-69a6.

213. BCA: 5.83c.

214. "Bodhisattvas living in the noble family" means that the monks are in a lineage defined by renunciation in that its members each have only one set of old patched clothes and one begging bowl, practice what they should adopt, and avoid what they should cast aside.

215. *Viniścaya-saṃgrahaṇī*, D4038: Zi 39a1-3. The three kinds of religious robes for a renunciate are the upper, lower, and outer garments for a monk or nun. Monks and nuns must always keep one set of these robes.

216. This citation of the *Bodhisattva-prātimokṣa-sūtra* is from *Śikṣā-samuccaya*, Vaidya 1961b: 80; D3940: Khi 81b4-5.

217. An example of a special case would be the explanation of how to lead a stingy person to become generous (LRCM: 378). This is a special case because usually you have to give with your own hands.

218. The citation of the *Ārya-gṛha-pati-ugra-paripṛcchā-nāma-mahāyāna-sūtra*, D63: Nga 264b5-265a4 is from *Śikṣā-samuccaya*, Vaidya 1961b: 14-15; D3940: Khi 14a1-15a4.

219. PS: 1.57-58; D3944: Khi 221b1-2.

220. *Catuḥ-śataka-śāstra-kārikā-nāma*, 5.95; D3846: Tsha 6a7.

221. Bbh, Wogihara 1971: 126; D4037: Wi 68b3-4.

222. *Subāhu-paripṛcchā-sūtra*, D70: Ca 156a4-b5.

223. Bbh, Wogihara 1971: 126; D4037: Wi 68b3-4.

224. *Subāhu-paripṛcchā-sūtra*, D70: Ca 157a6.

225. PS: 1.61; D3944: Khi 221b4.

Chapter Eleven *The Perfection of Ethical Discipline*

226. BCA: 5.11.

227. *Madhyamakāvatāra-bhāṣya* (MAVbh) on *Madhyamakāvatāra*: 2.1a; D3862: Ḥa 231a2-4. This is playing on the meaning of a number of Sanskrit roots that might produce the word *śīla* (here rendered "ethical discipline"): *śī* ("to lay down"), *śīl* ("to make a practice of") and *śyai* (cp. *śīta*) ("to cool down").

228. PS: 2.1, 2.48; D3944: Khi 221b4, 224a1-2.

229. PS: 2.49ab; D3944: Khi 224a2.

230. LRCM: 158-203; *Great Treatise* 1, Chapters 14 and 15.

231. LRCM: 269-270; *Great Treatise* 1: 342-343.

232. PS: 2.47; D3944: Khi 223b6-224a1.

233. PS: 2.60-61; D3944: Khi 224b3-5.

234. PS: 2.62-64; D3944: Khi 224b5-7.

235. PS: 2.49cd, 2.51c-52b; D3944: Khi 224a2-3, 224a4.

236. PS: 2.59, 2.65; D3944: Khi 224b2-3, 224b7.

237. The seven types of vows of individual liberation are listed according to the person receiving the vows: fully ordained monk or nun; novice monk or nun; layman and laywoman; and novice about to become a nun [a two-year observation period where special vows are taken to see if the aspirant is ready for full ordination].

238. The eleven types of living beings are: (1) those who need help, (2) those who are confused as to the proper method, (3) those who have given help, (4) those afflicted by fear, (5) those afflicted with sorrow, (6) those poor in goods, (7) those who want a dwelling, (8) those who want mental harmony, (9) those who proceed correctly, (10) those who proceed wrongly, and (11) those who need to be disciplined by supernormal powers.

239. *Byang chub sems dpa'i tshul khrims kyi rnam bshad byang chub gzhung lam*, Tatz 1986: 115, 121-132. The name here is *Tshul khrims le'u rnam bshad*.

240. *Viniścaya-saṃgrahaṇī*, P5539: 80.5.5-7.

241. PS: 2.8-9.

242. LRCM: 371.13.

Chapter Twelve *The Perfection of Patience*

243. BCA: 5.12-14.

244. Bbh, Wogihara 1971: 195-196; D4037: Wi 105b3-6.

245. PS: 3.3-5, 3.8bc; D3944: Khi 225a1-3, 225a5.

246. BCA: 6.6cd.

247. BCA: 6.1.

248. MAV: 3.6ac; D3861: Ḥa 203a5-6.

249. *Śikṣā-samuccaya*, D3940: Khi 84a2-7.

250. *Abhidharma-kośa-bhāṣya*, D4090: Khu 94b4-5, also cited at LRCM: 188.16; *Great Treatise* 1: 242.

251. LRCM: 199-200; *Great Treatise* 1: 255-256.

252. LRCM: 201-202; *Great Treatise* 1: 257.

253. LRCM: 334.

254. BCA: 6.3-5.

255. *Jātaka-mālā*: 21.29-33; D4150: Hu 73a1-4.

256. BCA: 6.2.

257. MAVbh, D3862: Ḥa 237a1.

258. *Catuḥ-śataka*: 109; D3846: Tsha 6a7-b1.

259. BCA: 6.31, 6.33-34, 6.37.

260. BCA: 6.39-40.

261. BCA: 6.41.

262. BCA: 6.42, 6.45-47.

263. BCA: 6.73.

264. *Jātaka-mālā*: 33.15; D4150: Hu 132a7-b1.

265. MAV: 3.5; D3861: Ḥa 203a4-5.

266. These two subheadings are not clearly presented in the text but are included in sTag-bu-yongs-'dzin's outline, p. 139.

267. BCA: 6.43-44, 6.67.

268. BCA: 6.90-91ab, 6.93.

269. BCA: 6.98.

270. BCA: 6.99-101.

271. BCA: 6.52-53.

272. BCA: 6.54.

273. BCA: 6.55-59.

274. BCA: 6.80-84.

275. BCA: 6.87-89.

276. BCA: 6.12ab.

277. BCA: 6.10, 6.16.

278. BCA: 6.12cd, 6.21. The same two citations appear at LRCM: 115.14; *Great Treatise* 1: 162.

279. BCA: 6.74-75.

280. BCA: 6.72.

281. BCA: 6.14.

282. *Śikṣā-samuccaya,* Vaidya 1961b: 101; D3940: Khi 101b6-7.

283. The citation of the *Gṛha-pati-ugra-paripṛcchā-sūtra,* D63: Nga 26b5-6 is from *Śikṣā-samuccaya,* D3940: Khi 101a6-7.

284. The citation of the *Gaṇḍa-vyūha-sūtra* is from *Śikṣā-samuccaya,* D3940: Khi 101a7.

285. BCA: 6.17-18ab.

286. These eleven activities are for the sake of the eleven types of living beings. See note 238 above.

287. LRCM: 371.13.

Chapter Thirteen *The Perfection of Joyous Perseverance*

288. BCA: 7.2a.

289. *Āryādhyāśaya-saṃcodana-nāma-mahāyāna-sūtra*, D69: Ca 147b5-7.

290. MSA: 16.65-66, 70.

291. Bbh, Wogihara 1971: 201; D4037: Wi 108a4-5.

292. PS: 4.2cd, 4.41cd-42; D3944: Khi 226b4-5, 228b3-4.

293. *Ārya-sāgaramati-paripṛcchā-nāma-mahāyāna-sūtra*, D152: Pha 40a5-7.

294. *Ārya-sad-dharmānusmṛty-upasthāna*, D287: Ya 128a6.

295. PS: 4.5-7; D3944: Khi 226b6-227a1.

296. BCA: 7.2b-d.

297. BCA: 7.3.

298. LRCM: 83, 98-132; *Great Treatise* 1: 124-125, 145-175.

299. BCA: 7.15.

300. BCA: 7.17-19.

301. *Ratna-megha-sūtra*, D231: Wa 21a3-6.

302. *Guṇāparyanta-stotra*, D1155: Ka 196b7-197a1.

303. BCA: 7.20-23.

304. BCA: 7.24-26.

305. BCA: 7.27-28, 7:30.

306. Rā: 3.25-27; Hahn 1982: 76-77.

307. Rā: 3.15-20; Hahn 1982: 74-75.

308. *Jātaka-mālā*, D4150: Hu 52b3 (story of Supāraga).

309. BCA: 7.39-40ab.

310. BCA: 7.40cd.

311. For karma and its effects in general, see *Great Treatise* 1: 209-242. For the benefits of the bodhisattva deeds and the faults of violating them, see LRCM: 365-371 for generosity; LRCM: 391-394 for ethical discipline; LRCM: 398-404 for patience; LRCM: 424-425 for joyous perseverance; LRCM: 448 and *Great Treatise* 3, Part One for meditative stabilization and meditative serenity; and LRCM: 450-459 and *Great Treatise* 3, Part Two for wisdom and insight.

312. BCA: 7.33-36.

313. BCA: 7.47-48.

314. BCA: 7.49ab.

315. BCA: 7.49cd.

316. *Suhṛl-lekha*, 52ab; D4182: Ṅe 43a4.

317. BCA: 7.50.

318. BCA: 7.51ab.

319. BCA: 7.51cd.

320. BCA: 7.55.

321. BCA: 7.52-53ab.

322. BCA: 7.53cd-54ab.

323. BCA: 7.54cd.

324. BCA: 7.62.

325. BCA: 7.63.

326. BCA: 7.64.

327. BCA: 7.65.

328. BCA: 7.66.

329. *Śata-pañcāsatka-nāma-stotra:* 2.21; Bailey 1951: 49.

330. At this point in the text (LRCM 442.7) there appears the heading from LRCM 428.3 and comment: (*de gnyis la brten nas brtson 'grus brtson pa lhur blang ba ni*) *'di ni par gzhan du chad* "(Based on the previous two sections, being intent on joyously persevering) This is missing in other editions." The heading is not included in the Ganden Bar Nying (220b.4).

331. BCA: 7.67.

332. BCA: 7.68.

333. *Suhṛl-lekha*, 54; D4182: Ṅe 43a5.

334. BCA: 7.69.

335. BCA: 7.70.

336. Ba-so-chos-kyi-rgyal-mtshan (*mChan*: 587.6) relates the story of the noble Kātyāyana, who was invited to teach by a border region king. When Kātyāyana and his disciples arrived there, the king greeted them lavishly with a great spectacle. When the king later asked Kātyāyana and his followers what they thought of the spectacle, the noble being answered that they had not noticed it, for he and his disciples practiced restraint of the sensory faculties (see *Great Treatise* 1: 101-102). The king did not believe this so he ordered a man to carry a vessel filled to the brim with mustard oil around the outside of the palace under the threat of death if he spilled so much as a drop. He also ordered the same spectacle to be reenacted before the man as he went. After the man succeeded in this task, the king asked him what he thought of the spectacle. When the man answered that he did not notice a thing, the king believed Kātyāyana and his followers.

337. BCA: 7.71.

338. BCA: 7.72.

339. BCA: 7.73.

340. BCA: 7.74.

341. BCA: 7.75.

342. *Śata-pañcāśatka-nāma-stotra*: 2.20; D1147; Bailey 1951: 49.

343. LRCM: 371.13.

Chapter Fourteen *The Perfections of Meditative Stabilization and Wisdom*

344. Bbh, Wogihara 1971: 206-207; D4037: Wi 111a1-3.

345. BCA: 8.1ab.

346. LRCM: 468ff; *Great Treatise* 3, Part One.

347. LRCM: 371.13.

348. Bbh, Wogihara 1971: 210; D4037: Wi 113a6-7.

349. LRCM: 564ff; *Great Treatise* 3, Part Two.

350. *Prajñā-śataka-nāma-prakaraṇa*, D4328: Ṅo 99b6-7.

351. *Ratna-guṇa-saṃcaya-gāthā*: 7.2; D13: Ka 6a5-6.

352. PS: 6.1-2; D3944: Khi 231b5-6.

353. PS: 6.4; D3944: Khi 231b7.

354. PS: 6.6, 6.12, 6.14-15ab, 6.17; D3944: Khi 232a1, 232a5-6, 232a6-7, 232b1-2.

355. PS: 6.43-45; D3944: Khi 233b5-7.

356. *Varṇāha-varṇe-bhagavato-buddhasya-stotre-śakya-stava:* 5.23a-b; Hartmann, 1987: 184.

357. Ibid.: 5.7.

358. PS: 6.39cd-42; D3944: Khi 233b3-5.

359. *Ratna-guṇa-saṃcaya-gāthā*: 7.1; D13: Ka 6a6.

360. PS: 6.5, 6.11, 6.13, 6.16, 6.18ab; D3944: Khi 231b7-232a1, 232a4-5, 232a6, 232b1, 232b2.

361. PS: 6.25, 28cd; D3944: Khi 232b7-233a1, 233a2.

362. PS: 6.52-53; D3944: Khi 234a4-6.

363. PS: 6.47ab; D3944: Khi 234a1.

364. PS: 6.48; D3944: Khi 234a2.

365. RGV: 5.14-15. P5525: 31.4.6-7.

366. *Śikṣā-samuccaya-kārikā*: 22a-c; D3939: Khi 2b4.

367. *Śikṣā-samuccaya*, Bendall and Rouse: 179; D3940: Khi 100b3-4.

368. *Nārāyaṇa-paripṛcchā-ārya-mahāmayā-vijaya-vāhinī-dhāraṇi*, D134: Na 92b2.

369. MSA: 9.60; D4020: Phi 15b4-5.

370. LRCM: 371.13.

371. Bbh, Wogihara 1971: 216; D4037: Wi 115b2-4.

Chapter Fifteen *Helping Others to Mature: The Four Ways to Gather Disciples*

372. LRCM: 364-390.

373. MSA: 16.73 ; D4020: Phi 24b6-7.

374. MSA: 16.74; Phi 24b7.

375. MSA: 16.75, Phi 25a1.

376. MSA: 16.78, Phi 25a2.

377. *Guṇāparyanta-stotra*, D1155: Ka 197a5-6.

378. MSA: 16.76, D4020: Phi 25a1.

379. MSA: 16.78, D4020: Phi 25a2-3.

380. Bbh, Wogihara 1971: 226; D4037: Wi 121a5-6.

381. *Hṛdaya-nikṣepa (Heart Summary)*, P5346: 47.2.3-4.

382. *Mahāyāna-patha-sādhana-varṇa-saṃgraha*, P5351: 51.4.1-3.

383. The eight similes of illusoriness are: all things are like (1) a magician's illusions, (2) dreams, (3) mirages, (4) reflections in a mirror, (5) shadows, (6) echoes, (7) reflections of the moon in water, and (8) emanations.

384. *Guṇāparyanta-stotra*, D1155: Ka 198a7-b1.

Abbreviations

AA	*Abhisamayālaṃkāra*
Bbh	*Bodhisattva-bhūmi*
BCA	*Bodhisattva-caryāvatāra,* Bhattacharya 1960
Bk1	First *Bhāvanā-krama*
Bk2	Second *Bhāvanā-krama*
Bk3	Third *Bhāvanā-krama*
D	*sDe dge* edition of the Tibetan translations of the sūtras and śāstras as found in Toh
Great Treatise 1	Cutler et al. 2000
Great Treatise 3	Cutler et al. 2002
LRCM	Tsong-kha-pa 1985 *sKyes bu gsum gyi rnyams su blang ba'i rim pa thams cad tshang bar ston pa'i byang chub lam gyi rim pa.* Zi-ling: Tso Ngön People's Press
MAV	*Madhyamakāvatāra*
MAVbh	*Madhyamakāvatāra-bhāṣya*
mChan	'Jam-dbyangs-bzhad-pa et al. *Lam rim mchan bzhi sbrags ma*
MSA	*Mahāyāna-sūtrālaṃkāra-kārikā*
P	Suzuki 1955-61
PS	*Pāramitā-samāsa*
RGV	*Ratna-gotra-vibhāga (Mahāyānottara-tantra-śāstra)*
Rā	*Rāja-parikathā-ratnāvalī*
Skt.	Sanskrit
Toh	Ui et al. 1934

Bibliography

Indian sūtras and tantras are listed alphabetically by title in the first section; Indian śāstras are listed alphabetically by title in the second section; both of these sections are in Sanskrit alphabetical order. In the third section, Tibetan commentaries are listed alphabetically by author in Tibetan alphabetical order. Works by modern writers are listed alphabetically by author in the fourth section.

A. Sūtras and Tantras

Ārya-akṣayamati-nirdeśa-nāma-mahāyāna-sūtra, 'Phags pa blo gros mi zad pas bstan pa zhes bya ba theg pa chen po'i mdo. D175; P842, vol. 34. According to Lamotte (1949: 342), it is also called the *Catuḥ-pratisaraṇa-sūtra.*

Ārya-adhyāśaya-saṃcodana-nāma-mahāyāna-sūtra, 'Phags pa lhag pa'i bsam pa zhes bya ba theg pa chen po'i mdo. D69; P760.25, vol. 24.

Ārya-ananta-mukha-nirhāra-dhāraṇī / Āryānanta-mukha-sādhaka-nāma-dhāraṇī, 'Phags pa sgo mtha' yas pas bsgrub pa zhes bya ba'i gzungs. D525; P539, vol. 11; P808, vol. 32.

Ārya-kāśyapa-parivarta-nāma-mahāyāna-sūtra, 'Phags pa 'od srung gi le'u zhes bya ba theg pa chen po'i mdo. D87; P760.43, vol. 24.

Ārya-gagana-gañja-paripṛcchā-nāma-mahāyāna-sūtra, 'Phags pa nam mkha' mdzod kyis zhus pa zhes bya ba theg pa chen po'i mdo. D148; P815, vol. 33.

Ārya-gayā-śīrṣa-nāma-mahāyāna-sūtra, 'Phags pa gayā mgo'i ri zhes bya ba theg pa chen po'i mdo. D109; P777, vol. 29.

Ārya-gṛha-pati-ugra-paripṛcchā-nāma-mahāyāna-sūtra, 'Phags pa khyim bdag drag shul can kyis zhus pa zhes bya ba theg pa chen po'i mdo. D63; P760.19, vol. 23.

Ārya-candrottama-dārikā-vyākaraṇa-nāma-mahāyāna-sutra, 'Phags pa bu mo zla mchog lung bstan pa zhes bya ba theg pa chen po'i mdo. D191; P858, vol. 34.

Ārya-tathāgata-jñāna-mudrā-samādhi-nāma-mahāyāna-sūtra, 'Phags pa de bzhin gshegs pa'i ye shes kyi phyag rgya'i ting nge 'dzin zhes bya ba theg pa chen po'i mdo. D131; P799, vol. 32.

Ārya-tathāgatācintya-guhya-nirdeśa-nāma-mahāyāna-sūtra, 'Phags pa de bzhin gshegs pa'i gsang ba bsam gyis mi khyab pa bstan pa zhes bya ba theg pa chen po'i mdo. D47; P760.3, vol. 22.

Ārya-tri-skandhaka-nāma-mahāyāna-sūtra, 'Phags pa phung po gsum pa zhus pa zhes bya ba theg pa chen po'i mdo. D284; P950, vol. 37.

Ārya-daśa-dharmaka-nāma-mahāyāna-sūtra, 'Phags pa chos bcu pa zhes bya ba theg pa chen po'i mdo. D53; P760.9, vol. 22.

Ārya-dharma-saṃgīti-nāma-mahāyāna-sūtra, 'Phags pa chos yang dag par sdud pa zhes bya ba theg pa chen po'i mdo. D238; P904, vol. 36.

Ārya-brahma-viśeṣa-cinti-paripṛcchā-nāma-mahāyāna-sūtra, 'Phags pa tshangs pa khyad par sems kyis zhus pa zhes bya ba theg pa chen po'i mdo. D160; P827, vol. 33.

Ārya-bhadra-kalpika-nāma-mahāyāna-sūtra, 'Phags pa bskal pa bzang po zhes bya ba theg pa chen po'i mdo. D94; P762, vol. 27.

Ārya-mañjuśrī-buddha-kṣetra-guṇa-vyūha-nāma-mahāyāna-sūtra, 'Phags pa 'jam dpal gyi sangs rgyas kyi zhing gi yon tan dkod pa zhes bya ba theg pa chen po'i mdo. D59; P760.15, vol. 23 .

Ārya-mañjuśrī-vikrīḍita-nāma-mahāyāna-sūtra, 'Phags pa 'jam dpal rnam par rol pa zhes bya ba theg pa chen po'i mdo. D96; P764, vol. 27.

Ārya-mahā-karuṇā-puṇḍarīka-nāma-mahāyāna-sūtra, 'Phags pa snying rje chen po'i pad ma dkar po zhes bya ba theg pa chen po'i mdo. D111; P779, vol. 29.

Ārya-ratna-cūḍa-paripṛcchā-nāma-mahāyāna-sūtra, 'Phags pa gtsug na rin po ches zhus pa zhes bya ba theg pa chen po'i mdo. D91; P760.47, vol. 24.

Ārya-ratna-megha-nāma-mahāyāna-sūtra, 'Phags pa dkon mchog sprin ces bya ba theg pa chen po'i mdo. D231; P897, vol. 35.

Ārya-rājāvavādaka-nāma-mahāyāna-sūtra, 'Phags pa rgyal po la dgams pa zhes bya ba theg pa chen po'i mdo. D221; P887, vol. 35.

Ārya-laṅkāvatāra-mahāyāna-sūtra, 'Phags pa lang kar gshegs pa'i mdo. P775, vol. 29.

Ārya-vimalakīrti-nirdeśa-nāma-mahāyāna-sūtra, 'Phags pa dri ma med par grags pas bstan pa zhes bya ba theg pa chen po'i mdo. D176; P843, vol. 34.

Ārya-vīradatta-gṛha-pati-paripṛcchā-nāma-mahāyāna-sūtra, 'Phags pa khyim bdag dpal byin gyis zhus pa zhes bya ba theg pa chen po'i mdo. D72; P760.28, vol. 24.

Ārya-sad-dharmānusmṛty-upasthāna, 'Phags pa dam pa'i chos dran pa nye bar gzhag pa. D287; P953, vol. 37.

Ārya-saṃdhi-nirmocana-nāma-mahāyāna-sūtra, 'Phags pa dgongs pa nges par 'grel pa zhes bya ba theg pa chen po'i mdo. D106; P774, vol. 29.

Ārya-sarva-vaidalya/vaipulya-saṃgraha-nāma-mahāyāna-sūtra, 'Phags pa rnam par 'thag pa thams cad bsdus pa zhes bya ba theg pa chen po'i mdo. D227; P893, vol. 35.

Ārya-sāgaramati-paripṛcchā-nāma-mahāyāna-sūtra, 'Phags pa blo gros rgya mtshos zhus pa zhes bya ba theg pa chen po'i mdo. D152; P819, vol. 33.

Ārya-siṃha-paripṛcchā-nāma-mahāyāna-sūtra, 'Phags pa seng ges zhus pa zhes bya ba theg pa chen po'i mdo. D81; P760.37, vol. 24.

Upāli-paripṛcchā-sūtra: Ārya-vinaya-viniścaya-upāli-paripṛcchā-nāma-mahāyāna-sūtra, 'Phags pa 'dul ba rnam par gtan la dbab pa nye bar 'khor gyis zhus pa zhes bya ba theg pa chen po'i mdo. D68; P760.24, vol. 24.

Karmāvaraṇa-viśuddhi- sūtra: Ārya-karmāvaraṇa-viśuddhi-nāma-mahāyāna-sūtra, 'Phags pa las kyi sgrib pa rnam par dag pa zhes bya ba theg pa chen po'i mdo. D218; P884, vol. 35.

Gaṇḍa-vyūha-sūtra, sDong pos brgyan pa/ sDong po bkod pa'i mdo. Section 45 of the *Buddhāvataṃsaka-nāma-mahā-vaipulya-sūtra, Sangs rgyas phal po che shes bya ba shin tu rgyas pa chen po'i mdo.* D44; P761, vol. 26.

Catuḥ-pratisaraṇa-sūtra. See *Ārya-akṣayamati-nirdeśa.*

Candra-pradīpa-sūtra. See *Samādhi-rāja-sūtra.*

Tathāgatotpatti-saṃbhava, De bzhin gshegs pa skye 'byung bstan pa'i le'u. Section 43 of the *Buddhāvataṃsaka-nāma-mahāvaipulya-sūtra.* D44; P761, vol. 26.

Daśa-bhūmika-sūtra, Sa bcu pa'i mdo. Section 31 of the *Buddhāvataṃsaka-nāma-mahāvaipulya-sūtra.* D44; P761, vol. 25.

Nāga-rāja-bherī-gāthā, Klu'i rgyal po rnga sgra'i tshig su bcad pa. D325; P991, vol. 39.

Nārāyaṇa-paripṛcchā-ārya-mahāmayā-vijaya-vāhinī-dhāraṇī, Sred med kyi bus zhus pa 'phags pa sgyu ma chen mo rnam par rgyal ba thob par byed pa zhes bya ba'i gzungs. D684. This work is not found in P.

Praśanta-viniścaya-prātihārya-sūtra: Ārya-praśanta-viniścaya-prātihārya-samādhi-nāma-mahāyāna-sūtra, Rab tu zhi ba rnam par nges pa'i cho 'phrul gyi ting nge 'dzin ces bya ba theg pa chen po'i mdo. D 129; P797, vol. 32.

Buddhāvataṃsaka-nāma-mahāvaipulya-sūtra, Sangs rgyas phal po che zhes bya ba shin tu rgyas pa chen po'i mdo. D44; P761, vols. 25-26.

Bodhisattva-prātimokṣa-catuṣka-nirhāra-nāma-mahāyāna-sūtra, Byang chub sems dpa'i so so thar pa chos bzhi sgrub pa zhes bya ba theg pa chen po'i mdo. D248; P914, vol. 36.

Mahā-vairocanābhisaṃbodhi-vikurvitādhiṣṭhāna-vaipulya-sūtrendra-rāja-nāma-dharma-paryāya, rNam par snang mdzad chen po mngon par rdzogs par byang chub pa rnam par sprul pa byin gyis rlob pa shin tu rgyas pa mdo sde'i dbang po'i rgyal po zhes bya ba'i chos kyi rnam grangs. D494; P126, vol. 5.

Ratna-kūṭa: Ārya-mahā-ratna-kūṭa-dharma-paryāya-śata-sāhasrika-grantha, 'Phags pa dkon mchog brtsegs pa chen po'i chos kyi rnam grangs le'u stong phrag brgya pa. P760, vols. 22-24.

Ratna-guṇa-saṃcaya-gatha: Ārya-prajñāpāramitā-ratna-guṇa-saṃcaya-gāthā, 'Phags pa shes rab kyi pha rol tu phyin pa sdud pa tshigs su bcad pa. D13; P735, vol. 21.

Vajrapāṇy-abhiṣeka-mahā-tantra: Ārya-vajrapāṇy-abhiṣeka-mahā-tantra, 'Phags pa lag na rdo rje dbang bskur ba'i rgyud chen mo. D496; P130, vol. 6.

Śraddhā-balādhānāvatāra-mūdra-sūtra: Ārya-śraddhā-balādhānāvatāra-mūdra-nāma-mahāyāna-sūtra, 'Phags pa dad pa'i stobs bskyed pa la 'jug pa'i phyag rgya zhes bya ba theg pa chen po'i mdo. D201; P867, vol. 34.

Śrī-paramādya-nāma-mahāyāna-kalpa-rāja, dPal mchog dang po zhes bya ba theg pa chen po'i rtog pa'i rgyal po. D487; P119, vol. 5.

Satyaka-parivarta, bDen pa po'i le'u: the fourth chapter of the *Ārya-bodhisattva-gocaropāya-viṣaya-vikurvāṇa-nirdeśa-nāma-mahāyāna-sūtra, 'Phags pa byang chub sems dpa'i spyod yul gyi thabs kyi yul la rnam par 'phrul ba bstan pa zhes bya ba theg pa chen po'i mdo*. D146; P813, vol. 32.

Samādhi-rāja-sūtra: Sarva-dharma-svabhāva-samatā-vipañcita-samādhi-rāja-sūtra, Chos tham cad kyi rang bzhin mnyam pa nyid rnam par spros pa ting nge 'dzin gyi rgyal po'i mdo. D127; P795, vol. 31.

Subāhu-paripṛcchā: *Ārya-subāhu-paripṛcchā-nāma-mahāyāna-sūtra, 'Phags pa lag bzangs kyis zhus pa zhes bya ba theg pa chen po'i mdo*. D70; P760.26, vol. 24.

Suvarṇa-prabhāsa-sūtra: Ārya-suvarṇa-prabhāsottama-sūtrendra-rāja-nāma-mahāyāna-sūtra, 'Phags pa gser 'od dam pa mdo sde'i dbang po'i rgyal po shes bya ba theg pa chen po'i mdo. D556; P176, vol. 7.

B. Śāstras

Abhidharma-kośa: Abhidharma-kośa-kārikā, Chos mngon pa'i mdzod kyi tshig le'ur byas pa. Vasubandhu. D4089; P5590, vol. 115.

Abhidharma-kośa-bhāṣya, Chos mngon pa'i mdzod kyi bshad pa. Vasubandhu. D4090; P5591, vol. 115.

Abhidharma-samuccaya, Chos mngon pa kun las btus pa. Asaṅga. D4049; P5550, vol. 112.

Abhisamayālaṃkāra: Abhisamayālaṃkāra-nāma-prajñāpāramitopadeśa-śāstra-kārikā, mNgon par rtogs pa'i rgyan. Maitreyanātha. D3786; P5184, vol. 88.

Ārya-aṣṭa-sāhasrikā-prajñāpāramitā-vyākhyā Abhisamayālaṃkārālokā, 'Phags pa shes rab kyi pha rol tu phyin pa brgyad stong pa'i bshad pa mngon par rtogs pa'i rgyan gyi snang ba zhes bya ba. Haribhadra. D3791; P5189, vol. 90.

Uttara-tantra-śāstra. See *Mahāyānottara-tantra-śāstra*.

Kāśyapa-parivarta-ṭikā: Ārya-mahā-ratna-kūṭa-dharma-paryāya-parivartta-śata-sāhasrika-kāśyapa-parivarta-ṭikā, 'Phags pa dkon mchog brtsegs pa chen po'i chos kyi rnam grangs le'u stong phrag brgya pa las 'od srungs kyi le'u rgya cher 'grel pa. Sthiramati. D4009; P5510, vol. 105.

Guṇāparyanta-stotra, Yon tan mtha' yas par bstod pa. Triratnadāsa. D1155; P2044, vol. 46.

Guru-kriyā-krama, Bla ma'i bya ba'i rim pa. Atisha. D3977; P5374, vol. 103.

Catuḥ-śataka: Catuḥ-śataka-śāstra-kārikā-nāma, bsTan bcos bzhi brgya pa zhes bya ba'i tshig le'ur byas pa. Āryadeva. D3846; P5246, vol. 95.

Cittotpāda-saṃvara-vidhi-krama, Sems bskyed pa dang sdom pa'i cho ga'i rim pa (*krama* is not found in the title at the start of the work). Atisha. D3969; P5364, vol. 103.

Jātaka-mālā, sKyes pa'i rab kyi rgyud. Āryaśūra. D4150; P5650, vol. 128.

Deśanā-stava, bShags pa'i bstod pa. Candragomin. D1159; P2048, vol. 46.

Pāramitā-samāsa-nāma, Pha rol tu phyin pa bsdus pa zhes bya ba. Āryaśūra. D3944; P5340, vol. 103.

Prajñā-pāramitā-stotra, Shes rab kyi pha rol tu phyin ma'i bstod pa. Nāgārjuna. D1127; P2018, vol. 46.

Prajñā-śataka-nāma-prakaraṇa, Shes rab brgya pa zhes bya ba'i rab tu byed pa. Nāgārjuna. D4328; P5820, vol. 144.

Pramāṇa-vārttika-kārikā, Tshad ma rnam 'grel gyi tshig le'ur byas pa. Dharmakīrti. P5709, vol. 130.

Bala-gotra-parivarta, sTobs kyi rigs kyi le'u. Eighth chapter of *Yoga-caryā-bhūmau-bodhisattva-bhūmi, rNal 'byor spyod pa'i sa las byang chub sems dpa'i sa.* Asaṅga. D4037; P5538, vol. 110.

Bodhicitta-vivaraṇa, Byang chub sems kyi 'grel pa. Nāgārjuna. D1801; P2666, vol. 61.

Bodhicittotpāda-samādāna-vidhi, Byang chub kyi sems bskyed pa dang yi dam blang ba'i cho ga (*yi dam* should be emended to *du*). Jetāri. D3968; P5363, vol. 103.

Bodhi-patha-pradīpa, Byang chub lam gyi sgron ma. Atisha. D3947; P5343, vol. 103.

Bodhi-mārga-pradīpa-pañjikā-nāma, Byang chub lam gyi sgron ma'i dka' 'grel. Atisha. D3948; P5344, vol. 103.

Bodhisattva-caryāvatāra, Byang chub sems dpa'i spyod pa la 'jug pa. Śāntideva. Skt. and Tibetan ed., Bhattacharya 1960. P5272, vol. 99.

Bodhisattva-bhūmi: Yoga-caryā-bhūmau-bodhisattva-bhūmi, rNal 'byor spyod pa'i sa las byang chub sems dpa'i sa. Asaṅga. D4037; P5538, vol. 110.

Bodhisattvādikarmika-mārgāvatāra-deśanā, Byang chub sems dpa' las dang po pa'i lam la 'jug pa bstan pa. Atisha. D3952; P5349, vol. 103.

Bhāvanā-krama, sGom pa'i rim pa. Kamalaśīla. D3915-3917; P5310-5312, vol. 102.

Madhyamaka-hṛdaya-kārikā, dBu ma'i snying po'i tshig le'ur byas pa. Bhāvaviveka. D3855; P5255, vol. 96.

Madhyamakāvatāra-nāma, dBu ma la 'jug pa zhes bya ba. Candrakīrti. D3861; P5262, vol. 98.

Madhyamakāvatāra-bhāṣya, dBu ma la 'jug pa bshad pa zhes bya ba. Candrakīrti. D3862; P5263, vol. 98.

Mahāyāna-patha-sādhana-varṇa-saṃgraha, Theg pa chen po'i lam gyi sgrub thabs yi ger bsdus pa. Atisha. D3954; P5351, vol. 103.

Mahāyāna-saṃgraha, Theg pa chen po bsdus pa. Asaṅga. D4048; P5549, vol. 112.

Mahāyāna-sūtrālaṃkāra-kārikā, Theg pa chen po'i mdo sde'i rgyan gyi tshig le'ur byas pa. Maitreyanātha. D4020; P5521; vol. 109.

Mahāyānottara-tantra-śāstra, Theg pa chen po rgyud bla ma'i bstan bcos. Also called *Ratna-gotra-vibhāga, dKon mchog gi rigs rnam par dbye ba.* Maitreyanātha. D4024; P5525, vol. 108.

Yoga-caryā-bhūmi, rNal 'byor spyod pa'i sa. Sa'i dngos gzhi, the Tibetan name for the first part of the *Yoga-caryā-bhūmi* (D4034; P5536, vols. 109-110) (and perhaps for all parts except the *Viniścaya-saṃgrahaṇī, Śrāvaka-bhūmi,* and *Bodhisattva-bhūmi*) is rendered *Yoga-caryā-bhūmi* in the translation.

Viniścaya-saṃgrahaṇī: Yoga-caryā-bhūmi-nirṇaya-saṃgraha / Yoga-caryā-bhūmi-viniścaya-saṃgrahaṇī, rNal 'byor spyod pa'i sa rnam par gtan la dbab pa bsdu ba. Asaṅga. D4038; P5539, vols. 110-111.

Ratna-gotra-vibhāga. See *Mahāyānottara-tantra-śāstra.*

Ratnāvalī: Rāja-parikathā-ratna-mālā/ratnāvalī, rGyal po la gtam bya ba rin po che'i phreng ba. Nāgārjuna. D4158; P5658, vol. 129.

Varṇāha-varṇe-bhagavato-buddhasya-stotre-śakya-stava, Sangs rgyas bcom ldan 'das la bstod pa bsngags par 'os pa bsngags pa las bstod par mi nus par bstod pa. Āryaśūra/ Matricita/ Mātṛceṭa. P2029, vol. 46.

Śata-pañcāśatka-nāma-stotra, brGya lnga bcu pa zhes bya ba'i bstod pa. Mātṛceṭa/Aśvaghoṣa. D1147; P2038, vol. 46.

Śikṣā-samuccaya, bSlab pa kun las btus pa. Śāntideva. D3940; P5336, vol. 102.

Śikṣā-samuccaya-kārikā, bSlab pa kun las btus pa tshig le'ur byas pa. Śāntideva. D3939; P5335, vol. 102.

Śiṣya-lekha, Slob ma la springs pa'i spring yig. Candragomin. D4183; P5683, vol. 129 and P5410, vol. 103.

Sūtra-samuccaya, mDo kun las btus pa. Nāgārjuna. D3934; P5330, vol. 102.

Suhṛl-lekha, bShes pa'i spring yig. Nāgārjuna. D4182; P5682, vol. 129.

Hṛdaya-nikṣepa, sNying po nges par bsdu ba. Atisha. P5346, vol. 103.

C. Tibetan Works

Anonymous. 1964. *Byang chub lam rim chen mo'i sa bcad.* Dharamsala: Sherig Parkhang.

Ngag-dbang-rab-brtan (sDe-drug-mkhan-chen-ngag-dbang-rab-brtan). See 'Jam-dbyangs-bzhad-pa et al.

'Jam-dbyangs-bzhad-pa et al. 1972. *mNyam med rje btsun tsong kha pa chen pos mdzad pa'i byang chub lam rim chen mo'i dka' ba'i gnad rnams mchan bu bzhi'i sgo nas legs par bshad pa theg chen lam gyi gsal sgron* (abbreviated title *Lam rim mchan bzhi sbrags ma*). New Delhi: Chophel Lekden.

sTag-bu-yongs-'dzin Ye-shes-rgya-mtsho. 2002. *Byang chub lam rim chen mo'i sa bcad kyi thog nas skyes bu gsum gyi rim pa'i man ngag gi gnad bsdus gsal ba'i sgron me.* Varanasi: Ladakh Atisha Dharma Center.

Dol-pa-rog-shes-rab-rgya-mtsho/Dol-pa-dmar-zhur-pa. *Be'u bum sngon po.* Bo-do-wa's (Po-to-ba) *Be'u bum sngon po* (*Be'u bum*) arranged by Dol-pa Shes-rab-rgya-mtsho.

Bo-do-wa's (Po-to-ba) *Be'u bum sngon po* (*Be'u bum*) arranged by Dol-pa Shes-rab-rgya-mtsho.

Pha-bong-kha (Pha-bong-kha-pa-byams-pa-bstan-'dzin-'phrin-las-rgya-mtsho). 1973. *Byang chub lam rim chen mo mchan bu bzhi sbrags kyi skor dran gso'i bsnyel byang mgo smos tsam du mdzad pa.* In *The Collected Works of Pha-boṅ-kha-pa Byams-pa-bstan-'dzin-phrin-las-rgya-mtsho.* Vol. 5. New Delhi: Chophel Lekden.

Ba-so-chos-kyi-rgyal-mtshan. See 'Jam-dbyangs-bzhad-pa et al.

Bra-sti (Bra-sti-dge-bshes-rin-chen-don-grub). See 'Jam-dbyangs-bzhad-pa et al.

Tsong-kha-pa. 1985. *sKyes bu gsum gyi rnyams su blang ba'i rim pa thams cad tshang bar ston pa'i byang chub lam gyi rim pa/ Byang chub lam rim che ba.* Zi-ling (Xining): Tso Ngön (mTsho sngon) People's Press.

Also: Ganden Bar Nying, early fifteenth century; and Dharamsala, 1991.

———. *dBu ma la 'jug pa'i rnam bshad dgongs pa rab gsal*. In *The Complete Works of Tsong-kha-pa*. Vol. Ma: 1-267. dGa' ldan phun tshogs gling woodblocks, gTsang, Tibet, n.d.

———. *dBu ma rtsa ba'i tshig le'ur byas pa'i rnam bshad rig pa'i rgya mtsho*. Also called *rTsa she ṭik chen*. In *The Complete Works of Tsong-kha-pa*. Vol. Ba: 1-282. dGa' ldan phun tshogs gling woodblocks, gTsang, Tibet, n.d.

———. *Byang chub lam gyi rim pa chung ba*. Also called *Lam rim 'bring*. In *The Complete Works of Tsong-kha-pa*. Vol. Pha: 1-201. dGa' ldan phun tshogs gling woodblocks, gTsang, Tibet, n.d.

———. *Byang chub gzhug lam*. In *Collected Works*. Vol. 2. (Gedan Sungrab Minyam Gyunphel Series, vol. 80.) New Delhi: N. G. Demo, 1975.

bLo-ldan-shes-rab. *sPring yig bdud rtsi'i thigs pa*.

Sha-ra-ba/Shar-ba-pa Yon-tan-grags. *Be'u bum dmar po*.

gSer-mdog-pan-chen Shakya mChog ldan. *sPring yig bdud rtsi'i thigs pa'i rnam bshad dpag bsam yong 'du'i ljon phreng*.

A-kya-yongs-'dzin, dByangs-can-dga'-ba'i-blo-gros. 1971. *Byang chub lam gyi rim pa chen mo las byung ba'i brda bkrol nyer mkho bsdus pa* (abbreviated title *Lam rim brda bkrol*). In *The Collected Works of A-kya Yoṅs-ḥdzin*. Vol. 1. New Delhi: Lama Guru Deva.

D. Modern Works

Bagchi, S., ed. 1967. *Suvarṇaprabhāsottamasūtra*. Darbhanga: Mithila Institute.

———. 1970. *Mahāyāna-Sūtrālaṅkāra of Asaṅga*. Darbhanga: Mithila Institute.

Bareau, André. 1955. *Les sectes bouddhiques du Petit Véhicule*. Paris: École française d'Extrême-Orient.

Bendall, C., ed. 1903-1904. "*Subhāṣita-saṃgraha*: An Anthology of Extracts...." *Le Muséon* 4 (1903): 375-402 and 5 (1904): 5-46.

Bendall, C., and W.H.D. Rouse. 1971. *Śikṣā Samuccaya*. 1922. Reprint, Delhi: Motilal Banarsidass.

Bhattacharya, Vidhushekhara. 1931. *The Catuḥśataka of Āryadeva*. Calcutta: Visva-bharati Book-shop.

———, ed. 1960. *Bodhicaryāvatāra*. Calcutta: The Asiatic Society.

Buescher, John. 1982. "The Buddhist Doctrine of Two Truths in the Vaibhāṣika and Theravāda Schools." Ph.D. diss., University of Virginia.

Chandra, Lokesh. 1982. *Tibetan-Sanskrit Dictionary*. Indo-Asian Literature, 3. 1959-61. Reprint, Kyoto: Rinsen Book Co.

Conze, Edward. 1954. *Treatise on Reunion with the Absolute*. Serie Orientale Roma, 6. Rome: Istituto Italiano per il Medio ed Estremo Oriente.

———. 1973. *The Perfection of Wisdom in 8,000 Lines and Its Verse Summary*. Bolinas: Four Seasons Foundation.

———, ed. and trans. 1979. *The Large Sūtra on Perfect Wisdom*. Delhi: Motilal Banarsidass.

Cozort, Daniel. 1986. *Highest Yoga Tantra*. Ithaca, NY: Snow Lion Publications.

Crosby, Kate, and Andrew Skilton. 1995. *The Bodhicaryāvatāra*. Oxford and New York: Oxford University Press.

Cutler, Joshua W.C., et al. 2000 and 2002. *The Great Treatise on the Stages of the Path to Enlightenment*. Vols. 1 and 3. Ithaca, NY: Snow Lion Publications.

Das, Sarat Chandra. 1985. *Tibetan-English Dictionary*. 1902. Reprint, New Delhi: Motilal Banarsidass.

de Jong, J.W. 1978. "Textcritical Notes on the *Prasannapadā*." *Indo-Iranian Journal* 20: 25-59 and 217-252.

———. 1987. *A Brief History of Buddhist Studies in Europe and America*. 2nd rev. ed. Bibliotheca Indo-Buddhica, 33. Delhi: Sri Satguru Publications.

———, ed. 1977. *Madhyamaka-kārikā*. Adyar: Theosophical Society.

Dreyfus, Georges. 1997. *Recognizing Reality: Dharmakīrti's Philosophy and Its Tibetan Interpretations*. Albany: State University of New York Press.

Driessens, Georges, trans. 1990 and 1992. *Le grand livre de la progression vers l'éveil*. 2 vols. Jujurieux and Saint-Jean-le-Vieux: Editions Dharma.

Dunne, John, and Sara McClintock. 1997. *The Precious Garland: An Epistle to a King*. Boston: Wisdom Publications.

Dutt, Nalinaksha, ed. 1966. *Bodhisattva-bhūmi*. Tibetan Sanskrit Works Series, 7. Patna: K.P. Jayaswal Research Institute.

Eckel, Malcolm David. 1987. *Jñānagarbha's Commentary on the Distinction Between the Two Truths*. Albany: State University of New York Press.

Edgerton, F. 1972. *Buddhist Hybrid Sanskrit Grammar and Dictionary*. 2 vols. 1953. Reprint, Delhi: Motilal Banarsidass.

Ferrari, A., ed. 1946. "Il 'Compendio delle Perfezioni' di Āryaśūra." *Annali Lateranensi* 10: 9-101.

Garfield, Jay. 1995. *The Fundamental Wisdom of the Middle Way*. New York: Oxford University Press.

Gokhale, V.V. 1946. "The Text of the *Abhidharmakośa* of Vasubandhu." *Journal of the Bombay Branch, Royal Asiatic Society* 22: 73-102.

———. 1947. "Fragment of the *Abhidharma-samuccaya* of Asaṅga." *Journal of the Bombay Branch, Royal Asiatic Society* 23: 13-38.

Gunaratana, Henepola. 1985. *The Path of Serenity and Insight: An Explanation of the Buddhist Jhānas*. Columbia, Missouri: South Asia Books.

Hahn, Michael. 1982. *Nāgārjuna's* Ratnāvalī. Vol. 1. Bonn: Indica et Tibetica Verlag.

Hartmann, Jens-Uwe, ed. and trans. 1987. *Das* Varṇārhavarṇastotra *des Mātṛceṭa*. Göttingen: Vandenhoeck & Ruprecht.

Hirakawa, A. 1990. *A History of Indian Buddhism: From Śākyamuni to Early Mahāyāna*. Asian Studies at Hawaii, 36. Honolulu: University of Hawaii Press.

Hopkins, Jeffrey. 1980. *Compassion in Tibetan Buddhism*. London: Ryder and Co.

———. 1996. *Meditation on Emptiness*. Rev. ed. Boston: Wisdom Publications.

———. 1998. *Buddhist Advice for Living and Liberation: Nāgārjuna's* Precious Garland. Ithaca, NY: Snow Lion Publications.

Horner, I.B. 1938-1966. *The Book of Discipline*. Vols. 1-3. London: Humphrey Milford. Vols. 4-6. London: Luzac and Company, Ltd.

Hurvitz, Leon. 1976. *Scripture of the Lotus Blossom of the Fine Dharma*. New York: Columbia University Press.

Johnston, E.H., ed. 1950. *Ratna-gotra-vibhāga-mahāyānottara-tantra-śāstra*. Patna: Bihar Research Society.

Johnston, E.H., and Kunst, A. 1990. "The *Vigrahavyvārtanī* with the author's commentary." *Mélanges chinois et bouddhiques* 9 (1951): 99-152. Reprinted in *The Dialectical Method of Nāgārjuna*. Third edition. Delhi: Motilal Banarsidass.

Kanakura, Yenshō, et al., eds. 1953. *A Catalogue of the Tōhoku University Collection of Tibetan Works on Buddhism*. Sendai: Tohoku University.

Khangkar, Tsultrim Kelsang, ed. 2001. *rJe tsong kha pa'i lam rim chen mo'i lung khungs gsal byed nyi ma*. Japanese and Tibetan Culture Series, 6. Kyoto: Tibetan Buddhist Culture Association.

Krang-dbyi-sun et al., eds. 1985. *Bod rgya tshig mdzod chen mo*. 3 vols. Beijing: Mi-rigs-dpe-skrun-khang.

La Vallée Poussin, Louis de, ed. 1970a. *Mūla-madhyamaka-kārikā de Nāgārjuna avec la Prasannapadā Commentaire de Candrakīrti*. Bibliotheca Buddhica, 4. 1903-1913. Reprint, Osnabrück: Biblio Verlag.

———. 1970b. *Madhyamakāvatāra par Candrakīrti*. Bibliotheca Buddhica, 9. 1907. Reprint, Osnabrück: Biblio Verlag.

———. 1971. *L'Abhidharmakośa de Vasubandhu*. Vol. 3. Brussels: Institut belge des hautes études chinoises.

Lamotte, Étienne. 1949. "La critique d'interprétation dans le bouddhisme." *Annuaire de l'Institut de philologie et d'histoire orientales et slaves* 9: 341-361.

———, ed. and trans. 1935. *Saṃdhinirmocana Sūtra: L'explication des mystères*. Louvain: Bureaux de recueil, Bibliothèque de l'Université.

Lang, Karen. 1986. *Āryadeva's Catuḥśataka*. Indiske Studier, 7. Copenhagen: Akademisk Forlag.

———. 1990. "sPa tshab Nyi ma grags and the Introduction of Prāsaṅgika Madhyamaka into Tibet." In *Reflections on Tibetan Culture*, edited by Lawrence Epstein and Richard Sherburne. Lewiston, NY: The Edwin Mellen Press.

Lévi, Sylvain, ed. and trans. 1983. *Mahāyāna-Sūtrālaṃkāra, exposé de la doctrine du Grand Véhicule selon la système Yogācāra*. Tome 1. 1907. Reprint, Kyoto: Rinsen Book Co.

Lindtner, Christian. 1986. *Nagarjuniana*. 1982. Reprint, Delhi: Motilal Banarsidass.

Lopez, Donald S., Jr. 1988. *The Heart Sūtra Explained: Indian and Tibetan Commentaries*. Albany: State University of New York Press.

Meadows, Carol. 1986. *Āryaśūra's Compendium of the Perfections: Text, Translation and Analysis of the Pāramitāsamāsa*. Ed. Michael Hahn. Indica et Tibetica, 8. Bonn: Indica et Tibetica Verlag.

Mimaki, K. 1982. *Blo Gsal Grub Mtha'*. Kyoto: University of Kyoto.

———. 1983. "The *Blo Gsal Grub Mtha'* and the Mādhyamika Classification in Tibetan grub mtha' Literature." In *Contributions on Tibetan and Buddhist Religion and Philosophy*, ed. E. Steinkellner and H. Tauscher. Vienna: Arbeitskreis für Tibetische und Buddhistische Studien Universität Wien.

Miyasaka, Y., ed. 1971-1972. *Pramāṇavārttika-kārikā: Sanskrit and Tibetan. Acta Indologica*, 2.

Monier-Williams, M. 1984. *A Sanskrit-English Dictionary*. 1899. Reprint, Delhi: Motilal Banarsidass.

Mookerjee, S., and H. Nagasaki, trans. 1964. *The Pramāṇavārttika of Dharmakīrti*. Patna: Nava Nālandā Mahāvihāra.

Nakamura, Hajime. 1989. *Indian Buddhism: A Survey with Bibliographical Notes*. 1980. Reprint, Delhi: Motilal Banarsidass.

Namdol, Gyaltsen. 1985. *Bhāvanā-krama*. Varanasi: Institute of Higher Tibetan Studies.

Ñāṇamoli, Bhikkhu, trans. 1991. *The Path of Purification*. Fifth edition. Kandy: Buddhist Publication Society.

Napper, Elizabeth. 1989. *Dependent-Arising and Emptiness*. London and Boston: Wisdom Publications.

Obermiller, E. 1931 "Sublime Science of the Great Vehicle to Salvation." *Acta Orientalia* 9: 81-306.

———. 1935. "A Sanskrit Ms. from Tibet—Kamalaśīla's *Bhāvanā-krama*." *The Journal of the Greater Indian Society* 2: 1-11.

Pagel, Ulrich. 1995. *The Bodhisattvapiṭaka*. Buddhica Britannica Series Continua, 5. Tring, U.K.: Institute of Buddhist Studies.

Pandeya, J.S., ed. 1994. *Bauddhastotrasaṃgraha*. Varanasi: Motilal Banarsidass.

Pfandt, Peter. 1983. *Mahāyāna Texts Translated into Western Languages: A Bibliographical Guide*. Köln: E.J. Brill.

Powers, John. 1995a. *Introduction to Tibetan Buddhism*. Ithaca, NY: Snow Lion Publications.

———, trans. 1995b. *Wisdom of Buddha: The Saṁdhinirmocana Sūtra*. Berkeley: Dharma Publishing.

Pradhan, P., ed. 1975. *Abhidharmasamuccaya of Asaṅga*. 1950. Reprint, Shantiniketan: Visva-Bharati.

Pruden, Leo M., trans. 1988. *Abhidharmakośabhāṣyam/ by Louis de La Vallée Poussin*. 4 vols. Berkeley: Asian Humanities Press.

Rabten, Geshe. 1988. *Treasury of Dharma*. London: Tharpa Publications.

Rahula, Walpola. 1980. *Le compendium de la super-doctrine (philosophie) (Abhidharmasamuccaya) d'Asaṅga*. 2nd ed. Publications de l'École française d'Extrême-Orient, 78. Paris: École française d'Extrême-Orient.

Rhoton, Jared Douglas, trans. 2002. *A Clear Differentiation of the Three Codes: Essential Distinctions among the Individual Liberation, Great Vehicle, and Tantric Systems. The* sDom gsum rab dbye *and Six Letters* by Sakya Pandita Kunga Gyaltshen. Albany: State University of New York Press.

Rinchen, Geshe Sonam, and Ruth Sonam. 1994. *Yogic Deeds of Bodhisattvas*. Ithaca, NY: Snow Lion Publications.

———. 2001. *Eight Verses for Training the Mind*. Ithaca, NY: Snow Lion Publications.

Roerich, George N. 1979. *The Blue Annals*. 1949-1953. Reprint, Delhi: Motilal Banarsidass. [This is a translation of 'Gos-lo-tsā-ba-gzhon-nu-dpal's *Bod kyi yul du chos dang chos smra ba ji ltar byung ba'i rim pa deb ther sngon po*.]

Ruegg, David Seyfort. 1963. "The Jo naṅ pas: A School of Buddhist Ontologists according to the *Grub mtha' śel gyi me loṅ*." *Journal of the American Oriental Society* 83: 73-91.

———. 1969 *La Théorie du Tathāgathagarbha et du Gotra*. Paris: École française d'Extrême-Orient.

———. 1981. *The Literature of the Madhyamaka School of Philosophy in India*. A History of Indian Literature, vol. 7, fasc. 1. Wiesbaden: Otto Harrassowitz.

———. 1983. "On the Thesis and Assertion in the Madhyamaka/dBu ma." In *Contributions on Tibetan and Buddhist Religion and Philosophy*, ed. E. Steinkellner and H. Tauscher. Vienna: Arbeitskreis für Tibetische und Buddhistische Studien Universität Wien.

———. 1989. *Buddha-nature, Mind and the Problem of Gradualism in a Comparative Perspective: On the Transmission and Reception of Buddhism in India and Tibet*. Jordan Lectures, 1987. London: SOAS, University of London.

———. 2000. "Introduction." *The Great Treatise on the Stages of the Path to Enlightenment*. Vol. 1. Ithaca, NY: Snow Lion Publications.

Sakaki, Ryōzaburō, ed. 1962. *Mahāvyutpatti*. Tokyo: Kokusho Kankōkai.

Shackleton Bailey, D.R. 1951. *Śata-pañcāśatka of Mātṛceṭa*. Cambridge: University Press.

Shastri, Swami Dwarikadas, ed. 1968. *Pramāṇavārttika of Ācārya Dharmakīrti*. Varanasi: Bauddha Bharati.

———. 1972. *Abhidharma-kośa and Bhāṣya of Ācārya Vasubandhu with Sphūṭārthā Commentary of Ācārya Yaśomitra*. Varanasi: Bauddha Bharati.

Shukla, Karunesha, ed. 1973. *Śrāvakabhūmi of Ārya Asaṅga*. Patna: K.P. Jayaswal Research Institute.

Sopa, Geshe Lhundup, and Jeffrey Hopkins. 1989. *Cutting Through Appearances: The Practice and Theory of Tibetan Buddhism*. Ithaca, NY: Snow Lion Publications.

Staël-Holstein, A. von, ed. 1977. *Kāśyapaparivarta, A Mahāyānasūtra of the Ratnakūṭa Class/ Edited in the Original Sanskrit, in Tibetan and in Chinese*. 1926. Reprint, Tokyo: Meicho-Fukyū-Kai.

Stcherbatsky, Th., and E. Obermiller, eds. 1970. *Abhisamayālankāra-prajñāpāramitā-upadeśa-śāstra: The Work of Bodhisattva Maitreya*. Fasc. 1: Introduction, Sanscrit Text and Tibetan Translation. Bibliotheca Buddhica, 23. 1929. Reprint, Osnabrück: Biblio Verlag.

Stearns, Cyrus. 2000. *The Buddha from Dolpo*. Albany: State University of New York Press.

Suzuki, D.T. 1932. *The Lankavatara Sutra*. London: Routledge and Kegan Paul.

———, ed. 1955-61. *The Tibetan Tripitaka, Peking Edition*. Reprinted under the Supervision of the Otani University, Kyoto. 168 volumes. Tokyo and Kyoto: Tibetan Tripitaka Research Institute.

Tatz, Mark. 1986. *Asaṅga's Chapter on Ethics with the Commentary of Tsong-Kha-Pa, The Basic Path to Awakening, The Complete Bodhisattva.* Studies in Asian Thought and Religion, 4. Lewiston/Queenston: The Edwin Mellen Press.

Thurman, Robert A.F. 1984. *Tsong Khapa's Speech of Gold in the* Essence of True Eloquence. Princeton: Princeton University Press.

———, ed. 1981. *The Life and Teachings of Tsong Khapa*. Dharamsala: Library of Tibetan Works and Archives.

Tucci, Giuseppe. 1958. *Minor Buddhist Texts*. Parts 1 and 2. Rome: Is.M.E.O.

———. 1971. *Minor Buddhist Texts*. Part 3. Rome: Is.M.E.O.

Tulku, Tarthang. 1982. *The Nyingma Edition of the sDe-dge 'Ka'-'gyur and bsTan-'gyur Research Catalogue and Bibliography.* Oakland, California: Dharma Press.

Ui, Hakuju, et al., eds. 1934. *A Complete Catalogue of the Tibetan Buddhist Canons (Bkah-hgyur and Bstan-hgyur).* Sendai: Tohoku Imperial University.

Vaidya, P.L., ed. 1961a. *Samādhirājasūtra.* Darbhanga: Mithila Institute.

———. 1961b. *Śikṣāsamuccaya.* Darbhanga: Mithila Institute.

———. 1963. *Laṅkāvatārasūtra.* Darbhanga: Mithila Institute.

Vajirañāṇa, Paravahera. 1975. *Buddhist Meditation in Theory and Practice.* Kuala Lumpur, Malaysia: Buddhist Missionary Society.

van der Kuijp, Leonard W.J. 1983. *Contributions to the Development of Tibetan Buddhist Epistemology from the Eleventh to the Thirteenth Century.* Alt- und Neu-Indische Studien, 26. Franz Steiner Verlag.

Wayman, Alex. 1961. *Analysis of the* Śrāvakabhūmi *Manuscript.* Berkeley: University of California Press.

———. 1978. *Calming the Mind and Discerning the Real.* New York: Columbia University Press.

———. 1980. "The Sixteen Aspects of the Four Noble Truths and Their Opposites." *Journal of the International Buddhist Association* 3: 67-76.

Wogihara, Unrai, ed. 1971. *Bodhisattvabhūmi.* 1930-1936. Reprint, Tokyo: Sankibo Buddhist Book Store.

———. 1973. *Abhisamayālaṃkārālokā Prajñā-pāramitā-vyākhyā: The Work of Haribhadra.* 1932-35. Reprint, Tokyo: Sankibo Buddhist Book Store.

Wylie, T. 1959. "A Standard System of Tibetan Transcription." *Harvard Journal of Asiatic Studies* 22: 261-267.

Yamaguchi, S., ed. 1966. *Madhyāntavibhāga-ṭikā; Exposition systématique du Yogācāravijñāptivāda*. 1934. Reprint, Tokyo: Suzuki Gakujutsu Zaidan.

Yuyama, A., ed. 1976. *Prajñā-pāramitā-ratna-guṇa-samcaya-gāthā: Sanskrit Recension A*. Cambridge: University Press.

Zahler, Leah, ed. 1983. *Meditative States in Tibetan Buddhism*. London and Boston: Wisdom Publications.

INDEX